CALIFORNIA STUDIES IN 19TH-CENTURY MUSIC

Joseph Kerman, *General Editor*

Music in Other Words

Edward Burne-Jones, *The Golden Stairs*. © Tate, London
2002.

Music in Other Words

Victorian Conversations

RUTH A. SOLIE

University of California Press

BERKELEY   LOS ANGELES   LONDON

The following publishers have generously given permission to reprint
excerpts from copyrighted works: a version of chapter 1, from *Explorations in Music, the Arts, and Ideas: Essays in Honor of Leonard B.
Meyer,* ed. Eugene Narmour and Ruth A. Solie, 1–42 (Stuyvesant, N.Y.:
Pendragon Press, 1988); portions of chapter 3, "Gender, Genre, and the
Parlor Piano," *The Wordsworth Circle* 25 (1994): 53–56; portions of
chapter 5, from *Yearbook of Comparative and General Literature* 45–46
(1998): 87–104; and a version of chapter 6, from *The Work of Opera:
Genre, Nationhood, and Sexual Difference,* ed. Richard Dellamora and
Daniel Fischlin, 185–208 (New York: Columbia University Press, 1997).

University of California Press
Berkeley and Los Angeles, California

University of California Press, Ltd.
London, England

Library of Congress Cataloging-in-Publication Data

Solie, Ruth A.
    Music in other words : Victorian conversations / Ruth A. Solie.
        p.   cm.—(California studies in 19th-century music ; 12)
    Includes index.
    ISBN 0-520-23845-1 (alk. paper)
    1. Music—19th century—Social aspects.   I. Title.   II. Series.

    ML196.S65   2004
    780' .9'034—dc21   2003003889

Manufactured in the United States of America
13 12 11 10 09 08 07 06 05 04
10 9 8 7 6 5 4 3 2 1

The paper used in this publication is both acid-free and totally chlorine-
free (TCF). It meets the minimum requirements of ANSI/NISO
Z39.48–1992 (R 1997) (*Permanence of Paper*).

For Penner

Contents

Prelude

Who are they, and what are they up to, these lissome young women in their Fortuny pleats, winding down the golden stairs, carrying their improbable musical instruments out of one enigmatic doorway and into another? Perhaps we should not ask, but simply enjoy their grace and their sinuous progress, vaguely medieval and at the same time so quintessentially Victorian. Even in Edward Burne-Jones's own time, his works were considered mysterious and resistant to interpretation, but evocatively beautiful and somehow reminiscent of the patterns and rhythms of music. In its inscrutable narrative, its beauty, and its musicality, the painting serves to remind us not only of the strangeness inherent in all historical distance, but also of the degree to which the Victorian world was saturated with music.

The various topics taken up in these essays are, in a sense, similarly inscrutable narratives. Nearly forty years ago I learned from Leo Treitler what has become a central preoccupation of my historical thought, the cardinal importance of "what goes without saying": the evidence we will never find is just that information that our historical subjects considered too obvious to be worth mentioning, its very centrality marked by its absence. Far from occasioning the discouragement it might have, this warning spurred my interest in nearly-dead metaphors, informal modeling systems, persistent but unscrutinized cultural tropes—language in general, especially the most casual—for glimmerings of what might be in those blank spaces, legible traces of the unsaid.

Another early and extremely important teacher, Leonard Meyer, once offhandedly described those traces as "cultural scuttlebutt"—a light-hearted but prescient characterization of what we later learned to call "discourses" that, long afterwards, helped to clarify for me the kinds of texts I was looking for and the kinds of evidence I might hope to find. Casual texts, quotidian or oblique references to music made in nonmusical contexts, might help me to find out more about those aspects of musical practice and experience that went without saying in more formal contexts.

Musicology, I have come to believe, has looked too exclusively to professionals (composers, scholars, music critics) for its evidence, thereby unwittingly missing the unspoken information about music and musical experience that is most central to a culture. Largely this has happened because of musicology's penchant, by now well understood and thoroughly deconstructed, for viewing music as a product rather than a behavior. But a culture's musical practices, its attitudes toward music, every aspect of what Christopher Small has taught us to call its "musicking," are revealed more by the ubiquitous and everyday conversations of music's users than by the rulings of the experts and professionals, often to the chagrin of the latter.[1]

In earlier approaches to this historiographic problem I explored metaphoric and figurative language used to talk about music. It is not surprising that communities use the same language to describe music that they use for other aspects of life: in 1850 the talk was of organisms and evolution, in 1900 of egos and psyches or of stock speculation, in 2000 of networks and virtuality. The dominant images of daily life and thought pervade our vocabularies, so music-talk reflects the central preoccupations of any cultural moment. The first chapter here represents this sort of undertaking, an exploration of the interpretive tropes most consistently used over the course of the nineteenth century; it is some twenty years old and only lightly revised to reflect its changed context within current scholarship.

But the reverse is also true: since musical practices help to make social realities what they are, aspects of the experience people have with music, and the beliefs they have about its uses and powers, may in turn be brought to bear in other arenas of life. To unearth these vocabularies and meanings, it helps to look away from the professional discourse of musicians and toward other arenas in which ordinary "cultural scuttlebutt" is regularly going on: in the rest of the essays in this volume I use sources as disparate and unlikely as journalism, novels, and teenagers' diaries to find glimpses of the muffled, even subterranean, conversations that tell us so much about what musical experience was like among the Victorians, what music actually meant to them—to fill in, that is, some of those blanks in our understanding of music's history.

---

1. Christopher Small, *Musicking: The Meanings of Performing and Listening* (Hanover: Wesleyan University Press for the University Press of New England, 1998).

I should say a word about my use of the term "Victorian," which may surprise in two different dimensions. Geographically, I follow a number of historians, most prominently Peter Gay, in applying it freely across Europe and North America: some of these essays concern England, but others range more widely, as do the attitudes and ideas I am exploring.[2] Temporally, "Victorian" has never been a style-term in music history as it has in literature and art (although it might serve us better than the attempt to fit the music of the whole nineteenth century to the Procrustean bed of romanticism), and I don't attempt to press it into that service here. Nonetheless, it is the case that this book is largely concerned with the variety of non-, post-, and antiromanticisms that the nineteenth century yielded up.

I am grateful to the many colleagues who suggested, discussed, edited, and sometimes harassed these essays into the best shape I am capable of giving them, reminding me daily of the extent to which scholarship is, happily, a sociable endeavor; they are named and duly acknowledged in the notes accompanying each separate chapter. I would like to express particular thanks to Joseph Kerman and William Weber for their very thoughtful and helpful responses to the book as a whole, and to Mary Francis, Rachel Berchten, and Edith Gladstone at the University of California Press for their deft and graceful work in bringing it into being. I owe a special and very happy debt to Elizabeth Harries, Helen Lefkowitz Horowitz, Ellen Rosand, and Elizabeth Spelman for their sustaining intellectual friendship.

2. In the third volume of his *The Bourgeois Experience: Victoria to Freud,* Gay comments that "'Victorian' is used in this book as a synonym for 'nineteenth-century'" (*The Cultivation of Hatred* [New York: W. W. Norton, 1993], 3).

1 Beethoven as Secular Humanist

Ideology and the Ninth Symphony in Nineteenth-Century Criticism

> This symphony is one of those intellectual watersheds which, visible from afar, and inaccessible, separate the currents of antagonistic beliefs.
> EDUARD HANSLICK, *The Beautiful in Music* (1885)

> The spirit of Beethoven is as humanising as the spirit of Sophocles.
> EDWARD DANNREUTHER. "Beethoven and His Works" (1876)

In recent years musicologists have been energetic in their efforts to demonstrate that the history of music in Europe has participated in the history of ideas more widely understood.[1] Although instinct suggests that this must be so, exploration of the relationship has been difficult because the attribution of intellectual or political meaning-content to musical compositions is a notoriously slippery business. Here I want to address the question through a side door, as it were: I argue that the link between music and other aspects of European intellectual life can be made visible by studying music's place in the general cultural conversation. The critical language in which music is described and evaluated derives from a common pool applicable to all subjects of discussion and therefore reveals common concerns and ideological presuppositions of the period.

There are reasons why the nineteenth century proves a particularly revealing arena for this kind of study. As has frequently been observed (and was recognized at the time), music played a central role in artistic and cultural life during most of that century. Especially in Germany and German-dominated areas (including England) it was considered the paradigmatic art, and its current events made headlines. And as Peter Gay has commented in

---

1. An elegant study making use of the same piece I deal with here is Leo Treitler's "History, Criticism, and Beethoven's Ninth Symphony," *19th-Century Music* 3 (1980): 193–210. The chapter epigraphs' sources are Eduard Hanslick, *The Beautiful in Music* (1854), trans. Gustav Cohen (London: Novello, Ewer, 1891), 96; and Edward Dannreuther, "Beethoven and His Works: A Study," *Macmillan's Magazine* 34 (1876): 194.

a discussion of Hanslick, music criticism in his time was "something like a boxing match, a political maneuver, or a military campaign"[2]—controversial, contentious, and a matter of great public interest. In the absence of a highly professionalized class of scholars of music and, in particular, of an "analytic" tradition in the sense in which we know it, music was a regular part of general cultural discourse; serious discussions of it found their way not only into the general literature—music criticism was as likely from George Eliot or Friedrich Nietzsche as from Robert Schumann or George Grove—but even, as we shall see, into works of popular fiction.

What made this broad cultural conversation possible was primarily an underlying set of assumptions about music and its role in individual and social life. It was taken for granted that, at least among the intelligentsia, people both enjoyed contemporary music and understood it[3]—although that latter assertion requires some qualification, to which I shall return below. Furthermore, it was expected that music had certain fundamental relationships to "real life," both as part of the social fabric and in connection with individual experience. In the commentaries discussed throughout this essay these preconceptions are evident: whatever the political, aesthetic, or other polemical position adopted by a given writer, there is virtually always the assumption that personal and social meanings are resident in whatever music is under scrutiny, and that uncovering those meanings is one of the commentator's primary tasks. Despite Heinrich Schenker's assertion that he was among the first to discuss the "real content" of music, earlier writers—many of them part musician, part social critic—had an equally firm and equally distinct notion of "content," different as it was from Schenker's later vision, and were equally persuaded that they were demonstrating it.

My essential subject here is not Ludwig van Beethoven or the Ninth Symphony. Rather, I take that piece and its attendant commentary as exemplary of the ways in which religious, philosophical, and political ideologies are reflected in the interpretation of music during the nineteenth century; these reflections, of course, come in turn to shape future perceptions of the piece and its place in the canon. That the Ninth Symphony yields a

---

2. Peter Gay, *Freud, Jews, and Other Germans: Masters and Victims in Modernist Culture* (New York: Oxford University Press, 1978), 258.

3. William Weber describes the process by which, during the course of the century, bourgeois taste gradually fixated on "dead composers" ("Mass Culture and the Reshaping of European Musical Taste, 1770–1870," *International Review of the Aesthetics and Sociology of Music* 8 [1977]: 5–21). Nonetheless, "men of letters" (as the English had it) retained their lively interest in current musical events and their right to comment on them.

particularly rich harvest of such allusions will surprise no one: I have chosen it primarily because it is so very much discussed. It looms large during the three-quarters of the century after its composition, undergoing symbolic readings that vary enormously (often contradicting one another) but never slacken either in frequency or polemical force. We might imagine the piece as a reflecting glass or, better, something like the monolith of Stanley Kubrick's *2001*—always present, hugely, at the center of discourse, inviting the attachment of meanings, almost as though it were a blank surface. In the nineteenth century only the music of Richard Wagner was as central to conversation and as passionately argued over.[4]

THE IMAGE OF BEETHOVEN

First and foremost there is the legendary Beethoven, the composer above all others for whom the nineteenth century wrote what Roland Barthes has called a "bio-mythology." He was created, says Barthes, "a complete hero, granted a discourse (rare for a musician), a legend (a good score of anecdotes), an iconography, a race (that of the Titans of art: Michelangelo, Balzac), and a fatal flaw (deafness in one who created for the ear's pleasure)."[5] The names "Titan" and "Prometheus" are rampant in the literature about him, granting him mythic status early on; godlike images abound, in a confused hodgepodge of pagan and Christian references that represents romanticism in distilled form. A mere decade after the composer's death, Robert Schu-

4. And it continues to be so, in ever-widening circles. David B. Levy comments on Chinese and Japanese responses to the symphony in *Beethoven: The Ninth Symphony* (New York: Schirmer Books, 1995). Robin Wallace provides helpful historical information on contemporary reviews (*Beethoven's Critics: Aesthetic Dilemmas and Resolutions during the Composer's Lifetime* [Cambridge: Cambridge University Press, 1986]); and Michael C. Tusa's "*Noch einmal:* Form and Content in the Finale of Beethoven's Ninth Symphony" (*Beethoven Forum* 7 [1999]: 113–37) surveys nineteenth- as well as twentieth-century attempts to come to grips with the form of the finale, a question that has recently been taken up anew by numerous scholars. Richard Taruskin offers a provocative meditation on the hermeneutic anxiety the piece provokes, in "Resisting the Ninth," *19th-Century Music* 12 (1989): 241–56.

5. Roland Barthes, "Music Practica," *L'Arc* 40 (1970): 16; my translation. The diverse recent studies of Beethoven's persistent cultural dominance and the development of his image include Scott Burnham, *Beethoven Hero* (Princeton: Princeton University Press, 1995); David B. Dennis, *Beethoven in German Politics, 1870–1989* (New Haven: Yale University Press, 1996); and Tia De Nora, *Beethoven and the Construction of Genius: Musical Politics in Vienna, 1792–1803* (Berkeley: University of California Press, 1995).

mann heard in the Adagio of the Ninth the heavens opening "to receive
Beethoven like a soaring saint" so that "it was impossible not to forget the
pettiness of this world and not to feel a presentiment of the Beyond thrilling
the beholders," and his fellow *Davidsbündler* Feski heard the "Seid umschlungen" passage in the finale as an irresistible invitation to throw himself into the composer's open arms.[6] Nor, of course, was the frenzy merely
local. In 1856 a statue of Beethoven was installed in the Boston Music Hall,
and its inauguration marked by the reading of a long poem by William Wetmore Story.[7] Momentarily at a loss for words, Story says,

> We can only say, Great Master, take the homage of our heart;
> Be the High Priest in our temple, dedicate to thee and Art.
> Stand before us, and enlarge us with thy presence and thy power,
> And o'er all Art's deeps and shallows light us like a beacon tower.

Story's poem continues for forty-seven couplets and, it will be noted, mim-
ics the metric scheme of Schiller's "Ode to Joy."

There is more here than mere overheated rhetoric, or such fevered quotes
would be of little interest. What underlay the intense and ongoing fascination with the Ninth Symphony was the persistent belief—apparently quite
earnest—that Beethoven, like any other saint, had messages to convey from
beyond the grave. Wagner described the symphonies point-blank as "a revelation from another world." Edward Dannreuther, a serious writer in a
serious journal, described the music of the late period as touching upon
"the domain of the seer and the prophet; when, in unison with all genuine
mystics and ethical teachers, he delivers a message of religious love and
resignation—of identification with the sufferings of all living creatures, dep-
recation of self, negation of personality, release from the world."[8] It is because the figure of Beethoven, his character and his life as well as his music, was invested with religious and moral content that his works were pored
over so earnestly in search of oracles.

We learn something else about the popular view of Beethoven from the

6. Robert Schumann, *On Music and Musicians*, ed. Konrad Wolff, trans. Paul
Rosenfeld (New York: W. W. Norton, 1969), 223; J. Feski, "Gedanken unter die neunte
Symphonie von Beethoven," *Neue Zeitschrift für Musik* 4 (1836): 126.

7. Story, an American sculptor and writer, is the subject of Henry James's 1903
book *William Wetmore Story and His Friends*, and his career is the basis of
Nathaniel Hawthorne's fictional tale *The Marble Faun*.

8. Richard Wagner, "Music of the Future" (1860), in *Three Wagner Essays*, trans.
Robert L. Jacobs (London: Eulenberg, 1979), 77; Dannreuther, "Beethoven and His
Works," 197.

fact that his name is so often coupled with those of Dante and Shakespeare, not merely as great creators but as definitively established avatars of national genius.[9] This habit may in part account for Wagner's problematic relationship to Beethoven, creating as it did the suspicion that there was room for only one permanent embodiment of the German spirit, or in any event only one in music. (When Beethoven shared this place of honor it was invariably with Goethe.) Many later arguments about Wagnerism were fought out on this battlefield—the personification of genuine German art—and at the same time the Beethoven myth helped generate the perception, continentwide by the end of the century, that serious music in a very real sense *was* German music.[10]

The ideology of genius has its own byways and ramifications, of course, and many of them participate in the creation here of an oracular symphony whose message has continually to be divined. The romantic creator is one whose work "is initiated by the idea." That is, there is something transcendental at the core, underneath the eye's or ear's surface perception.

> And the purport of this idea, the dream picture of which [the artist] carries in his mind, determines the form in which it is to be realised. . . . And if ever genius has demonstrated the truth of this fact, Beethoven is that one. . . . Beethoven's most profound compositions [the last quartets and the first and third movements of the Ninth Symphony] . . . serve to prove that the highest ideas cannot be adequately realised in the types mentioned. And upon the idea everything depends; for it is the Eternal, the Infinite.[11]

This is pure idealism, Hegel out of Coleridge; it clearly invites exegesis, whose pursuit is not discouraged but rather spurred on by the concomitant realization that it can probably never be fully satisfactory: "When any work of Beethoven's is called an organism, it is obvious that if the phrase is to

9. Elaine Sisman writes about such a coupling as a similar barometer of cultural placement and reception ("Haydn, Shakespeare, and the Rules of Originality," in *Haydn and His World*, ed. Elaine Sisman [Princeton: Princeton University Press, 1997], 3–56).

10. When in 1874 George Eliot created her quintessential musician, Klesmer, her description of him as "a felicitous combination of the German, the Sclave, and the Semite" both recognized this tradition and responded provocatively to the anti-Semitic polemics rampant at the time (*Daniel Deronda*, ed. Barbara Hardy [Harmondsworth: Penguin, 1967], 77); see chapter 5. On the general topic of music and Germanness, see David Gramit, *Cultivating Music: The Aspirations, Interests, and Limits of German Musical Culture, 1770–1848* (Berkeley: University of California Press, 2002).

11. Elterlein (pseud. Ernst Gottschald), *Beethoven's Symphonies in Their Ideal Significance* (1853), trans. Francis Weber (London: W. Reeves, 1893), 87.

convey any meaning, it must signify that in point of form and musical contents Beethoven's works are as perfect as any product of nature. That is to
say, so far above any product of traditional or teachable art as to be only in-
tuitively and not logically comprehensible."[12] As we shall see further on,
later and particularly American forms of idealism took a different view of
the discoverability of nature's (and Beethoven's) secrets, as scientific advance
gave credence to prevailing mores of social progressivism.

THE IMAGE OF THE NINTH

In addition to the aura that surrounded the name of Beethoven, there are
features of the symphony itself that invited the development of a mystique
of its own.[13] From the beginning its sheer size astonished critics. At first the
length of the piece was routinely cited as a flaw; critics of the first London
performance in March 1825 complained that "the author has spun it out to
so unusual a length, that he has 'drawn out the thread of his verbosity finer
than the staple of his argument'"[14] and, in another case, that "its length alone
will be a never-failing cause of complaint to those who reject monopoly in
sounds, as it takes up exactly one hour and twenty minutes in performance."[15] But this latter critic intuited, as well, the relationship between the
piece's length and its sheer bigness of sound; he refers to "so much ram-
bling and vociferous execution given to the violins," to the "deafning bois-
terous jollity" of the concluding section in which "all the known acousti-
cal missile instruments I should conceive" are employed, and in general to
"the obstreperous roarings of modern frenzy" that the symphony typified
for him. In the long run, of course, his perception of the link between du-
ration and size of musical conception proved more prophetic than, for ex-

12. Dannreuther, "Beethoven and His Works," 197.
13. Since this essay was written, the mystique of the Ninth has continued to be
a topic of much interest to musicologists and other scholars. See in particular Scott
Burnham's review article "Our Sublime Ninth," *Beethoven Forum* 5 (1996): 156–63;
Nicholas Cook, *Beethoven: Symphony No. 9* (Cambridge: Cambridge University
Press, 1993); and David Levy, *Beethoven: The Ninth Symphony.*
14. "C," "Some Contemporary English Criticisms of Beethoven, *Monthly Musical Record* 42 (1912): 91. Apparently the original of this review was written by
William Ayrton and appeared in *Harmonicon* for March–April 1825 (see *The At-
tentive Listener: Three Centuries of Music Criticism,* ed. Harry Haskell [Princeton:
Princeton University Press, 1996], 84). The internal quotation draws on *Love's
Labour's Lost* 5.1.16–17.
15. "Beethoven's New Symphony," *The Quarterly Musical Magazine and Review* 7 (1825): 81.

ample, the German critic Herrmann Hirschbach's opinion that the piece was "zu lang ausgesponnen" simply through sheer monotony and excessive repetition.[16]

As later nineteenth-century compositions gradually became larger, as audiences became accustomed to concert-going as a mass social activity and to awed reverence as the appropriate mien in a concert hall,[17] the size of the Ninth took on a different connotation, giving it the lineaments of monumentality and making it appear prophetic. I would even argue that in a psychological sense the symphony continued to grow during the latter decades of the century. When Wagner writes in 1873 of the reorchestrations he used in his Leipzig performance of the work, his apologia rests upon the "opulence" of Beethoven's conception and suggests (reverently, of course) that the work is even larger than its composer realized it was, arguing that his deafness "led him at last to an almost naive disregard of the relation of the actual embodiment to the musical thought itself."[18] The greater number of his changes in orchestration were made to enlarge the sound of the piece in what he saw as the correct proportion to its length and spiritual conception. It is well known that this tradition, once established, was continued with ever-increasing grandiosity by other conductors, including both von Bülow and Mahler.[19]

The many references to this symphony as a message from beyond the grave, like occurrences of the term "swan song," indicate that the Ninth's position as a late work in Beethoven's oeuvre is also important to its mystique. Again and again writers make casual reference to its status as a kind of last will and testament (although they must have been aware of the later origin of the last quartets) and seem to be attempting to read it as we have lately seen Mozart's *Requiem* cinematically read, as the dramatic last utterance from a deathbed. There is a certain intrinsic quality to a late piece, perhaps based on what Janet Levy has described as the covert valuing of "maturity" in music criticism. Certainly the idea is supported by Alexandre Ouli-

16. "Beethoven's neunte Symphonie: eine Ansicht," *Neue Zeitschrift für Musik* 9 (1838): 32.

17. See Weber, "Mass Culture," passim.

18. "The Rendering of Beethoven's Ninth Symphony" (1873), in *Richard Wagner's Prose Works*, trans. William Ashton Ellis (1892; reprint, New York: Broude, 1966), 5:232, 241.

19. See Walter Damrosch, "Hans von Bülow and the Ninth Symphony," *Musical Quarterly* 13 (1927): 280–93; and Denis McCaldin, "Mahler and Beethoven's Ninth Symphony," *Proceedings of the Royal Musical Association* 107 (1980–81): 101–10.

bicheff's curious characterization of Beethoven as "old for his age" when he worked on the piece.[20]

Since present-day audiences and scholars of music history have been bequeathed a traditional account of the Ninth Symphony dominated by incomprehension of its formal innovations and outrage at the appending of a choral movement to a symphony, it may come as a surprise that not all of its contemporary critics were troubled by these anomalies. Rather, such questions were themselves at the core of the debate about the deeper meaning of the piece, and the debating parties lined up in ways quite consistent with other aspects of their ideological posture. A characterization of those who found the piece unproblematic and clearly based on traditional classical forms—this is not to say that they agreed about what those forms were—reveals the lie of the land: they were French, or anti-Wagnerians, or orthodox religionists, or what we might call "protoformalists," explicators of notes instead of messages. The anti-Wagnerian Selmar Bagge characterizes Beethoven's forms as fairly usual with some modifications, identifying the finale as a fantasy to which the composer has joined aspects of variation form. The primary category, fantasy, is significant since as a genre it has been marked by formal freedom from its beginning; thus the extreme irregularity of this movement is contained within a fixed historical tradition. Revealingly, Bagge bolsters his analysis with evidence that the symphony Beethoven left unfinished, the projected tenth, appeared from extant sketches to be purely instrumental. The contrary Wagnerian argument, of course, required the assumption that in the Ninth Beethoven had brought purely instrumental music to the limit of its possibilities, an apocalyptic arrival that in turn required the reading of the finale as innovative and entirely unprecedented, a new birth.[21] True to form, Bagge reads the spiritual message of the piece in purely orthodox terms: Beethoven's message, he says, is that only religion can bring us from earthly pain into joy—indeed, the shape of the symphony as a whole makes it clear that only those who have seen extreme pain and suffering will be rewarded on this magnificent scale (71).

An exactly similar web of argumentation is presented by Vincent d'Indy

---

20. Janet M. Levy, "Covert and Casual Values in Recent Writings about Music," *The Journal of Musicology* 5 (1987): 3–27; Alexandre Oulibicheff [or Aleksandr Ulybyshev, in the Library of Congress's transliteration], *Beethoven, ses critiques et ses glossateurs* (Leipzig: Brockhaus, 1857), 269; my translation.

21. "L. van Beethoven's Neunte Symphonie," *Allgemeine Musikalische Zeitung*, 3d ser. 12 (1877): col. 49–53, 65–71. For more on the aftermath of this interpretive dispute, see Mark Evan Bonds, *After Beethoven: Imperatives of Originality in the Symphony* (Cambridge, Mass.: Harvard University Press, 1996).

as late as 1911. He discusses the Ninth together with the *Missa solemnis*, prefacing all with an account of the religious underpinnings of Beethoven's late style: "wishing to have done with a wretched existence which no longer offers him a single exterior attraction, he turns his gaze inward, to that soul which he has ever striven to raise toward God, the Source of all that is good and beautiful. . . . And thus he comes to lead a purely introspective life, an almost monastic life, contemplative, intense, fruitful."[22]

From this reading it seems naturally to follow that "the entire aesthetics of his third manner are founded on ancient forms theretofore unemployed by him . . . a solid ancestral basis. . . . These forms are the Fugue, the Suite, the Chorale with Variations" (97). There is perhaps a touch of overkill in d'Indy's subsequent easy classification of the first movement as "constructed after an impeccable sonata plan" (114), the third as "a prayer" (115), and the "Seid umschlungen" passage as "a liturgical chant, a psalm constructed on the eighth Gregorian mode (with—possibly—a trifle less delicacy in the use of the tritone than was observed by the monkish composers of the middle ages)" (116). The point, I need not stress further, is not who was "right" about the generic assignment of this movement, but that from a particular sort of orthodox religious commitment a particular kind of analysis follows, and that is because conversations about the Ninth Symphony had been going on for so long and in such a tangled but thoroughly familiar contextual web.

Among French commentators, Berlioz provides what at first appears to be a counterexample. His discussion of the piece begins with a different—though elsewhere familiar—trope of this discourse: "To analyze such a composition is a difficult and dangerous task, and one we have long hesitated to undertake."[23] As one reads on, however, it becomes apparent that the sort of difficulty he has in mind is of the workshop variety. Beethoven's formal novelties, he argues, must occur here by "an intention as reasonable and as beautiful for the fervent Christian as for the pantheist or the atheist—in fact an intention purely musical and poetical" (44), and he then proceeds to explore the formal, harmonic, and melodic structures of the piece with a professional eye toward understanding its inner workings. This is a notion of "difficulty" and "innovation" quite distinct from that intended by the camp for whom these terms are philosophically value-laden.

---

22. Vincent d'Indy, *Beethoven: A Critical Biography*, trans. Theodore Baker (Boston: Boston Music, 1911), 92.

23. Hector Berlioz, *Beethoven: A Critical Appreciation of Beethoven's Nine Symphonies and His Only Opera*—Fidelio—*with Its Four Overtures*, comp. and trans. Ralph De Sola (Boston: Crescendo, 1975), 43.

In this latter group, deeply committed to the mystification of the symphony, are Wagnerians, romantic idealists, American transcendentalists, and those inclined to radical politics—frequently, indeed, and here is the core of the argument I expand upon below, they were apologists for a growing secular philosophy they referred to as "humanism." It is, among other things, an orientation toward a moralistic ideology of "art" as opposed to "entertainment," so that the difficulty of the piece is an important mark of moral seriousness. In a famous passage on hearing this symphony, Schumann noted a comment he attributed to Karl Voigt: "I am the blind man who is standing before the Strasbourg Cathedral, who hears its bells but cannot see the entrance."[24] By its mysteriousness, the work is elevated to a status above or beyond the comprehension of mere mortals. Lowell Mason's 1862 review of a Birmingham performance begins in this manner—"We are entirely incompetent to give any description of this composition"—and goes on to detail the implications of his disclaimer: "Who comprehends immensity and eternity? But does it follow that, therefore, these may not fill the mind with aspirations after the Infinite, the source of all perfection and happiness? We may not understand, and yet may derive great pleasure and good from the musical forms of truth, which Beethoven or others have discovered."

Difficulty is important, then, because it suggests that the piece has something to teach or convey that will repay effort, and it assures that one is not merely enjoying oneself. Perhaps the quintessential confessional statement in this mode comes from an anonymous London correspondent, "P.," to *Dwight's* in 1852: "Then came the last movement, about which I stay my pen. I did not understand it, and reverently stand in hope and faith, that its secrets may at some future day be revealed to me." So entrenched was this position vis-à-vis music that it went beyond simple spiritual experience to develop its own Puritan work ethic. Thus the British clergyman and amateur musician H. R. Haweis: "German music is . . . a truer expression, and a more disciplined expression, of the emotions. To follow a movement of Beethoven is, in the first place, a bracing exercise of the intellect."[25]

In some critical circles, however, where the complexities and formal innovations of the piece as a whole were not valued but viewed as flaws, a different tone was taken. The symphony was frequently dubbed a "mon-

24. Schumann, *On Music and Musicians*, 98.

25. Lowell Mason, "Beethoven's Ninth Symphony," *Dwight's Journal of Music* 20 (1862): 13; "P.," report from London on a performance of the Ninth conducted by Berlioz, *Dwight's Journal of Music* 1 (1852): 109; H. R. Haweis, *Music and Morals* (1871; New York: Harper and Bros., 1904), 59.

strosity," and its critics were particularly fond of inventing clever metaphors of incongruity to describe it. David Friedrich Strauss's entire reading of the piece is focused on this issue, and in a single two-page article he develops some half-dozen such images to drive home the point. He compares the piece to the dog-headed gods and man-beast creatures of myth and antiquity; he likens Beethoven to a sculptor who places a colored head atop a white marble torso; he characterizes the choral finale as a "vocal *deus ex machina*" used to rescue the composer from a musical dilemma. Hanslick called the finale "the gigantic shadow of a gigantic body," and Oulibicheff dismissed the whole as "two works joined only by a catalogue number."[26]

These epithets are prompted by the ever-present ideology of organicism, which demanded a sort of biological trueness to nature that would naturally prohibit any appearance of arbitrary constructedness. But it is an organicism folded back upon itself, belying its idealist origins (and what Stackelberg has called idealism's "contempt for material evidence")[27] and producing a criticism redolent of formalism. These writers are talking about the music, not about its message. Indeed, it is clear that the practice of quasi-biblical exegesis in connection with the Ninth enabled critics who indulged in it to construct narratives that accounted for the symphony's formal puzzlements and thus domesticated them; it was writers dealing only with the notes who had the problem, and they recognized it. David Strauss, who was a theologian and historian of religion, saw clearly that in invoking pagan images like dog-headed gods he was acknowledging "monsters" of undeniably powerful symbolic meaning to human beings; nonetheless, he says, what is symbolic and psychologically important is not necessarily artistically successful (col. 130).

For these essentially conservative writers Beethoven's mixed-media event violated not only organic principles but also tenets of the earlier (but still powerful) pure form of romanticism. In 1810, well before the composition of the Ninth, E. T. A. Hoffmann claimed Beethoven for romanticism in a gesture, Rosen and Zerner explain, designed "first, to appropriate an already acknowledged classicism and assimilate it into Romantic art; and, second, to take pure, instrumental music, the most abstract of the arts, as a model

26. David Friedrich Strauss, "Beethoven's Neunte Symphonie und ihre Bewunder: Musikalische Brief eines beschränkten Kopfes," *Allgemeine Musikalische Zeitung* 12 (1877), col. 129–33 (first published anonymously in 1853, in *Augsburger Allgemeine Zeitung*); Hanslick, *Beautiful in Music*, 57; Oulibicheff, *Beethoven*, 287; my translation.

27. Roderick Stackelberg, *Idealism Debased: From* Völkisch *Ideology to National Socialism* (Kent, Ohio: Kent State University Press, 1981), 2.

of Romantic poetry, and to claim for poetry the ability of music to create an independent world of its own—a visionary world, whose relation to the real world is always ironic, as the absolute purity of instrumental music is finally unattainable for the poet."[28] In the 1850s conservative critics could hardly help seeing at least partial failure in a symphony that Wagnerians were citing as proof of the expressive limitations of purely instrumental music.[29]

The genre confusion into which the piece threw its commentators can often be spotted in the varying constellations of names with which Beethoven's was associated by different writers as they pondered to what tradition the piece belonged.[30] The association most natural to us—Haydn, Mozart, Beethoven—appears less frequently than we might expect, not, I think, because its historical force was unrecognized but because nineteenth-century critics were less interested than we in the bald "facts" of music history and stylistic evolution. Then too, they saw the classical proportions of the two earlier composers in sharp contrast to the gigantism that had become a regular feature of Beethoven hagiography. The pseudonymous Elterlein specifically contrasts Beethoven to his two great predecessors on the grounds that, while their symphonic messages can more or less be viewed collectively—Haydn's is "pure, childlike ideality" and Mozart's "noble, harmonious humanity"—"each [of Beethoven's symphonies] represents a world in itself, with an ideal centre of its own."[31] Haydn is frequently invoked in fictional accounts of the symphony's genesis, as we shall see below, but there he appears as "Papa Haydn," clearly in the role not of professional precursor but of spiritual guide and mentor. Mozart's name is infrequent except in the most technical discussions of *thematische Arbeit;* in some circles he was suspected of too great a love of sensuous beauty.[32] British writers, not surprisingly, often couple Beethoven's name with Handel's (see, for instance, Grove), suggesting that for them the symphony could most easily be taken in in terms of the English oratorio tradition—thus si-

28. Charles Rosen and Henri Zerner, *Romanticism and Realism: The Mythology of Nineteenth-Century Art* (New York: Viking, 1984), 34.

29. See Bonds, *After Beethoven,* ch. 5.

30. Treitler's article ("History, Criticism") discusses the ways in which Beethoven's extraordinary mix of genres in the symphony functions as a set of codes for the listener. For Beethoven's contemporaries, apparently, the signals were often crossed.

31. Elterlein, *Ideal Significance,* ix.

32. A marked exception is presented by Bernard Shaw, who links Mozart and Beethoven in a particular way, as writers of what he considered serious religious music (*Shaw's Music: The Complete Musical Criticism in Three Volumes,* ed. Dan H. Laurence [New York: Dodd, Mead, 1981], 1:356).

multaneously accounting for the chorus, for the tone of moral uplift, and for the grandiosity of the spectacle.[33] This same habit of categorizing by association provided a perhaps unexpected forum for working out disputes as to the purpose and function of music. Among the most provocative of links, for example, is Dannreuther's of "Palestrina, Bach, and Beethoven"—a genealogy clearly designed to fix the piece in a religious or didactic framework.[34] The English late-century insistence upon art as primarily an instrument of moral education comes strongly to the fore here. K. R. Hennig adds a different polemical twist by speaking of "Beethoven, Schumann, Wagner"—that is, by projecting Beethoven's lineage into a specifically Wagnerian future.[35]

Hennig thus reminds us that the Ninth not only has ancestors but, in proper organic fashion, generates offspring. The monumentality and prophetic status granted the piece made its place in history a matter of serious import that was much argued over. Through the 1830s the Ninth Symphony still passed for "contemporary music," and contemporary music was still the principal concert fare, although partisan and nationalist quarrels were the order of the day. As time went on and the shift in repertory began— becoming fixed at the classical masters—language changed to reflect a set of values higher than "cutting-edge" contemporaneity: that is, Beethoven and his masterpiece gradually came to represent not only German music as a whole but the spirit of the nineteenth century as well. Teetgen says that "Beethoven ushered in the nineteenth century; he was the Napoleon of its better half,"[36] and Dannreuther makes clear some of the background and socially based reasons why this matters:

> The whole distance of the revolution and the birth of the modern spirit
> in poetry and philosophy lies between him and his predecessors. He
> was the first among musicians who distinctly felt the influence of the
> literary and social fermentation of his time. He is the first to become

33. George Grove, *Beethoven and His Nine Symphonies* (London: Novello, 1896), 369. However, the fact that the first London performances were sung in Italian perhaps suggests an early attempt to hear it in the context of opera.

34. The notorious Houston Stewart Chamberlain invokes Palestrina's name in a political context, considering him a sort of honorary German: "Palestrina follows closely in the footsteps of the men of the north" and is thus ultimately related to Beethoven (*The Foundations of the Nineteenth Century*, trans. John Lees [London: John Lane, 1912], 2:511 ff.).

35. K. R. Hennig, *Beethoven's neunte Symphonie: eine Analyse* (Leipzig: F. C. Leuckart, 1888), 8; my translation.

36. Alexander Teetgen, *Beethoven's Symphonies Critically Discussed* (London: W. Reeves, 1879), 117.

conscious of the struggles and aims of mankind *en masse*, and he is
the first musician, if not the first poet, who consciously offers himself
as the singer of humanity. Essentially a man of the 19th century, his
music reflects modern life quite as much, if not more, than Goethe's
Faust does.[37]

By the 1870s, the formerly fluid repertory having begun to congeal in
various ways around the Gibraltar that the Ninth by then presented, local
disputes and stylistic shifts had themselves become part of history. Haweis
writes that history shows us two kinds of music.

> Between the spirit of the musical Sentimentalist and the musical
> Realist there is eternal war. The contest may rage under different
> captains. At one time it is the mighty Gluck who opposed the ballad-
> mongering Piccini; at another it is the giant Handel versus the melo-
> dramatic Bononcini; or it is Mozart against all France and Italy; or
> Beethoven against Rossini, or Wagner against the world: . . . [in each
> case the issues are] false emotion, or abused emotion, or frivolous
> emotion versus true feeling, disciplined feeling, or sublime feeling.[38]

Talented at capsulizing various but related ideological strands, Haweis here
makes it clear that as of 1871 the canon is firmly in place, that its heroes are
without exception German, and that the famous Beethoven-Rossini rivalry
has become part of a consistent and intelligible teleology, one moreover that
legitimizes Wagner's claim to the historical succession. Elsewhere he deftly
brings together several of the threads of this rhetorical web—racial characterization, the moral purpose of art, the habit of reading extramusical content into musical compositions, and the need to work at it all—in one summary sentence: "It would not be difficult to show in great detail the
essentially voluptuous character of Italian music, the essentially frivolous
and sentimental character of French music, and the essentially moral,
many-sided, and philosophical character of German music" (61).

Because of Beethoven's formal innovations, and largely on the strength
of the choral finale, it was very early predicted that the Ninth would play a
decisive role in music history as the efficient cause of the demise of the instrumental symphony since it was thought to have outrun the artistic and
expressive possibilities of the genre. Sometimes Wagner is credited with
originating this notion because he harped so relentlessly on the piece as
prophetic of his *Gesamtkunstwerk*, but indeed some version of this rhetor-

---

37. Dannreuther, "Beethoven and His Works," 195.
38. Haweis, *Music and Morals*, 57. On the sense of "realism" intended here, an
essentially avant-garde aesthetic, see Rosen and Zerner, *Romanticism and Realism*.

ical trope had been around almost from the beginning, and it was often enough invoked by those who had little interest in seeing the music-drama as the symphony's natural successor. Schumann already had to contend with it in his 1835 review of Berlioz's *Symphonie fantastique*, remarking that "after Beethoven's Ninth Symphony, outwardly the greatest instrumental work, limit and proportion appeared to be exhausted." Elterlein makes use of a convenient accident of history, arguing that "there was no climax possible beyond this; the tenth symphony had, of necessity, to remain a myth."[39] Echo after echo sounds this theme: "Such was the Ninth Symphony. . . . *It had to be the last one.* . . . Another symphony could have been only a retrogression to a previous standpoint"; the piece was "un chef-d'oeuvre qui a tué le genre." Even Claude Debussy, who had little sympathy with "Wagner's highly-spiced masterpieces," remarked that "it seems to me that the proof of the futility of the symphony has been established since Beethoven."[40] It was, of course, precisely this notion that Wagner capitalized upon in his claim that the instrumental symphony was but a way-station along the evolutionary road to his *Gesamtkunstwerk*, that the Ninth proved Beethoven's acquiescence to the claim that further artistic progress could be achieved only through a new union of music and poetry: "The Last Symphony of Beethoven is the redemption of Music from out her own peculiar element into the realm of *universal Art*. . . . Beyond it no forward step is possible; for upon it the perfect Art-work of the Future alone can follow, the *universal Drama* to which Beethoven has forged for us the key."[41]

Despite the irritable dismissal of this argument by stubbornly sensible critics like Edmund Gurney—who found the idea that "Beethoven, tottering on the final Pisgah-peak of the Symphony, pointed on to the Wagnerian Opera . . . a real curiosity in the way of finding a text for a theory"[42]— nonetheless the vehemence of the controversies surrounding Wagner and the frequency with which his disciples took up this interpretation of the Ninth made this the most significant and most frequent historical assertion about the symphony's influence. It was, to a great degree, the argument that

39. Schumann, *On Music and Musicians*, 165; Elterlein, *Ideal Significance*, 79.

40. A. B. Marx, in A. E. Kroeger, "Marx's Characterization of Beethoven's Ninth Symphony," *Dwight's Journal of Music* 30 (1871): 413; Charles Vimenal, "La Neuvième symphonie de Beethoven," *L'Art* 1 (1875): 21 (my translation); Claude Debussy, *Monsieur Croche the Dilettante-Hater*, trans. B. N. Langdon Davies, in *Three Classics in the Aesthetic of Music* (New York: Dover, 1962), 17.

41. "The Artwork of the Future" (1849), in *Wagner's Prose Works*, 1:126.

42. Edmund Gurney, *The Power of Sound* (1880; New York: Basic Books, 1966), 514.

made the piece famous. Wagner's familiar call to arms is couched in the images of sexuality that were favorites of his. "Music is a woman," he said, and poetry the male begetter.[43] Therefore Beethoven's "most decisive message, at last given us by the master in his *magnum opus,* is the necessity he felt *as Musician* to throw himself into the arms of the Poet, in order to compass the act of *begetting* the true, the unfailingly real and redeeming Melody" (107). It is this generative act that produces universal "patriarchal" melody. Having thought this over for some years, Nietzsche—by now on the way to turning *contra* Wagner—responded strongly:

> What therefore shall we think of that awful aesthetic superstition that Beethoven himself made a solemn statement as to his belief in the limits of absolute music, in that fourth movement of the Ninth Symphony, yea that he as it were with it unlocked the portals of a new art . . . ? And what does Beethoven himself tell us when he has choir-song introduced by a recitative? "Alas, friends, let us intone not these tones but more pleasing and joyous ones!" More pleasing and joyous ones? For that he needed the convincing tone of the human voice, for that he needed the music of innocence in the folk-song. Not the word, but the "more pleasing" sound.[44]

READING THE NINTH AS IDEOLOGICAL TEXT

Throughout the century, writers continually commented on the fact that exegesis of the Ninth was the standard procedure; those more inclined to "analysis" (there were some, although they were relatively rare compared to readers of "ideal content") naturally abhorred it, and it is clear from their bitter complaints that they heard a lot of it. In 1835 Schumann satirized the practice—already rampant—in the well-known "Mardi-Gras Speech by Florestan":

> these Beethovenians . . . said "That was written by our Beethoven, it is a German work—the finale contains a double fugue. . . . " Another chorus joined in: "The work seems to contain the different genres of poetry, the first movement being epic, the second comedy, the third lyric, the fourth (combining all), the dramatic." Still another bluntly began to praise the work as being gigantic, colossal, comparable to the Egyptian pyramids. And others painted word pictures: the symphony expresses the story of mankind—first the chaos—then the call of God

43. *Opera and Drama* (1851), in *Wagner's Prose Works,* 2:111.
44. "On Music and Words" (1871), trans. M. A. Mügge, in *The Complete Works of Friedrich Nietzsche* (Edinburgh: Foulis, 1909–13), 2:38.

"there shall be light"—then the sunrise over the first human being, ravished by such splendor—in one word, the whole first chapter of the Pentateuch in this symphony.

I became angrier and quieter.[45]

A few years later, Berlioz insisted upon attempting to discuss the piece "without prying" into the composer's mind. As might be expected, the ever-growing exegetic literature provided a natural target for the acid-tongued Hanslick, who described one such account as giving "an exhaustive description of the significance of the 'subject' of each of the four parts and their profound symbolism—but about the *music itself* not a syllable is said. This is highly characteristic of a whole school of musical criticism, which, to the question whether the music is beautiful, replies with a learned dissertation on its profound meaning." By Debussy's time it was no exaggeration to say, as he did, that the piece "has been subjected to such transcendental interpretations, that even such a powerful and straightforward work as this has become a universal nightmare."[46]

Exegeses or "programs" of the Ninth fall roughly into four categories: search narratives, creation myths, accounts that interpret the piece as autobiographical on Beethoven's part, and those that content themselves with more general assessments of moral instruction. There are several features, though, that all have in common. For one thing, they assume a phenomenal stance: all are focused tightly on the experience of hearing the piece, not on "score study." Second, it can be argued, as I will below, that all of them finally belong to that last category—that is, all reflect ideological commitments of one sort or another, and these are overwhelmingly of a moral or religious nature.

The most familiar type is generally psychological narratives of varying degrees of sophistication; this bent seems fitting to the depth and seriousness of the piece and accords with the belief that the composer is the bearer of an important message for the listener. Most of them resemble literary quest narratives and appear to be retrospectively prompted by the opening of the last movement.[47] That is, Beethoven's search for "more pleasing and joyous tones" was generalized backward to the symphony as a whole, as John Sullivan Dwight somewhat ingenuously explains:

45. Schumann, *On Music and Musicians,*100.
46. Berlioz, *Beethoven,* 143; Hanslick, *Beautiful in Music,* 179; Debussy, *Monsieur Croche,* 62.
47. But Anthony Newcomb identifies such a plot archetype as common in discussions of nineteenth-century symphonies ("Once More 'Between Absolute and Program Music': Schumann's Second Symphony," *19th-Century Music* 7 [1984]: 233–50).

It is in this first movement that one feels the pledge and prophecy
of something grand, extraordinary, that is yet to come. We know no
music which seems so pregnant with a future as this, teeming with
more than it has means to utter, and foreshadowing a solution, such
as came to Beethoven in that fourth or Choral movement. It is this first
Movement that requires and justifies the last and finds its explanation
there.[48]

Because of this feature, the narrative format could usually serve to explain
many of the symphony's formal anomalies. The technique, however, cut both
ways. Berlioz's refusal to engage in such interpretation enabled him to see—
though not to solve—the problem of the finale's double exposition, a mystery that remains opaque in most programs because it seemed to make no
sense in terms of a psychological or spiritual quest. Consequently it was usually ignored altogether except, ironically, by the universally recognized father of the entire genre. It was Wagner's absolute confidence in his own theory of the *Gesamtkunstwerk* that enabled him to describe that first successful
arrival at the "Ode to Joy" tune as "the ultimate attempt to phrase by instrumental means alone a stable, sure, unruffled joy: but the rebel rout appears incapable of that restriction; like a raging sea it heaps its waves, sinks
back, and once again, yet louder than before, the wild chaotic yell of un-
slaked passion storms our ear."[49]

While all the narrative accounts are profoundly moralistic in tone, sharp
religious and political differences turn up in the definition of *what* joy is
found at the end of the search. Wagner's 1846 program is unquestionably
the prototype and often acknowledged as such by subsequent writers (it was
widely translated, available in English and French fairly soon after publication and in Italian by the 1890s). His story—the bulk of whose content, interestingly, is contained in quotations from *Faust*—is of the "Titanic struggle" of a heroic soul. In the first movement the soul wrestles defiantly against
fate; in the second, momentarily fleeing from despair, it participates in an
orgy of ultimately futile earthly jollities. In the slow movement the soul
muses on the innocent joys of early childhood and is gradually able to move
from melancholy to a new resolve to continue the struggle. Finally, urged
on by the instrumental hint of what prize might be won, the soul determines to join battle afresh and is ultimately rewarded with the attainment
of ecstasy "with God to consecrate our universal love."

48. [John Sullivan Dwight], "Mr. Zerrahn's Beethoven Night," *Dwight's Journal of Music* 14 (1859): 414.
49. "Report on the Performance of Beethoven's Ninth Symphony at Dresden"
(1846), in *Wagner's Prose Works*, 7:252; it includes the program.

Elterlein provides a very close paraphrase of this program, though his is even more combative in tone. His stubborn "soul" is throughout hungry for fresh battle; in the finale he hears "stalwart youths . . . eager to perform heroic deeds," and their reward is "sublime ecstasy in the beatitude of God's presence." In these accounts we hear the romantic cult of personal suffering along with a markedly militaristic tone, but they are religiously traditional, interpreting Schiller's text as though with a singular God instead of plural gods, beatitude instead of dithyrambic celebration. G. A. Schmitt, however, follows the familiar path to a different, quintessentially secular, conclusion. He makes the pattern of his narrative explicit, describing each middle movement as not satisfying the problems raised by the first, because "not devotion alone can make us happy . . . but more is wanted. An active religion of good works to all men being the leading idea of all the subsequent parts, the motive of the Hymn to Joy is now stated." The governing idea of the piece, Schmitt says, is "an idea which is the polar star of all human aspirations: HUMANITY; human happiness, brotherly love to all men," and the choral finale thus represents "the apotheosis of Humanity by an invocation of its tutelar deity: JOY."[50]

What is particularly interesting about Schmitt's discussion of the piece, which extended over several issues of *Dwight's Journal*, is that these programmatic and hortatory assertions appear freely interwoven among purely technical sentences whose purpose is the dissection of theme from motive, phrase from section; to Schmitt, as apparently to his audience, there was no distinction between the two modes of approach that would accord superior explanatory status or validity to one over the other. Willy Pastor's 1890 account—more purely programmatic—is particularly detailed, matching individual themes, phrases, and modulations to individual lines in the interior monologue; a psychodrama with a pungent fin-de-siècle flavor: "Various fates befall [the] hero. That eternally unsolved, painful riddle of creation, doubt in God and longing after inner peace, lead him to seek solitude. But there he finds only despair. In order to deaden his pain, he throws himself into the maelstrom of life. But that too cannot satisfy him. Disconsolate, he turns again to solitude and now, finally, he finds what he sought." The name of this psychological drama, Pastor says, is *Der Mensch unter den Menschen*, and its hero is the human spirit.[51]

50. Elterlein, *Ideal Significance*, 74; G. A. Schmitt, "The Motives and Themes of Beethoven's Ninth Symphony," *Dwight's Journal of Music* 14 (1859): 411, 410.
51. Willy Pastor, "Beethoven's 'Neunte': Versuch einer Deutung," *Musikalisches Wochenblatt* 21 (1890): 313. I am grateful to Philipp Naegele for assistance with the translation.

Sir George Grove's book on the Beethoven symphonies, read to this day by students and music lovers, focuses on thematic analysis; but, like Schmitt, Grove is perfectly comfortable supporting and explaining his technical description with programmatic evidence:

> a remarkable passage occurs in which Beethoven passes in review each of the preceding three movements, as if to see whether either [sic] of them will suit for his *Finale*. . . . Hitherto, in the three orchestral movements, Beethoven has been depicting "Joy" in his own proper character: first, as part of the complex life of the individual man; secondly, for the world at large; thirdly, in all the ideal hues that art can throw over it. He has now to illustrate what Schiller intended in his Ode.[52]

Continuing on, he describes the so-called *Schreckensfanfare* as "an impersonation of the opposite to all that is embodied in the 'Ode to Joy.' But this time the rebuke of the prophet finds an articulate voice, and Beethoven addresses us in his own words." It is as though the elaborately worked-out midcentury narratives have been distilled into a set of capsule associations so taken for granted that they serve as synonyms for structural description.

In the catalog of exegetic excess mentioned by Schumann in connection with the Ninth Symphony, the creation myth is a prominent one. Although at times its language turns up in other narrative accounts, still it forms a distinct type in the literature searching for the meaning of the piece. Thayer first heard the symphony in Berlin in 1854, the three instrumental movements alone in two separate performances and, shortly thereafter, the whole.[53] From the beginning, he described the opening movement as a void, a "strange, empty humming" across which electrical sparks shoot, "awakening life in the mass." His program, as it develops, follows the life cycle of a kind of homunculus or created being that, starting as a clod of earth, reaches full manhood by Beethoven's creative genius. Like other critics, Thayer uses the structure of his narrative to account for certain formal aspects of the piece, in particular the sequence of emotional states that seems to him appropriate for the development of the newly vivified being: "Poor humanized clod! Beaten back in all quarters, he may well despair of finding that Joy which he seeks. The trouble how-

---

52. Grove, *Beethoven and His Nine Symphonies*, 372.

53. This unsigned article in *Dwight's Journal* is identified by Michael Ochs as being the work of Thayer ("A. W. Thayer, the Diarist, and the Late Mr. Brown: A Bibliography of Writings in *Dwight's Journal of Music*," in *Beethoven Essays: Studies in Honor of Elliot Forbes*, ed. Lewis Lockwood and Phyllis Benjamin [Cambridge, Mass.: Harvard University Press, 1984]: 78–95).

ever is in himself. He must pass through still another state before he attains the goal." (124)

At the arrival of the finale, Thayer exults: "This clod is now capable of Joy. Is this not Beethoven's philosophy? Could Kant desire a better?" Thayer here develops at full length a metaphor more casually introduced by A. B. Marx, who likened the opening of the symphony to "lightning-flashes of a new birth." A similar story is tartly reported by Chrysander in his description—part of a review—of a program published in 1870:

> In the first movement Hr. Hoffman is led down a primeval path. The second and third movements "represent the destinies of the world" which, of course, ultimately represents a dying one. . . . [W]e enter "the region of the beyond" . . . the author seeks a speculative philosophy of life in Beethoven, and in taking that path he confuses metaphysics with fantasy.[54]

Another school of thought considered the work to represent the reflection, more or less unmediated, of the composer's biography or psychic experience—as Ambros put it, Beethoven's works were seen as "types of the powerful life of his soul." This is a pattern of thought into which the more guarded assessments of the piece naturally fell, since biographical facts could be used to explain or account for idiosyncrasies of compositional strategy. Oulibicheff, although he appreciated the magnitude of Beethoven's torments and remarked that the late works show him engaged in a "constant tortured self-interrogation," like Hamlet, ultimately judged that the tortures overcame the musical genius. Not all agreed, however. It was also possible to read Beethoven's message itself as autobiographical : that is, the symphony became his way of acting as a spiritual model for his admirers. Here is Vimenal's account:

> It is not surprising that the idea of joy should stir in Beethoven's mind at this time, if one imagines how little of it was his to savor. . . . Deafness, isolation, family troubles, lack of money, artistic deceptions, the indignation of a genius if not unrecognized at least abandoned, anger at the crowds who enthusiastically pursued Italian music, preferring *Tancred* to *Fidelio*, such were Beethoven's joys at this date. . . . Thence, doubtless, the joyous finale which crowns a symphony where melancholy dominates; thence these three first parts darkened in design and anticipating only blackness, not only to give by contrast more intensity

54. Kroeger, "Marx's Characterization," 394; [Chrysander, Friedrich], "Ein Programm zu Beethovens Neunter Symphonie [in Berlin, 1870]," *Allgemeine Musikalische Zeitung*, 3d ser. 6 (1871): 72–73.

to the joy of the finale, but also to oppose to this ideal tableau the aspirations of the unhappy poet . . . the real tableau of his life.[55]

I include one lengthy quotation from Marx, in order to make clear the seriousness of this interpretive pursuit. The artistic and moral role Beethoven played during the later nineteenth century, coupled with the secularization of society and the ubiquity of religious skepticism, made the great symphony as obvious and significant a source of moral instruction as the lives of the saints had once been.

> The first movement of every Symphony is decisive as to the thought of the whole work; it is particularly so decisive in the Ninth. And what has it uttered? The endless complaint of everlasting dissatisfaction, which accompanies in his own realm of the world of instruments Him, who filled and invigorated it with his mighty soul! Even though those voices of the instruments charm all nature together, even though they whisper into our ears sweet spirit tones, or sweep down from heaven like the greeting of angels to men: still man always needs, above all, Man; and the voice of man is to man the most dear, most deeply felt, most comprehensible music. This is universal truth; and this truth arose to the consciousness of Beethoven in the world of instruments that he had so mightily peopled.
>
> Then came the time to separate. And if, mayhap—as we cannot know—a presentiment of his death touched the noble man, it must have helped to awaken that consciousness and united with it. Was not he solitary in the loud world of man as he was solitary in the world of his instruments and musical visions? And his open, loving, altogether harmless soul so yearned for the dear companionship of man! This sense of brotherhood and love of men, how it penetrates all his works, his letters, and even shines through his attacks of suspicion, jealousy and injustice!
>
> Thus the external resolve to give to his Symphony a new formation by appending to it a final chorus, became an internal necessity. That which was a general truth and a particular life experience of Beethoven, became now the ruling idea of the Ninth Symphony.[56]

Somewhat in this same vein, the Ninth gave rise to an apparently unique fictional genre, a collection of originary myths focusing on that work itself. What is remarkable about these stories—apart from the fact that they were written for adult readers and published in journals specific to the mu-

55. August Wilhelm Ambros, "The Ethical and Religious Force in Beethoven," trans. KGW, *Dwight's Journal of Music* 30 (1871): 417; Oulibicheff, *Beethoven* (my translation); Vimenal, "La Neuvième symphonie," 21.
56. Kroeger, "Marx's Characterization," 395.

sically literate—is their reliance upon fictions of divine intervention to explain the genesis of the symphony. In one, Beethoven is visited in his room by a procession of "good and evil spirits," at one extreme Satan, who offers to aid in the composition for his usual fee—Beethoven marks crosses in his manuscript to ward him off—and at the other a benign father who "bears a remarkable resemblance to papa Haydn" and does finally prove helpful.[57] Another (also featuring Haydn prominently) hangs upon Beethoven's temptation to the sin of despair and his rescue by the brief, miraculous restoration of his hearing; as the sounds of spring momentarily surround him, a shepherd's pipe plays the chorale "Freu' dich sehr," and the idea for the great symphony is born.[58] A third tale symbolizes Beethoven's compositional genius with an apparently withered rosebush that miraculously flowers when the composer's hand touches it, thus reassuring him that his great gift still lives. A year later, says the author, the symphony was performed.[59]

The reader will have observed that all of these programmatic accounts, despite their varying narrative types or degree of particularity of imagery, all ultimately concern themselves with moral polemics of one sort or another. There seem to be, among these writers, both the assumption and the deep-seated hope that the great soul of Beethoven has lessons to teach that modern man would ignore at his peril. The programs may have served to "coat the pill" or make the moral message apparently inarguable through coordinated musical analysis, but some writers preferred to go right to the heart of the matter, moral instruction undiluted by fable. These discussions tend to come late in the century and have a slight air of desperation. By the 1870s, it was impossible to ignore the serious crisis in which orthodox religious practice found itself, or the pervasive feeling of moral rootlessness it left behind. Conservative critics by and large gave up efforts at subtlety, straightforwardly marching Beethoven into the pulpit. Niecks is said to have characterized the symphony as "a musical exposition of Beethoven's phi-

---

57. "Die 'Neunte Sinfonie' von Beethoven: eine phantastische Definition," *Neue Musik-Zeitung* 6 (1885): 105.

58. "Die Neunte: eine Phantasie." *Deutsche Musiker-Zeitung* 20 (1889): 35–63, 47–48. This story appeared in a separate "women's section" of the journal, a regular feature titled *Mildwide: Für die Frauen, durch die Frauen*. Tusa observes that this chorale tune was frequently mentioned as a source or reference for the "Ode to Joy" melody (*"Noch einmal,"* 116).

59. M. Frey,"Zur Vorgeschichte von Beethovens neunter Sinfornie," *Bär: Berlinische Blätter für vaterländische Geschichte und Alterthumskunde* 24 (1898): 31–34.

losophy."[60] Bagge in 1876 offers a rather detailed reading of the pictures painted by the symphony, in the traditional programmatic mode, but concludes that the piece is not merely or fundamentally a musical experience but a spiritual one; Beethoven demonstrates, he says, that religion lifts us from pain to joy. K. R. Hennig, whose aesthetic approach involves the discovery and explication of a *Gesamtidee* for each musical work, expresses the core idea of the Ninth as a set of commandments or "precepts," one provided in each movement:

I. Man's life should be a noble struggle for virtue, despite all the powers of fate.

II. Man can with discretion enjoy the delights of life but not become too caught up in them.

III. Man should be submissive even before the loss of whatever love he finds on earth.

IV. Above the stars lives a loving father who calls us his children and who wants us all to reach out the hand of reconciliation to one another in brotherly love. This is the greatest happiness.[61]

As late as 1911 Vincent d'Indy still expresses his certainty that the piece is not "a revolutionary apology for liberty," as some were claiming, but that religious faith and the presence of God in one's life are "what one must see in the Choral Symphony, if it be considered with the eyes of the soul."[62] What matters is what the alternatives were, as seen by one who was a professional composer himself: politics or religion, an orthodox or a secular moral message, but never merely music.

THE NINETEENTH-CENTURY SITUATION AND THE CONFLICTING MESSAGES OF THE NINTH

Interpretive traditions such as these grew up during the nineteenth century because the pervasive spirit of romantic and idealist aesthetic philosophies suggested that works of art bore hidden meanings behind their surfaces and carried important messages for the conduct of human life. They grew up in particularly luxuriant proliferation around the Ninth Symphony because,

---

60. Quoted without reference by Edith A. H. Crashaw in "Wagner and the Ninth Symphony," *Musical Times* 66 (1925): 1090–91.

61. Bagge, "L. van Beethoven," 71; Hennig, *Beethoven's neunte*, 88.

62. D'Indy, *Beethoven*, 116.

as we have seen, it had certain formal properties that confirmed its oracular status and because it occupied a particularly portentous place in the oeuvre of the composer who came to be both saint and hero to the century as a whole. I would like now to elaborate upon the issues that were debated within the criticism of the piece: that is, the ideological principles, often at great variance with one another, to which Beethoven was called as witness. As is well known, the century was one of enormous and continual upheaval in all the arenas in which humans customarily act according to received beliefs and common assumptions—politics, social relations, religion, standards of ethical behavior. For my present purposes, I argue that all ultimately boiled down to religious faith and matters of morality; this is so because the arts themselves tended during the nineteenth century to be viewed religiously and became, for some, a substitute for religious orthodoxies they considered outworn. Houston Chamberlain wrote that "music alone has made possible the natural religion of the soul, and that in the highest degree by the development which culminated at the beginning of the nineteenth century in Beethoven."[63]

The Challenge from Science

In many respects the intellectual challenges of the period focused on religious traditions. The discoveries of science seemed to conspire in destabilizing the authority of scripture; the names of Charles Darwin and Charles Lyell are those most frequently mentioned, but evolutionary explanations gradually appeared in all disciplines, perhaps most strikingly in the social sciences. Herbert Spencer and August Comte, beginning from different contexts, both ended by asserting that human societies were evolving even as the biological species and predicated their views of the future on the eventual, inevitable transformation of theistic religion into a new "religion of humanity." Thus belief in social "progress" came to imply atheism. One of George Eliot's critics, defending her against charges of immorality provoked by her expressed atheism, explains this connection quite clearly:

> She is perhaps the first great *godless* writer of fiction that has appeared in England; perhaps, in the sense in which we use the expression, the first that has appeared in Europe. . . . Now among the vast changes that human thought has been undergoing, the sun that we once all walked by has for many eyes become extinguished; and every energy has been bent upon supplying man with a substitute. . . . The new object of our

63. Chamberlain, *Foundations of the Nineteenth Century*, 561.

duty is not our Father which is in Heaven, but our brothers and our children who are on earth.[64]

For a while, it was possible to retain a relatively orthodox religious stance in the face of scientific challenge, seeing "natural philosophy" as working in the service of religious revelation, but the posture was a tenuous one. An anonymous correspondent to *Dwight's Journal* in October 1852 complained of German bias in the publication and demanded that the editor purge the journal of "German mysticism and Boston transcendentalism"—a juxta-position right on the mark, of course, since both were offspring of the same idealist philosophical tradition.[65] Nor is it insignificant that the letter was signed "Giustizia," written no doubt by a disgruntled Rossini fan playing out in yet another forum the fanatic rivalry between north and south that pervaded musical conversations everywhere at midcentury.

Dwight's editor answered, somewhat huffily, that these charges were mere "vulgar catchwords" and that the paper espoused no metaphysical po-sition, a rather disingenuous response given his own connection with Brook Farm and his writings for its journal, *The Harbinger*.[66] Indeed, a year later *Dwight's* carried an account of the Ninth Symphony by Lowell Mason that went far to substantiate "Giustizia's" charge. Judging the piece to be as yet inexplicable, Mason invokes other similarly imponderable entities—the sun and moon, electricity, the ocean, a tempest—that nonetheless "have great moral power over man," and he manages to work truth, beauty, and good-ness all into the next two sentences. That inclusion of "electricity" gives a typically American flavor to this discussion; Mason three times invokes the benevolent face of science in the course of his essay, once as the force that will eventually reveal God to us and once, by analogy, as that which Beethoven had discovered in the realm of music. This is the language that Leo Marx has called "the rhetoric of the technological sublime," as it occurs in the writings of Whitman and Emerson. Like Mason, Emerson believed,

64. Unsigned review in the *Edinburgh Review* 150 (1879): 557–86, quoted in David Carroll, ed., *George Eliot: The Critical Heritage* (London: Routledge and Kegan Paul, 1971), 453.

65. "P.," report from London, 109. Leo Marx comments that "Germanic" was a common epithet in America during this period, "calculated to evoke memories of Goethe and other vaguely disreputable poets with curious manners and an unreal-istic, freewheeling, metaphysical turn of mind" (*The Machine in the Garden: Tech-nology and the Pastoral Ideal in America* [New York: Oxford University Press, 1964], 218).

66. In this connection, see Christopher Hatch, "The Education of A. W. Thayer," *Musical Quarterly* 42 (1956): 355–65.

according to an 1843 entry in his journal, that "Machinery and Transcendentalism agree well."[67]

It was Mason's contemporary, the great American Beethoven apologist Alexander Wheelock Thayer, who fixed this imagery in its most vivid form in the course of the creation scenario we have encountered above—though, as so often happens in this literature, using a similar argument to come to the opposite philosophical stance, abandoning Mason's theistic conclusion. It is in the mysterious opening of the first movement, "like the humming of a wheel in a room full of machinery," that the miracle happens:

> Mark how the animal becomes vivified, how passion arises, how troubles encompass him, and he finds himself surrounded with difficulties against which he must struggle. The clod is a man![68]

Is there a reader of English anywhere for whom these words are not redolent of another, more familiar text, one in its way as canonic in our culture as the Ninth itself?

> It was on a dreary night of November, that I beheld the accomplishment of my toils. With an anxiety that almost amounted to agony, I collected the instruments of life around me, that I might infuse a spark of being into the lifeless thing that lay at my feet. It was already one in the morning; the rain pattered dismally against the panes, and my candle was nearly burnt out, when, by the glimmer of the half-extinguished light, I saw the dull yellow eye of the creature open; it breathed hard, and a convulsive motion agitated its limbs.[69]

For this "modern Prometheus," as for *his* hapless clod, we know that there was no final transcendence into joy. The change in tone is created by both geographical and temporal distance, as well as by a pronounced shift in religious commitment. Mary Shelley's is a cautionary tale about scientific overreaching, a "tower of Babel" story of human hubris, written in 1818 and reflecting conventional Christian values as well as early-romantic unease about the darkly secret activities behind laboratory doors. By 1854, and particularly across the Atlantic, scientific advance had been comfortably accommodated into current visions of a universal social and spiritual progress based upon human learning and accomplishment. Thayer does not use this imagery disparagingly—for him it does not render the piece "artificial" or "monstrous," as other commentators so colorfully had it. Rather, the im-

67. Leo Marx, *Machine in the Garden*, 222, 232.
68. Mason, "Beethoven's Ninth," 124.
69. Mary Wollstonecraft Shelley, *Frankenstein, or The Modern Prometheus* (1818 text) (New York: Pocket/Simon and Schuster, 1976), 58–59.

agery excites him, and he is filled with the same salvific optimism in whose grip Mason assures us that science will one day reveal to us the face of God. Beethoven, we gather, had already acquired this understanding.

The Challenge from Politics

Not only scientific progress and social evolutionary theories but political developments had religious implications, as various socialisms and communal living experiments arose at least partially in response to the perceived failures of orthodox Christianity to solve social ills. Again, Beethoven faithfully continued to provide the necessary moral perspective. Berlioz noticed a new feature appearing in French attitudes toward Beethoven in the 1840s: "A certain religious element appears [in Beethoven criticism], dimly indicated, but of so special a kind that it seems to point to new implications. This strain of thought appears to be influenced by ideas originating in the circle of Saint-Simon."[70] That the connection of music to political commitment and activism was taken quite seriously is revealed in Ford Madox Ford's comment about Wagnerian music, that in some circles it was suspect as "atheistic, sexually immoral, and tending to further socialism and the throwing of bombs."[71]

The ideology of "difficulty," a feature of late-romantic aesthetic philosophy I noted above, presents some complications in a school of thought that at the same time bore a commitment to democratic or even socialist values. How could the writer with such values avoid the charge of elitism, of creating a priestly inner circle uniquely capable of penetrating music's mysteries? To put it the other way round, how could one attribute high artistic value to a piece of music that anybody could understand and enjoy? Richard Wagner prefaced his programmatic description of the piece by explaining that he would not even try to help the audience to a real understanding of the piece "since that could come from nothing save an inner intuition" but that he would offer some hints since its scheme "might easily escape the less-prepared and therefore readily-bewildered hearer." When the New York correspondent for *Dwight's Journal* reported on a performance by Theodore Thomas in 1866, his pleasure in the piece seems to have been genuinely disturbed by worries about "how many among the audience were capable of really comprehending the work they had just heard?"[72] The priestly ideology of romanticism is summed up in a comment of Leo Schrade expressing a view largely, but by no means exclusively, French: "The French romantics never attributed to Beethoven's work an appeal to the masses, precisely because of their view of music and what constituted the power to be moved by it. Such appeal was reserved for the political interpretations to come."[73]

Even so, as late as 1893 so politically inclined a figure as George Bernard Shaw still had trouble reconciling the exalting of difficulty with democratic social commitments. "Mass taste" was not yet quite so easily dismissed as it later became. Shaw wrote of the Ninth:

> How far the work has become really popular it would be hard to determine, because . . . so many people come whenever it is in the bills, not to enjoy themselves, but to improve themselves. To them the culmination of its boredom in an Ode to Joy must seem a wanton mockery, since they always hear it for the first time; for a man does not sacrifice himself in that way twice, just as he does not read Daniel Deronda twice, and consequently . . . he never becomes sufficiently familiar with it to delight in it.[74]

His observation sounds the familiar theme of the piece's difficulty, but at the same time acknowledges the social grounding of bourgeois concert-going and the regnant ideology of self-improvement through art. Simply complaining about philistinism did not acknowledge the complexity of the situation. His reference to *Daniel Deronda* is telling: not only is George Eliot's last novel intimately concerned with fashions and polemics in music, but it was received with language remarkably like that addressed to the Ninth. Also a late work, a particularly large one, and one instantly tagged as formally incoherent and difficult, it served as a locus for the same arguments we have been encountering. (Is its religious vision orthodox or humanistic? Does it rely on traditional formal types or on radical innovation? What is its message, its moral lesson?) Among late-century English critics, it is not unusual to find Eliot's name linked to Beethoven's on the same grounds that Shaw invokes, as in this representative passage from an 1877 review:

> The manner of few great artists—if any—becomes simpler as they advance in their career, that is, as their ideas multiply, as their emotions

---

72. Wagner, "Report on the Performance," 247; F. L. Ritter, untitled concert review, *Dwight's Journal of Music* 25 (1866): 358.
73. Schrade, *Beethoven in France*, 43.
74. *Shaw's Music*, 2:825–26.

receive more numerous affluents from other parts of their being, and as the vital play of their faculties with one another becomes swifter and more intricate. The later sonatas of Beethoven still perplex facile and superficial musicians. The later landscapes of Turner still bewilder and amaze the profane . . . when the sustained *largo* of the sentences of *Daniel Deronda* is felt after the crude epigrammatic smartness of much of the writing in *Scenes of Clerical Life* we perceive as great a difference and as decided a preponderance of gain over loss.[75]

Ironically, the Ninth Symphony contains within itself an exemplary case of the elite/philistine conflict, in the "Ode to Joy" theme of its finale. Early in the century, that melody's anomalous character—deliberately archaic in style, closed, symmetrical, simpler than anything in its environment—proved problematic to the critics, who heard it as stylistically inappropriate.[76] An early English writer called it "one of the most extraordinary instances I have ever witnessed, of great powers of mind and wonderful science, wasted upon subjects infinitely beneath its strength." Writing satirically about critical reaction to a different piece, Robert Schumann indicates that he has heard this many times before; "you will think it common, unworthy of a Beethoven, like the melody to *Freude, schöne Gotterfunken* in the D minor symphony" (105). Later, the "political interpretations" mentioned by Schrade began to come to the fore and lent the tune's simplicity a different social meaning.[77] After midcentury, idealist philosophy began to appear in quasi-populist form in so-called *völkisch* political ideology (a particularly although not exclusively German phenomenon, as was idealism itself) that Roderick Stackelberg has described as "the marriage of idealism and nationalism," one of "diverse movements of cultural revitalization whose goal it was to eliminate foreign influence and revive traditional values."[78] We are perhaps only too familiar with the later political ramifications of this phenomenon; in the history of music, though, what seems to matter is that the currency of this ideology fed into a set of nationalistic musical controversies already long ongoing. They were not particularly sinister, but they were vociferous and easily heated to the boiling point. During and

75. Edward Dowden in *Contemporary Review* 39 (1877): 348–69, quoted in Carroll, *Critical Heritage*, 444.

76. Both of the interpretive traditions for the tune discussed by Tusa ("*Noch einmal,*" 116), folk melody or hymn, carry a populist flavor.

77. "Beethoven's New Symphony," 81; Schumann, *On Music and Musicians*, 105. Caryl Clark shows how the tune's social meaning continues to change with political circumstances, though never, apparently, to diminish ("Forging Identity: Beethoven's "Ode" as European Anthem," *Critical Inquiry* 23 [1997]: 789–98).

78. Stackelberg, *Idealism Debased*, 6, 9.

shortly after his lifetime Beethoven had been the standard-bearer in the struggle against the popularity of Italian music, especially the operas of Rossini and Bellini. George Eliot precisely captures the atmosphere of argumentation when she puts this polemic into the mouth of her musician, Klesmer:

> that music you sing [Bellini] is beneath you. It is a form of melody which expresses a puerile state of culture—a dandling, canting, see-saw kind of stuff—the passion and thought of people without any breadth of horizon. There is a sort of self-satisfied folly about every phrase of such melody: no cries of deep, mysterious passion—no conflict—no sense of the universal. It makes men small as they listen to it.[79]

The search for the national roots of a culture, in which its traditional values were presumably to be found, lent Beethoven's simple tune a newly prophetic and oracular aura. Wagner, whose politics with regard to populist values were unclear a best, led the way:

> That patriarchal melody—as I shall continue to call it, in token of its historic bearings . . . shows itself wholly confined to the tone-family ties which rule the movements of the old national *Volkslied*. It contains as good as *no* modulation, and appears in so marked a simplicity of key, that in it the aim of the musician, to go back upon the historic fount of Music, is spoken out without disguise.[80]

The same *völkisch* values are expressed in 1855 by Thayer,

> Again the simplicity of the tune which follows, and its perfectly popular character, was most striking and astonishing. But then as one reflects upon it, it is just what it should be, for it is the outpouring of the JOY of all the brotherhood of Man. Highly wrought, artistic (in the common acceptation) music would be out of place; but this, so popular in its form, may well be the expression of the universal feeling.[81]

and by A. B. Marx in 1859, who calls it "that simple people's melody. For that which is most profound and grand finds at all times its last sanctification and confirmation in the heart and mouth of the people."[82] And so, turn by turn, the tune and the politics provide support and context for each other.

The frequent invocation of "the people" brings to mind the nationalist

---

79. Eliot, *Daniel Deronda*, 79. See chapter 5.
80. Wagner, "Opera and Drama," 2:289.
81. [Alexander Wheelock Thayer,] "Diary Abroad, No. 8," *Dwight's Journal of Music* 6 (1855): 124.
82. A. B. Marx, *Ludwig von Beethoven: Leben und Schaffen* (Berlin: [Otto Janke?], 1859), 412.

strains so common in both aesthetics and politics during the century. As is well known, the argument sometimes turned vicious, particularly in its Wagnerian form. Beethoven, said Wagner, had been crucial in the struggle to rescue German music from Jewish and ultramontane corruption. He

> again raised music, that had been degraded to a merely diverting art, to the height of its sublime calling, he has led us to understand the nature of that art, from which the world explains itself to every consciousness as distinctly as the most profound philosophy could explain it to a thinker well versed in abstract conceptions. *And the relation of the great Beethoven to the German nation is based upon this alone.*[83]

In its classic form, the response to this polemic is that of Nietzsche, who thought little of what passed for German culture in his lifetime and was far more concerned to make of Beethoven a type of the universal human spirit.

> Beethoven is the intermediate event between an old mellow soul that is constantly breaking down, and a future over-young soul that is always coming; there is spread over his music the twilight of eternal loss and eternal extravagant hope—the same light in which Europe was bathed when it dreamed with Rousseau, when it danced round the Tree of Liberty of the Revolution, and finally almost fell down in adoration before Napoleon.[84]

The Challenge from Theology

Another challenge to religious orthodoxy in the nineteenth century came, ironically enough, from theology itself. Biblical scholars began to study scripture "scientifically" in keeping with modern historical and philological methods. When their investigations did not yield the sorts of authenticity that literal-minded religious faith required, some responded by taking an evolutionary view quite in keeping with Spencer's or Comte's. They began to characterize traditional religion as a phase through which humanity passed on its way to a more comprehensive, nonsectarian religion of moral probity. The works of Feuerbach and of David Freidrich Strauss—especially the latter's *Das Leben Jesu kritisch bearbeitet,* which appeared in 1836— created storms of controversy. This is the same Strauss whose characterization of the Ninth as "monstrous" we have encountered earlier; his critique of the piece first appeared anonymously in 1853 in the *Augsburger Allgemeine Zeitung.* His assessment of it rests on an extremely subtle con-

---

83. *Beethoven: With a Supplement from the Philosophical Works of Arthur Schopenhauer,* trans. Edward Dannreuther (1870; London: W. Reeves, 1880), 41.
84. Friedrich Nietzsche, *Beyond Good and Evil* (1886), trans. Helen Zimmern, in *Complete Works,* 12: 200–201.

nection between religion and aesthetics. Strauss objects to the symphony's formal flaws precisely because, to his ear, they interfere with the communication of Beethoven's real message, which is humanistic at heart. The choral finale, he says, is deeply symbolic of the composer's understanding that "only in men and with men does the solution to man's torments lie"; he fears that the sensationalistic aspects of the composition will obscure this important recognition, rendering the piece overpopular and trivial.[85] As his metaphors make clear, Strauss insisted on distinguishing religious meaningfulness from aesthetic value, a distinction with which the orthodox-minded were uncomfortable.

Strauss's odd little foray into music criticism had astonishing repercussions: it simply infuriated people. It was reprinted often, with editors often providing rejoinders and commentaries, as Chrysander did in 1877 in the *Allgemeine Musikalische Zeitung*. For the rest of the century it was repeatedly suggested, none too politely, that the great theologian stick to his own field.[86] The degree of furor is revealing, perhaps having less to do with the content of his article than to the intellectual position he stood for, one every bit as threatening as Darwin's or Karl Marx's. The critique as it stands seems a harmless enough mix of pedestrian formal puzzlement (although his language is more than usually vivid) and utopian social commentary. He took the eventual triumph of "secular humanism" for granted, and he took for granted as well Beethoven's espousal of it, though suggesting that the latter lacked sufficient fervor. This, I suspect, is what caused the difficulty. As Hanslick pointed out, polemicists for the symphony were more likely to talk about Beethoven's greatness of soul than about the music itself. Strauss, apparently rather knowledgeable about music, found both soul and symphony wanting.

The uncertainties and ambiguities of exegetic interpretation were compounded by the absolute requirement that the message being discerned here must be Beethoven's, not Schiller's—which is as much as to say that such secure verbal reference as was available was cheerfully ignored. A. B. Marx

85. Strauss, "Beethoven's Neunte," col. 130.
86. Strauss's "incompetence" was one of the last subjects on which Wagner and Nietzsche continued to agree, although their accord was not based on common arguments. In his 1869 appendix to "Judaism in Music" Wagner refers sarcastically, and in the context of a vicious racial slur, to "genuine" German artistic values as "a subject the famous bible-student, David Strauss, might presumably expound with just as great discernment as Beethoven's Ninth Symphony" (*Wagner's Prose Works*, 3:114), and Nietzsche published a notorious full-scale demolition of him in the first of his *Thoughts Out of Season* ("David Strauss, the Confessor and the Writer" [1873], trans. Anthony M. Ludovici, in *Complete Works*, vol. 4).

put it quite bluntly, arguing that thematic material bears the meaning of the piece and "precludes all supposition that the meaning of the Symphony might have a connection with the meaning of Schiller's Ode."[87] This viewpoint, or at least its echo by scores of later commentators, may actually be a byproduct of the great *Zukunftsmusik* controversy because the futurist debate was whether it was the presence of words or the introduction of human voices as such that constituted Beethoven's revolutionary move; the conservative argument, on the contrary, had merely to do with whether the piece could properly be called a symphony. None of the discussants seemed much concerned with what words were used.

But for purposes of religious argumentation, the text was inextricably part of the experience of the work, and there were circumstances in which it was not simply ignored but deliberately misread, turned into something more convincing as "Beethoven's own" text. Many critics suggested with greater or lesser degrees of subtlety that Beethoven had improved upon or clarified Schiller's meaning or had compensated for the poet's lapses of taste. There seems to be consensus now that the poetry is slight;[88] Nietzsche buttressed his own argument with that same judgment: "To the dithyrambic world-redeeming exultation of this music Schiller's poem . . . is wholly incongruous, yea, like cold moonlight, pales beside that sea of flame." Bagge used its weaknesses in support of an ingenious apologia for the hybrid form of the whole; the poem, he said, omits all of the human sorrows and struggles that must precede genuine joy, so Beethoven composed those in the first three movements. The acerbic Teetgen expostulated, "What made him in his grand old age (old for him) so harp upon Schiller's crude performance, we know not"; it was precisely the same "crudity" that provoked Grove's speculation as to why Beethoven chose the portions of the text that he did:

> In making his selection Beethoven has omitted, either by chance or intention, some of the passages which strike an English mind as most *risqués* in Schiller's Ode . . . and the omissions furnish an example

87. Kroeger, "Marx's Characterization," 394.
88. Maynard Solomon points out that Schiller himself did not think much of it ("Beethoven and Schiller," in *Beethoven, Performers, and Critics,* ed. Robert Winter and Bruce Carr [Detroit: Wayne State University Press, 1980], 166). That this assessment is still current is suggested by Robert Winter in "The Sketches for the 'Ode to Joy'" in ibid., 200. James Parsons writes about the interpretation of Schiller's text and its setting by other composers in "Footnotes, Fantasies, and Freude: Once More on Schiller's and Beethoven's *An die Freude,*" *Beethoven Newsletter* 9 (1994): 114 +; and in "'*Deine Zauber binden wieder*': Beethoven's Schiller and the Music of Enlightenment"(paper delivered at the 1996 annual meeting of the American Musicological Society, Baltimore).

of the taste by which his colossal powers were, with few exceptions, guided.[89]

Later, Grove worries at this topic some more, apparently feeling that those "few exceptions" needed to be accounted for.

> and if in the Finale a restless, boisterous spirit occasionally manifests itself, not in keeping with the English feeling of the solemnity, even the sanctity, of the subject, this is only the reflection, and by no means an exaggerated reflection, of the bad taste which is manifested in parts of the lines adopted from Schiller's Ode, and which Beethoven, no doubt, thought it was his duty to carry out in his music. That he did not entirely approve of such extravagance may be inferred from the fact that, in his selection of the words, he has omitted some of the more flagrant escapades. (389)

It is important, I think, that Grove's sense of taste here was based on "the solemnity, even the sanctity," of the event that the Ninth had become—that is, on the ways in which audiences had learned to hear the piece. In England, by Grove's and many other accounts, Natalia Macfarren's singing translation of the finale text was used in most performances, and its extensive and imaginative misrenderings of Schiller's original are not so much inept as symptomatic of certain predominant readings of the piece already in place. That is, she projected into her text a number of responses to the symphony that had become commonplace, readings that had by virtue of cultural and ideological trends overwhelmed the actual text of the original.

To begin with, "joy," a happy state of affairs but not a virtue to be dutifully practiced, is not really up to the level of religious solemnity people wished to hear in Beethoven's finale—not, at least, within an orthodox Christian tradition; Grove's comments reveal this unease. It has rather a pagan air about it, something of what Nietzsche called the Dionysian. Religious exegesis of the piece had long played down its selfish pursuit of "joy" in favor of the poem's emphasis on "brotherhood," and in many cases entirely supplanted it with nobler virtues like "love" and "hope." In Lady Macfarren's version, these mainstays of a more muscular Christianity become real.[90] From the opening stanza she removes both Elysium and the plural "gods"; the third

---

89. Nietzsche, "On Music and Words," 2:38; Bagge, "L. van Beethoven," 51; Teetgen, *Beethoven's Symphonies*, 104; Grove, *Beethoven and His Nine Symphonies*, 325.

90. My source for Macfarren's translation is Grove, confirmed however by the many other sources in which it is quoted. In *Symphony No. 9*, Cook points out (106) that Macfarren made two translations of the text, of which the second—somewhat truer to the original—is more widely encountered in miniature scores now.

line, "Wir betreten feuertrunken," is piously replaced with "Joy by love and hope attended." In one of the piece's most dramatic passages, she exchanges Schiller's gnomic and somewhat threatening interrogatives

> *Ihr stürzt nieder, Millionen?*
> *Ahnest du den Schöpfer, Welt?*

for hortatory statements direct from the pulpit:

> O ye millions, kneel before Him,
> Tremble, earth, before thy Lord

and goes on the replace the "Sternenzelt" that Beethoven so gorgeously set with the Lord's sword of vengeance stayed by "mercy"—another familiar virtue helping defend against hints of paganism.

English audiences apparently did not object to this bowdlerization because it accurately represented the way they already interpreted the piece. Grove does not comment upon it, and even the purist Tovey suggests only that Macfarren has reversed the poetic conception by urging prostration rather than rising to look upward to the stars,[91] as

> *Brüder—überm Sternenzelt*
> *Muss ein lieber Vater wohnen*

is replaced by

> To the power that here doth place ye,
> Brothers, let us prostrate fall.

Whereas German audiences, of course, continued to hear the poetry in its original language, there is considerable evidence in their narrative accounts of it to suggest that they read the music's message much as Macfarren did, or in other similarly adaptive ways. What such readings represent is a sort of middle stage in the evolution of the Ninth's meaning. As if in obedience to Comte's scheme of the spiritual evolution of mankind, the poet's text appeared first as rather "pagan," in keeping with the classicism of its eighteenth-century original, and then it was Christianized. Finally, however, by the last decades of the century, the text was put to the service of the new religion of mankind.[92]

---

91. Donald Tovey, *Essays in Musical Analysis* (London: Oxford University Press, 1935), 2:42.

92. On the relationship of pagan and Christian elements in the piece, and in Schiller's text, see Lawrence Kramer, "The Harem Threshold: Turkish Music and Greek Love in Beethoven's 'Ode to Joy,'" *19th-Century Music* 22 (1998): 78–90; and Maynard Solomon, "Beethoven and Schiller," in his *Beethoven Essays* (Cambridge, Mass.: Harvard University Press, 1998), 205–15.

Traditional religionists, ironically enough, continued to derive support from Wagner's poetic and ultimately orthodox reading, and for several generations they elaborated upon it. K. R. Hennig, facing up to what was by 1888 a familiar charge, stoutly insisted that "Beethoven maintained throughout his life the pure dogmatic position of his church"; the symphony, he argued, could be read straightforwardly as a statement of the composer's religious faith.[93] As d'Indy was to do later, Hennig projected his vision of orthodoxy onto his formal reading of the work, explaining the puzzling fourth movement as a rondo; with this formal design, it becomes clear, the recurrence of material aptly symbolizes doctrinal stability. Though this simply and usually rather clear-cut form bears little resemblance to the fantasy that Bagge heard in the same movement, both designations served to quiet their authors' anxiety about stability and orthodoxy.

CONCLUSION

In 1849 the revolutionary Michael Bakunin is reported to have said to Wagner, "All, all . . . will pass away; nothing will remain; not only music, the other arts as well . . . but one thing will endure for ever, the Ninth Symphony."[94] In a disturbed world, with political, social, and religious mores constantly shifting beneath the feet like sand, Beethoven's masterpiece stood firm as a source of secure knowledge, despite the evident fact that every commentator divined from the piece whatever message was necessary to his own inner quietude.

In his 1876 article, drawing upon the vivid sense of history that characterized the nineteenth century, Edward Dannreuther ponders the developing relationship between spirituality, scientific discovery, and culture.

> As the culture of ancient Greece was based upon a mythical creed and a religious embodiment thereof in art, so in all likelihood the culture of the distant future will be based upon science and music. . . . [I]n our century the antipoetical spirit of positive science and the flat prose of productive industrialism is balanced by the music of Beethoven and his disciples. . . . To read a string quartet, even taken merely in the light of a bracing intellectual exercise, seems on a par with the reading of a Platonic dialogue. Nay, one may affirm more than this—Beethoven is, in the best sense of the word, an ethical, a religious teacher.[95]

93. Hennig, *Beethoven's neunte*, 94.
94. William Ashton Ellis, *Life of Richard Wagner: Being an Authorised English Version of C. F. Glasenapp's "Das Leben Richard Wagners"* (London: K. Paul, Trench, Trubner, 1902), 2:321–22.
95. Dannreuther, "Beethoven and His Works," 193–94.

We recognize, of course, that even as early as 1838 discussion of this piece commonly took place in the context of religious debate, as when Berlioz insisted that the symphony was "as beautiful for the fervent Christian as for the pantheist or the atheist." Brendel, as quoted in Elterlein, could feel the tension or rather the coexistence in the piece of things that might have been thought mutually exclusive: "By the side of a pronounced secularism," he says, "there are contained in this music all the elements of deepest religiousness."[96]

The late century's awareness of itself as a period of change and uncertainty becomes more and more evident. In effect, after more than fifty years of struggle, the reading of the Ninth as an apologia for Christian orthodoxy is finally forced to give way. Alexander Teetgen couched his entire 1879 discussion of the symphony in terms of the conflict between pessimistic and optimistic philosophy. He heard in the piece a confusion, a paralysis of action he called "Hamletism," an appropriate frame of mind for the period and one that confirmed Beethoven's role as spokesman for the entire century. "The other centuries were centuries of belief or unbelief; this is one of doubt, with a soul—belief, groping after a new one." Although Teetgen does not finally judge the symphony successful, for formal reasons, he is clear enough about its ultimate message:

> the voice of peace—in modern dialect the voice of man; in the light
> of which reading, this entry of the human voice becomes portentous,
> as though it said, let the elements rage, let the arts stutter, the human
> voice alone can bring relief.[97]

Willy Pastor points in 1890 to a similar existential uncertainty, verging on despair. His entire discussion of the piece revolves around the question where spiritual consolation is to be found; it is a kind of epigrammatic remnant of the traditional "search narrative" program, of course, but its focus is interior, serious, and somewhat grim. The persistent "problem" of the finale's meaning he explains this way:

> The reconciliation of man with a world which, in its ideals, appears
> alien and repugnant to him, but which nonetheless draws near him
> if only he will not flee from it, that is the essential content of the last
> movement of the D minor symphony.[98]

He is clear, as these critics tend to be, that "joy" is to be taken purely as itself: "Freude—Freude! Dies Zauberwort löst alle Fesseln."

96. Elterlein, *Ideal Significance*, 78.
97. Teetgen, *Beethoven's Symphonies*, 100, 102.
98. Pastor, "Beethoven's 'Neunte,'" 314.

George Bernard Shaw wrote often about the Ninth in his days as a music critic, and often in the context of the spiritual pilgrimage of his century through its tangled web of religion, science, and social theory. In 1885 he observed that, "About the religious music of the xix century there is a desperate triviality" and declared his own response to the musical situation:

> The Zauberflöte was the first oratorio of the religion of humanity. Beethoven's setting of Schiller's Ode to Joy was the second. The inextinguishable vital spark which in Handel's day still dwelt in Lutheranism has passed into Positivism and Socialism.[99]

But it was much later and in quite another context that its full implications became clear. In a 1911 speech to the Heretics Society, pointedly titled "The Religion of the Future," Shaw cast his lot firmly with the moral framework provided by socialism, at the same time invoking the name of the composer who had become its timeless spokesman. "In democracy we are trying to get human nature up to a point where idolatry no longer appeals to us."[100] In this new world, he explained in answer to a questioner, "For its external expression the religion of the future might have the symphonies of Beethoven and the plays of GBS. They need not bother about the past."

99. *Shaw's Music*, 1:345, 356.
100. *The Religious Speeches of Bernard Shaw*, ed. Warren Sylvester Smith (University Park: Penn State University Press, 1963), 32.

2 Music in a Victorian Mirror

Macmillan's Magazine *in the Grove Years*

> For us in England just now music seems to be what the drama was in
> the Elizabethan age—the panegyric among the fine arts . . . the art that
> can bring the largest gathering of people into conscious and intelligent
> sympathy, increasing the pleasure of everyone by the sense that many
> other persons are sharing it at the same time.
>
> "Notes on Mr. Tennyson's 'Queen Mary,'" *Macmillan's Magazine*

In this essay I attempt to find a window onto the meanings that music held
in English Victorian culture, to understand how musical ideas and information, as well as feelings and attitudes toward music, may permeate a culture—
or at least a larger segment of the culture than we customarily encounter
when we simply take on faith what the music professionals tell us. And permeate they did: as one historian of the era remarks, "The Victorians, it
seemed, could do anything with music—except compose it. Nineteenth-
century Britain was awash with music."[1]

I take as a source of inspiration the work of Gillian Beer on the reflection of Victorian science in literature; as she explains in a recent book, she
studies not only the formulation of scientific ideas but also "their transforming reception by those living alongside, outside the scientific community."[2] The generalist journals like *Macmillan's* seem a fruitful place to look
for this nonspecialist reception precisely because in them, as Beer says,
"philosophers, lawyers, evolutionary theorists, politicians, astronomers,
physicists, novelists, theologians, poets, and language theorists all appeared

I would like to thank Lawrence Kramer, Roberta Marvin, Bonnie Wade, and William
Weber for reading an earlier draft of this essay and helping me enormously with
the process of clarifying and reorganizing it. It's my misfortune that I was not able
to carry my argument in all of the fascinating directions that they suggested, but I
am keeping those ideas in mind for future projects.

1. Anonymous author of "Notes on Mr. Tennyson's 'Queen Mary,'" *Macmillan's
Magazine* 32 (1875): 434; K. Theodore Hoppen, *The Mid-Victorian Generation,
1846–1886* (Oxford: Clarendon Press, 1998), 394.
2. Gillian Beer, *Open Fields: Science in Cultural Encounter* (Oxford: Clarendon
Press, 1996), v.

alongside each other, more often with the effect of bricolage than synthesis, true enough. But their lying alongside on the page encouraged the reader to infer connections between their activities by the simple scan of the eye and by the simultaneous availability of diverse ideas" (203). And similarly for music: in the magazines the professional writing of musicians lies alongside the same range of other discourses in which music is invoked for various purposes and to various effects, producing the same kind of "transforming reception" and offering us the opportunity for some insights into the percolation of musical ideas and beliefs through cultural discourse at large.

VICTORIAN JOURNALISM AND READERSHIP

Monthly magazines like *Macmillan's,* whose audience and range of cultural coverage might be very loosely likened to those of the *New Yorker* today, present to us, as Laurel Brake has commented, a "pithy conspectus" of Victorian writing—and therefore of reading—in which individual pieces of writing are "instantly and always contextualized" by the total contents of the issue and of the preceding and succeeding issues in which longer works are serialized.[3]

From the early nineteenth century on there had been an explosion of readership in Britain, and of periodical publication of all sorts, despite still strong opposition both from evangelical religion's suspicion of secular learning and from upper-class fears of mass literacy.[4] New magazines alone multiplied in almost incredible numbers: a tabulation of the numbers of new start-ups in London by decade chronicles an exponential growth from 20 in the 1800s to 170 in the 1860s and 140 in the 1870s—these figures take no account, of course, of the numbers that disappeared at the same time.[5] Early in the century these publications addressed a vast number of highly specialized audiences, defined by political affiliation, religious sect, profession, or craft; it would have been hard to find a single representative "cross-section" publication. But the 1850s marked a turning point in the history of

3. See Laurel Brake, "Writing, Cultural Production, and the Periodical Press in the Nineteenth Century," in *Writing and Victorianism*, ed. J. B. Bullen (London: Longman, 1997), 54–72; and also her *Subjugated Knowledges: Journalism, Gender and Literature in the Nineteenth Century* (New York: NYU Press, 1994).

4. An excellent source is Richard D. Altick, *The English Common Reader: A Social History of the Mass Reading Public 1800–1900* (Chicago: University of Chicago Press, 1957).

5. G. F. Barwick, "The Magazines of the Nineteenth Century," *Transactions of the Bibliographical Society* 11 (1909–11): 238.

readership, both a broadening of the size of the market for books and periodicals in general and a leveling out of the reading public—not that class differences in reading practices disappeared—as a more general audience developed and new publications reached beyond a particular political, occupational, or sectarian audience.[6] In 1859 both *Macmillan's Magazine* and *Cornhill* appeared, the first of the new "shilling monthlies" that gradually filled a gap in the market between the most egregious of the mass-market newspapers and the quarterlies that had been dominant earlier, journals with a drier, more aristocratic view of literary culture and oriented toward a classical Oxbridge interpretation of "literature" that did not include fiction (at least in English) and took a dim view of anything in popularized form.

The new monthlies, by contrast, defined their market largely through serialized fiction; they appealed to a middle-class readership that was not necessarily university educated and that included women.[7] One of their sources of appeal was that the practice of serialization made many books (fiction and nonfiction alike) available to a greatly enlarged readership by spreading the cost over several monthly installments. And there was considerable coverage of national and international affairs as well; Lucy Brown has suggested, in her history of Victorian journalism, that a sequence of particularly interesting news stories—including, among others, the American Civil War, the Franco-Prussian War, the siege of Paris and the commune, and the Ashanti wars—helped develop a public taste for news just during the 1860s and 1870s when economic and technological developments were making it more accessible.[8]

In order to give a more sharply focused image of *Macmillan's Magazine* itself, let me list some of its contributors. In fiction, authors who may be considered journal "regulars" during these years include Dinah Mulock, Charlotte Yonge, William Black, and Margaret Oliphant, joined occasion-

6. See *The Victorian Periodical Press: Samplings and Soundings,* ed. Joanne Shattock and Michael Wolff (Leicester: Leicester University Press, 1982).

7. This description should not mislead the twenty-first-century reader, however. From our perspective, the range of topics covered in these journals—from current political and international affairs, through recent literary and cultural events, to the most esoteric reaches of science, antiquarianism, and theology—is astonishing and bespeaks a reading public hungry for information and tolerant of a high degree of challenge. *Macmillan's* had no illustrations and no other distractions from densely printed text. (It is probable that each issue was accompanied by an advertising supplement, according to the common practice; but these were bound separately and are virtually nowhere preserved now.)

8. Lucy Brown, *Victorian News and Newspapers* (Oxford: Clarendon Press, 1985), 97.

ally by Bret Harte, Frances Hodgson Burnett, and Anthony Trollope. The two volumes (42–43) that cover the year 1880 mark a significant watershed in literary history, interweaving the closing chapters of Oliphant's *He That Will Not When He May* with the opening ones of Henry James's *Portrait of a Lady*. In poetry, there are regular contributions by Tennyson (the laureate, and a considerable literary lion of the moment), Christina Rossetti, George Eliot, and George Meredith; in science, by T. H. Huxley, Alfred Russell Wallace, and Francis Galton. Frequent music authors include John Hullah, Edward Dannreuther, Francis Hueffer, and Ferdinand Hiller (translated from the German). Other names that recur with frequency include Arthur Stanley (the dean of Westminster) on religious topics; the historian J. R. Seeley; the social activist Octavia Hill along with Arthur Helps, Samuel Smiles, Frances Power Cobbe, and Eliza Lynn Linton on various social issues; and Charles Kingsley, F. D. Maurice, W. Gifford Palgrave, Matthew Arnold, and Walter Pater as critics-at-large.[9] It is clear, then, that *Macmillan's* readers could expect to find the leading authorities of the day in each area of the journal's coverage; in addition, there were countless travel writers, many of them women, and from time to time members of government or of the military wrote on some aspect of their special expertise.[10]

Macmillan's had a particular role in the history of Victorian journalism as the first monthly magazine to do away with the long-standing (though by midcentury contested) practice of authorial anonymity. Authors were used to this traditional protection; the journalist and publisher Robert Chambers, sometime in the 1820s, described the freedom of anonymous publication in terms fascinatingly familiar from the discourse of present-day internet proselytizers: anonymity gave one, he said, the heady ability to speak "without gender, class, or status," with a neutrality that appeared to confer

9. Critics in Victorian periodicals did not specialize in a single area of expertise but were regarded rather as professional reviewers; see Laurel Brake, "Literary Criticism and the Victorian Periodicals," *Yearbook of English Studies* 16 (1986): 92–116. By the last decades of the century, however, a trend toward specialization was already visible.

10. Although there were certainly "regulars" associated with each Victorian magazine, on the whole authors were not bound by any sort of exclusive association with one publication. All the periodicals in the peer group of shilling monthlies drew on the same pool of authors. Among the few exceptions, we may assume that Dean Stanley's close personal relationship to George Grove accounted for the frequency of his contributions to *Macmillan's*. Ann Parry offers a "case study" of *Macmillan's* in its first eight years, under David Masson's editorship, in "The Intellectuals and the Middle Class Periodical Press: Theory, Method, and Case Study," *Journal of Newspaper and Periodical History* 4, no. 3 (1988): 18–32.

authority beyond challenge and to voice a universal judgment.[11] Anonymity, that is, had produced a kind of collective voice for each journal in the marketplace of opinion; conversely, it tended to make opinion appear more seamless and corporate than was really the case. By the time Alexander Macmillan founded his magazine, debate had become heated, with readers beginning to feel—and many authors agreeing with them—that they needed knowledge of authors' identities in order to be able to evaluate properly the burden of their arguments.

What is especially interesting is the number of fine distinctions that appear among different signature practices, making clear that no single sense of authorship prevailed, nor of the desirability of publicity. Pieces could be by-lined at the beginning (usually only "stars" were identified in this way), signed at the end, or identified only on the contents page of the volume; signatures could take the form of full names, initials, partial names ("Professor Seelye," "Miss Yonge"), classicizing pseudonyms ("Coelebs," "Presbyter Academicus"), or identities ("by the author of 'The Heir of Redclyffe,'" "by a clergyman of the Church of England," "by one who knew him"). Some dwindling percentage remained entirely anonymous.

George Grove served as the second editor of the magazine, from 1868 until 1883, following David Masson.[12] (Given *Macmillan's* activist role in ending journalistic anonymity, it is curious that Grove's editorship was itself anonymous: there is no mention of his name, or even the initial "G," in the magazine—which is not to say that his identity was any secret to readers.) The story of Grove's career is readily available and need not be detailed here,[13] except perhaps to place the editorship of the magazine

11. James A. Secord, *Victorian Sensation: The Extraordinary Publication, Reception, and Secret Authorship of* Vestiges of the Natural History of Creation (Chicago: University of Chicago Press, 2000), 367. Secord writes interestingly about Victorian reading practices in the chapter "Self-Development," and comments elsewhere (19) on the paradoxical effect of modern bibliographic guides that identify anonymous authors, thereby attaching their writing to an "authorial" tradition quite alien to the whole-journal context in which it originally appeared and diluting the force of the intertextuality stressed in Brake's work.

12. Grove's editorship is discussed in Ann Parry, "The Grove Years 1868–1883: A 'New Look' for *Macmillan's Magazine*?," *Victorian Periodicals Review* 19 (1986): 149–57.

13. Biographies of Grove include Charles L. Graves, *The Life and Letters of Sir George Grove, C.B.* (London: Macmillan, 1903); and Percy M. Young, *George Grove 1820–1900: A Biography* (Washington, D.C.: Grove's Dictionaries, 1980). A good brief summary of Grove's career, John Parry's "Sir George Grove," is in the pamphlet distributed by Grove's Dictionaries (London, 2000) to celebrate the second edition of *The New Grove Dictionary of Music and Musicians* (note, however, that all of these are in various ways "in-house" projects).

within the trajectory of his developing musical interests and expertise. By 1868 Grove had set aside his early engineering career; he had completed a major portion of the work on a *Dictionary of the Bible,* traveling to the Holy Land in pursuit of relevant research. Since 1850 he had been secretary to the Crystal Palace, or rather to the Society of Arts that managed it and its programming. These last two roles had introduced him to innumerable scholars, writers, and musicians, turning the affable Grove into one of the charmed group who "knew everyone" and providing him later on with a bottomless supply of authors for *Macmillan's.* He traveled fairly widely—in the Middle East, on the continent, in America—further increasing his circle of acquaintances and experts. In due course he became a member of the Macmillan inner circle, assisting David Masson in various ways with the magazine from its first issues, and was a natural successor to the editorship when Masson left to take up a professorial post. Most salient, of course, was the increasing (and increasingly knowledgeable) devotion to music that led Grove later to compile the great *Dictionary of Music and Musicians* and ultimately to become the founding head of the Royal College of Music.

The question must be asked to what extent the identity of this particular editor produced a monthly magazine that was more "music-friendly" than would have been the norm for Victorian journalism in general: how typical a "mirror" is this? It is true that Grove's own increasing absorption in music influenced the content of the magazine to some extent; Ann Parry's statistical survey shows an increase in musical topics over those offered by the previous editor, and her review of Grove's editorial correspondence reveals his efforts to induce Macmillan's publishing house to produce more books on music as well.[14] Nonetheless, it is not my sense that the attention the magazine gave to music differed substantially from the attention to music elsewhere in Victorian literate culture at the time. For one thing, given the enormously active role—serious interference, by today's standards—taken by Alexander Macmillan himself during both Masson's and Grove's editorships, Grove probably could not have skewed it very much even if he had wanted to. For another, and this is more to the point, most of the references to music I am interested in here, for a portrait of music's symbolic and suggestive position in Victorian culture, are not in the articles that are actually about music per se but crop up in all kinds of other writing—

14. Ann Parry, "The Grove Years," 151–52. However, Grove also increased coverage of politics, history, religion, and education over their representation during David Masson's editorship.

criticism, fiction, travel writing, social concerns, education, and others—as will be seen farther along.

A SNAPSHOT OF THE ERA, 1868–83

Asa Briggs offers the following tidbit to help locate us temporally: 1859, the year of the magazine's founding, had seen the publication of Darwin's *Origin of Species,* Samuel Smiles's *Self-Help* (that eponymous progenitor of a vast and still thriving genre), Fitzgerald's translation of the *Rubaiyat,* and John Stuart Mill's *On Liberty.*[15] One scholar has aptly identified "the optimistic, imperial, professional, and relatively secular public culture of the second half of the nineteenth century,"[16] but most historians also record what J. F. C. Harrison calls the "mood of doubt" that came to a head in the 1880s.[17] In particular, among the middle class there was vivid awareness of rapid social and industrial change going on; Victorians were bullish on scientific and technological progress, but they became increasingly skeptical about the changing society's ability to generate acceptable social conditions and to correct what were seen as desperate social problems—*Macmillan's,* like other magazines of the time, evidences a great deal of concern for poverty, housing, education, and related issues.

It is the era that saw the turn-by-turn alternation in the prime minister's office of two larger-than-life political figures: the conservative, empire-building Disraeli (who charmed Victoria) and the liberal, reform-minded Gladstone (whom Victoria loathed).[18] Both men were spellbinding orators, and both were deeply implicated in the popular press: Disraeli was one of the best-selling novelists of the day, and Gladstone—when out of office—had the habit of taking on government policies he detested in the pages of the newspapers and the shilling monthlies.

15. Asa Briggs, *A Social History of England* (London: Weidenfeld and Nicolson, 1983), 229.

16. Secord, *Victorian Sensation,* 5.

17. J. F. C. Harrison, *Late Victorian Britain, 1870–1901* (n.p.: Fontana, 1990), 120.

18. Disraeli served for part of 1868 and then from 1874–80; Gladstone from 1868–74 and then from 1880 on into the 1890s. Sources for the general history of the period, in addition to Briggs and Harrison, include Hoppen, *Mid-Victorian Generation;* Geoffrey Best, *Mid-Victorian Britain, 1851–70* (n.p.: Fontana, 1979); David Newsome, *The Victorian World Picture: Perceptions and Introspections in an Age of Change* (New Brunswick: Rutgers University Press, 1997); Esmé Wingfield-Stratford, *Those Earnest Victorians* (New York: William Morrow, 1930); and G. M. Young, *Victorian England: Portrait of an Age* (1936; London: Oxford University Press, 1953).

Ireland had become a bitter legacy that remained puzzling and divisive throughout the century; while certain religious reforms were on track by midcentury—the disestablishment of the Church of Ireland, for example— others, such as desperately needed land reform, remained elusive. Political disputes covered over much more primitive layers of sheer cultural distaste; as Hoppen says, early in the century the Irish were distrusted because they were Catholic; by the end, they were distrusted on cultural grounds.[19] Such distaste is dismayingly evident in the magazine: in fictional as well as nonfictional contexts, and even when individual authors protested a certain sympathy, the cultural otherness of the Irish was simply taken for granted; the "Celtic character"—while admittedly charming and always picturesque—was mercurial, self-interested, untruthful, ignorant, childish, and of course easy prey to drink.[20]

A number of persistent domestic issues fill pages of the magazine, all redolent of extraordinary pressures on the traditional English class structure. Proposals for the creation of a national school system were highly contentious because of religious denominational contests—in their turn governed by class interests—for control of the curriculum. University reform, primarily concerning Oxford and Cambridge, covered many kinds of issues from large-scale matters of curriculum to details of examination, celibacy, and the abolition of the required oath of subscription to the Thirty-Nine Articles of the Church of England. Here too, it is important to bear in mind that in Victorian England discussions of education at the two premier universities were actually discussions of the entire social structure of the country and revealed the persistence with which the Victorian drive toward betterment for all ran head-on into the equally strong determination to preserve class distinctions. Similar disputes prevailed about the nature of civil service and military examinations: traditionally they reflected the classical atmosphere of the Oxbridge education rather than having anything in particular to do with the skills and knowledge required for the positions being filled and therefore acted more as social filters than as predictors of professional aptitude, a problem identified by many an author. There were also scandals about military unpreparedness and disorganization, heated arguments about

19. Hoppen, *Mid-Victorian Generation*, 447.
20. These characterizations did not apply to the Anglo-Irish "plantation" class that had come to Ireland from England as part of its original annexation, but only to those of the "Celtic race." A particularly intriguing and provocative account of the English view of the Irish occurs in Catherine Gallagher and Stephen Greenblatt, "The Potato in the Materialist Imagination," in *Practicing New Historicism* (Chicago: University of Chicago Press, 2000).

temperance and prohibition, and endlessly arcane controversies about religion. (As with educational questions, "religion" covered more than met the eye. In a not-quite-secular society with an established church, matters of religious doctrine and practice came to general knowledge in the form of Parliamentary actions and were intensely public.)

It is a commonplace to observe that the most dominant intellectual trait of Victorian culture was its historicism, its obsession with time, the past, and temporal development.[21] Whatever the topic of any piece of writing in the magazine, it was sure to be approached from a historical viewpoint or some aspect of its history highlighted; archaeological and anthropological research, along with the discoveries of geology and other evolutionary sciences, fed and supported this preoccupation. Indeed, the pervasive historicism of Victorian thought has been suggestively linked to the very emergence of serial journalism, since these serials themselves enacted the sense of time, development, and history ("story," after all) itself.[22]

ARTICLES ABOUT MUSIC IN *MACMILLAN'S*

In the articles on music itself during the fifteen years of Grove's editorship, themes and attitudes appear that are quite consistent with music's more casual appearances in other kinds of texts and may therefore be perused as background to that larger and more diffuse investigation. For one thing, we get a clear idea of the degree of readers' musical literacy, along with their legendary attachment to a pair of adopted German composers. Joseph Bennett brings a variety of musicological perspective to "The Autograph of Handel's 'Messiah'" (August 1868), a sort of review of a recently issued photographic reproduction of the famous autograph housed in Buckingham Palace. Commenting on this reproduction as a beneficent example of the uses of current science, Bennett goes on to "read" the autograph for signs of Handel's character and moods, even extrapolating some notions about the physique and physical reality of "the burly Saxon." He moves on, then, to illustrate a number of differences between the autograph and the performed version, offering a large number of musical examples and addressing his

21. See, among others, Rosemary Jann, *The Art and Science of Victorian History* (Columbus: Ohio State University Press, 1985); and Philippa Levine, *The Amateur and the Professional: Antiquarians, Historians and Archaeologists in Victorian England, 1838–1886* (Cambridge: Cambridge University Press, 1986).

22. Linda K. Hughes and Michael Lund, *The Victorian Serial* (Charlottesville: University of Virginia Press, 1991), 59.

readers in ways that assume their ability to recognize departures from the version they knew so well.

Mendelssohn appears twice, first in the publication of some of his letters in June 1871, with the remark (presumably an editorial intervention by Grove) that they had somehow been omitted from the volumes published by the family; and then in the memoir by Ferdinand Hiller, translated (anonymously) by Grove's friend Mary Emilie von Glehn and spread over four issues between January and May 1874—later that year issued in book form by Macmillan.

Francis Hueffer's article "The Chances of English Opera" (May 1879) is a casual piece useful mostly as an indicator of the degree to which opera was a topic much on the minds of the public, but Hueffer also gives us a few diagnoses of the present state of musicality in England, as he sees it. There has been a sea change in recent years, he thinks.

> Not only does the interest taken in it exceed that granted to all the other arts in conjunction, but the character of this interest itself is becoming more and more divested of the attributes of a fashionable pastime.

What is more, Hueffer sees a broadening of taste and a weakening of the partisan allegiances that had so prominently marked musical discourse in England up to this point:

> The exclusive admiration of Handel and Mendelssohn, on the one hand, and of the school "of the future," on the other, is gradually being merged in an intelligent appreciation of all good music to whatever school or country it may belong. (57)

Victorian literate culture took an evolutionary view of music as of everything else.[23] John Hullah's "Popular Songs of the Last Half Century" (December 1869), mainly just a catalog of popular composers, offers itself up as a way to "trace the progress" of song in England. It takes the gendered nature of song performance entirely for granted—"the tastes and powers of our grandmothers" are compared to those suggested by "any contem-

---

23. Michael Musgrave provides a wonderful contemporary description by Samuel Phillips of the organization of the exhibit courts in the Crystal Palace, where visitors could "trace the course of art" from pre-Christian times to the present and obtain "an idea of the successive stages of civilization which from time to time have arisen in the world, flourished for a greater or less period, until overturned by the aggression of barbarians or the no less destructive agency of a sensual and degraded luxury" (Samuel Phillips, *Guide to the Crystal Palace and Park* [London, 1854], quoted in Michael Musgrave, *The Musical Life of the Crystal Palace* [Cambridge: Cambridge University Press, 1995], 17).

porary young lady's collection"—and Hullah ends with an observation about the evolution of musical style. Ironically, given the operatic debates swirling around him at this moment in music history, Hullah obliviously supposes that music is becoming less "vocal" now, because of the great dominance of instrumental music, and expresses the hope that singing will not be altogether forgotten in the "music of the future."[24]

As Hullah's usage suggests, there is no question that Wagner (or, at any rate, "Wagnerism") was the primary debate topic of the day as far as music was concerned, and that his music and his ideas were firmly connected in the public mind to just these ongoing discussions of development and evolution. The segment of the public that read *Macmillan's* was just the audience for current opera and theater, of course, and it was accustomed to this polemic and to encountering Wagner's name always more or less in the language of historical and evolutionary imperative. A schoolmaster from Winchester, C. Halford Hawkins, covered "The Wagner Festival at Bayreuth" (November 1876) in its first year of operation. His article is a minute and awe-struck description of the *Ring* by a self-styled Wagnerian. He manages to narrate the whole story, though he permits himself a little rhetorical gulp of apprehension before launching into it ("I must endeavour to sketch shortly and intelligibly the main story" [57]), and he has a number of insightful things to say about Wagner's innovations in musical style and in staging. What is perhaps most striking to a later reader is Hawkins's absolute conviction, reiterated frequently in the essay, that this "experiment will not be repeated," that he cannot imagine circumstances in which the entire *Ring* will ever be performed again. "Herein," he says, "is chronicled the euthanasia of the *magnum opus* of the advanced school" (63).

But the heavy hitter on Wagnerian topics is without question Edward Dannreuther, whose "The Opera: Its Growth and Decay" (May 1875) deploys the favorite developmental metaphor, with its whiff of a fate already too far along. The essay is a very complete, and very vivid and characteristic, statement of the contest between German and Italian opera as it was perceived in England in these years, and not from any pretended position of neutrality; he refers to the "sugar plums and fireworks" of Rossini, the "revolting *olla podrida* of Meyerbeer," "blatant and violent" Verdi, and so forth—commonly held, if seldom so outspokenly expressed, contemporary views among the literati—in constructing an operatic cosmos where "ideal

24. See chapter 5 for another exploration of the Victorian understanding of singing and melody.

drama on the Greek model" is in perpetual conflict with "vulgar theatrical amusement."

He harps on the "artificiality" of opera, due to its aristocratic origins, in contrast to the "organic" and "truly national" character of drama, which has its origin in "public life"; given the degradation opera has suffered over recent generations, at Italian and French hands, it has effectively reached its end.

> The opera, then, has ceased to live; and what we have now before us is the piteous spectacle of Monsieur Offenbach, with his friends, dancing the *can-can* around its dead body!
>
> In another paper we hope to pursue the history of its resuscitation. (72)

This *Dämmerung* only too evidently paves the way for a sequel, the Wagnerian apologetic that was Dannreuther's main business in life. And, indeed, "The Musical Drama" (November 1875)—pointedly not "opera"—completes the story by explaining how Wagner's later works constituted a "veritable musical drama" in which "all the absurdities and trivialities charged against the opera have been avoided, and . . . the full stream of Beethovenian instrumental music has been led into a dramatic channel" (80). Wagner's pedigree does not originate only in Beethoven, but in Sebastian Bach and the rise of instrumental music since his time, for the best of which, Dannreuther tells us, "the dramatic principle is the *punctum saliens*." He goes on in this second essay to detail several aspects of Wagner's mythic plots ("Wagner was led almost unconsciously by the spirit of music towards mythical and legendary subjects" [82]), his abandonment of traditional operatic forms, his alliterative verse, and the peculiar nature of his melodies.

It is everywhere evident in Victorian writing that the apparently innocent but oh-so-laden phrase "of the future" had become a universal preoccupation from midcentury on. I do not know whose use of it launched the tag—perhaps it was Ludwig Feuerbach's *Grundsätze der Philosophie der Zukunft*, first published in 1843 and widely known in Britain—but it subsequently turned up in every kind of discourse from government Blue Books to *Punch* cartoons. The coinage evidently captured the Victorian imagination, immersed as it was in the sense of an ongoing developmental stream of history and an intense concern as to where that stream would lead; witness Canon Kingsley's essay in *Macmillan's* for March 1871, "The Natural Theology of the Future." Needless to say, Wagner's music and his writings were always interpreted in terms of this trope and therefore always shadowed by all the anxieties attendant upon it.[25] Once in a while it even served as the fulcrum of a gentle parody, as in Mary A. Lewis's (anonymous) plaint in "Cheap Literature for Village Children" (July 1878) about the dreadful quality of the books available for poor children, which she found sanctimonious, pallid, and both smug and patronizing in language and diction:

> We have heard of late a great deal about "the music of the future," and we think that some of these tales must be written in the "language of the future," and be meant for children in those days of the "sweet by and by" when all boys and girls shall have passed "Standard VI," and be in a very different state of mental cultivation from any that they have reached at present. (217)

Apart from its role as Wagnerian apologetic, Dannreuther's article also provides an abbreviated philosophy of music that articulates aesthetic ideas many of his readers would have shared:

> Music is continually saying, *This is;* all other arts say, *This signifies.* Music gives the very impulse of passion; the other arts suggest it. The spirit of music is orgiastic; that of the plastic arts contemplative. Music is an immediate picture of volitions; it represents emotions in the most direct manner; and it tends to transport everything it touches into an ideal sphere. (81)

It is precisely because of this immediacy, music's uniquely direct connection to passion and volition, that it was invoked in so many social, political, and domestic contexts, as we shall see further on.

Another serious and quite challenging contribution by Edward Dannreuther, his "Beethoven and His Works" (July 1876), nearly strains our credulity about the patience, the musical knowledgeability, and the moral earnestness of the magazine's readers. This substantial and rather astonishing article is really too full of material to be accounted for adequately here; it would easily support an answering critical essay of its own. At least eleven of its seventeen pages are given over to a compact stylistic account of Beethoven's music, using musical examples and covering his formal innovations ("his principle of organic construction"), new types of key relationship, his use of counterpoint, the invention of the scherzo, his use of

25. See chapter 5 for further ramifications of this idea. In a *Macmillan's* article on "Russia and the East" in May 1869, Karl Blind reports having recently heard in Moscow the claim that Russian ought to be the "language of the future," a claim that Blind considers "disrespect to music" (38). In July 1770 Edward Nolan comments in an essay on Macaulay, "Even as Herr Wagner is giving us the music of the future, so might some one, surely, provide us with the words" (196).

very detailed performance indications, and some "blemishes" that resulted, the author thought, from Beethoven's deafness and from the inadequacy of the instruments—especially the pianos—available in his day. Dannreuther makes an attempt to specify the precise nature of Beethoven's religious faith, always a major issue for Victorian readers, which he characterizes as an "ecstatic humanitarian faith" and a "pantheistic abstraction," and he summarizes the composer's artistic conception as "always that of an *instrumental poem.*"

Dannreuther also offers here, as a setting for his discussion of Beethoven, a vivid picture of the general place of music within mid-Victorian thought. He comments that "by virtue of Beethoven, music has become *the* modern art" (193); here he echoes the frequently expressed sentiment that music was the essential or archetypal art of the period, an idea that had been famously epitomized just shortly earlier in Pater's dictum that "all art constantly aspires towards the condition of music."[26] In the same vein Grove himself characterized music as "at once so prominent and so eminently progressive" in his preface to the *Dictionary of Music and Musicians.*[27] Dannreuther's article furnishes this observation with its perhaps inevitable sequel: "As the culture of ancient Greece was based upon a mythical creed and a religious embodiment thereof in art, so in all likelihood the culture of the distant future will be based upon science and music." As good a prediction as any, I suppose, of the era of the Napster lawsuit, but from the author's point of view a classic expression of the Victorian faith in a kind of progress in which ever more elevated art and ever more benevolent science would go hand in hand.

This point is dramatized in another article that will provide a brief detour from writings exclusively on the topic of music. In February 1883 the magazine published a kind of paean to modern technology, Ernest Foxwell's "Express Trains—A Rhapsody." Foxwell goes through a number of familiar rhetorical gestures of the moment, including the nationalist/essentialist claim that " express trains are *par excellence* the expression of English nature" (264) and the assertion of awe at modern wonders: "distance is *felt* in the nineteenth century, instead of being assented to by figures or the lapse of days" (269). But, strikingly, he proceeds at considerable length to analogize the experience to that of listening to music, arguing that the feeling

26. Walter Pater, "The School of Giorgione," in his *Studies in the History of the Renaissance* (1873). By the mid-1870s many critics thought that the other arts were in fact approaching this condition.

27. (London: Macmillan, 1879), v.

induced by the express is the same kind we experience at a great performance of Beethoven: "both music and expresses feed the disposition to be enthusiastic, by affording public instances of what can be done when conditions are accurately grappled" (273). "This illusion of infinite capability, bred
by such sights as expresses and such music as Beethoven's, is invaluable for
giving men buoyancy" (274). Notice that music is, again, quintessentially
modern, part of a brave new world of high technology, peace, and general
well-being; here we encounter the "panegyric" in action.

This remarkable extended simile brings us back to the moral effects of
music: both those it might have if the proper music were listened to in the
proper manner by those who most need to hear it and, conversely, the accurate diagnostic tool for revealing character that personal response to music can provide. These are most conventional attitudes of the day and certainly most conventionally expressed in the pages of the magazine, and yet
this idea may perhaps turn out to have the most far-reaching consequences
for the general understanding of music in Victorian culture. So Joseph Bennett's "The Condition of Opera in England" (July 1869—opera again!)
dwells on the perfectly pedestrian points that opera ought to be a force for
popular refinement instead of mere entertainment, and that the subscription system denies access to just those people who need it most, the un-
refined poor.

Julian Marshall gives us, in "Some Traits of Composers" (February 1876),
a fairly silly, disorganized spate of breezy anecdotes about composers' eccentric compositional practices, filled with dinner guests, cats, tears, and
champagne glasses. But the foundation on which Marshall builds his essay
is not without interest. "At a time when art and literature are daily taking
a stronger hold on all classes of society," he begins, echoing a by now familiar theme, it is understandable that the public is curious to know more
about the personalities of great artists. "To understand an artist's character
cannot but help us to understand his works," he suggests, for "as no human
action can be properly valued for good or bad, unless we clearly see the motives which dictated it, so no work of art can ever be truly appreciated except with a clear comprehension of its author's purpose" (340). This comprehensive interweaving of artwork with character, and of moral evaluation
with the whole, meant that musical practices—and indeed musicality itself,
in the hands of writers on a myriad of other topics—could stand in for the
moral nature of individuals and of whole communities.

Sometimes the exploration of these moralizing topics was elaborated
seriously and at length. There could be no more evocative and detailed com-

pendium of Victorian beliefs about music than Henry Leslie's article "Music in England," which appeared in the magazine in July 1872. Rueing the high levels of stress and pressure in modern life, due to "the hurried pace to which railways and telegraphs have brought us" and "the enormous flood of information" to be dealt with every day, Leslie prescribes the "humanizing, elevating, and refining influence" that music would have if provided more liberally for the British public and "especially [for] its least wealthy portion" (245). The burden of his argument is to "demonstrate how great is the social influence of music"—and impressive indeed his claims are, from the reduction of drunkenness to the fostering of family togetherness—and to argue for government support for music education in order to "elevate the national taste" (246).[28]

Leslie's essay is a meliorist exercise, to be sure, embodying the general view of music as one of the more significant means of improving both mind and soul; it is not, however, entirely devoid of equally typical worries. Along with bracing doses of optimism and social fervor, Leslie also expresses with unusual candor the two anxieties that so frequently accompanied discussions of music in Britain: the suspicion that England really might be "das Land ohne Musik," and the fear that music study was "effeminate" and would prove an "enervating" influence on young English boys.[29] He raises both issues here, of course, in order to dismiss them—to disarm potential critics with upfront reassurance. These themes from Leslie's essay, both the faith and the anxiety, are reflected and refracted throughout the magazine over these fifteen years, in pieces of writing of every type from fiction and poetry to political, scientific, and religious contributions.

These are not the only articles on musical topics that *Macmillan's* offered during the Grove years, but among them they seem to cover the pri-

28. Good support is offered to Leslie's argument by articles such as "The People's Concert Society," by Florence Marshall, in the April 1881 issue. Marshall details the good effects in various British cities of the "undertakings started for the benefit of the poor, [and] the reformation, or recreation, or edification of the working man" (433). She is shrewd about the difficulties encountered in some places and judges overall that music is still too expensive and inaccessible. And she insists that the poor, when given the opportunity to attend free concerts, listen more attentively and with more appreciation than their social betters.

29. Leslie expresses as well another familiar concern, the perennially troublesome need to take account of German leadership in all things musical: how could the great masterworks of the musical tradition be rescued from identification with the socially distrusted and at the moment politically inimical force of Germany in the current world?

mary issues and topics of interest that we will see, much elaborated and ramified, in other kinds of writing in the magazine.[30]

THE MUSICALIZATION OF THE WORLD: MUSIC IN OTHER WRITING

Gillian Beer makes a most interesting suggestion that may help explain the extraordinary frequency of these musical references. As developments in Victorian science continued to call into question the validity and authenticity of the eye's powers, she says, aspects of sound began to "assume the status as ideal function that sight had earlier held," and "the ear became the chosen arbiter of refined discriminations." There is evidence in the scientific writing of the time of attempts to find equivalence between visible and auditory experience: Beer cites work in the journal *Nature* during the 1870s that proposed the acoustic octave and the color spectrum as natural homologies.[31] And indeed, J. Norman Lockyer's *Macmillan's* article "Ears and

---

30. A bland and anonymous essay on "Covent Garden and the Royal Italian Opera" (January 1879) testifies to the reading public's devotion to opera as a topic; in "A Conservatoire of Music for England" (December 1879) Charles Sumner Maine discusses the report of the proceedings of Prince Christian's executive committee on the establishment of a national school of music (in 1883 it became the Royal College of Music). In July 1873 Ferdinand Hiller contributed a fairly informal and anecdotal essay on Cherubini. Finally, *Macmillan's* printed both of Eliot's long poems on musical topics, *The Legend of Jubal* in May 1870 and *Armgart* in July 1871; for further critical discussion of the latter, see Rebecca A. Pope, "The Diva Doesn't Die: George Eliot's Armgart," in *Embodied Voices: Representing Female Vocality in Western Culture*, ed. Leslie C. Dunn and Nancy A. Jones (New York: Cambridge University Press, 1994), 139–51; and Wendy Bashant, "Singing in Greek Drag: Gluck, Berlioz, and George Eliot," in *En Travesti: Women, Gender Subversion, Opera*, ed. Corinne E. Blackmer and Patricia Juliana Smith (New York: Columbia University Press, 1995), 216–41. On *Jubal*, see my "'Music Their Larger Soul': George Eliot's *The Legend of Jubal* and Victorian Musicality," forthcoming in *The Figure of Music in Nineteenth-Century Poetry*, ed. Phyllis Weliver (Aldershot: Ashgate Press).

A review of Schumann's *On Music and Musicians*, in the translation by Fanny Ritter (September 1878), gives Edmund Gurney the opportunity to lay out the themes that preoccupy him in his major work on musical aesthetics, *The Power of Sound* (1880)—both of which he saw as necessary to clear away predominant misconceptions in the culture surrounding him—first, that science does not and cannot explain music, only the relatively lifeless physical elements of music; and second, that music is not about the representation of things or of emotions but has its own meaning and power. Gurney finds corroboration of both points of view in Schumann's writing.

31. Gillian Beer, "'Authentic Tidings of Invisible Things': Vision and the Invisible in the Later Nineteenth Century," in *Vision in Context: Historical and Con-*

Eyes" (January 1878), a general discussion of the physics of sound and sight, pursues just such an analogy between the color spectrum and pitch scale by way of introducing the idea of "wavelength." Spectrum analysis of a single element, says Lockyer, is like pushing down one key of the piano at a time: you get one wavelength instead of the whole spectrum. The article comes complete with quasi-musical examples showing, for instance, a B for thallium, a D for sodium.

Frances Power Cobbe uses Tartini's "Devil's Sonata" (as she calls it) in support of her theory of dreaming as a kind of thought, "Dreams as Illustrations of Unconscious Cerebration" (April 1871), and the science teacher George Farrer Rodwell cites Pythagorean ideas about the music of the spheres in his discussion "On the Perception of the Invisible" (August 1874). The pioneering anthropologist E. B. Tylor offers an extended discussion of ancient cosmologies in which the planets (then seven) represent the seven notes of the octave, in the course of introducing the magazine's readers to "The Study of Customs" (May 1882). Francis Galton published part of his later infamous work on hereditary genius in the issue for March 1869, promising a later volume of "somewhat elaborate and extensive inquiry" that would include painters, poets, and musicians among its subject categories.

All of these surely offer support to Beer's suggestion about the emergence of a sort of auditory epistemology in Victorian culture. But perhaps the most striking example comes from no less a scientific figure than T. H. Huxley. In "Bishop Berkeley on the Metaphysics of Sensation" (June 1871), Huxley uses the following metaphor, as charming as it is effective, to expose the weaknesses of Berkeley's famous reasoning and his philosophy's fatal inability to imagine anything beyond the limits of human faculties:

> Suppose that a piano were conscious of sound, and of nothing else? It would become acquainted with a system of nature entirely composed of sounds, and the laws of nature would be the laws of melody and of harmony. It might acquire endless ideas of likeness and unlikeness, of succession, of similarity and dissimilarity, but it could attain to no conception of space, of distance, or of resistance; or of figure, or of motion.
>
> The piano might then reason thus: All my knowledge consists of sounds and the perception of the relations of sounds; now the being of sound is to be heard; and it is inconceivable that the existence of

temporary Perspectives on Sight, ed. Teresa Brennan and Martin Jay (New York: Routledge, 1996), 90–91. Lawrence Kramer suggested "musicalization of the world" as an appropriate description of the ubiquity of musical references, both literal and metaphoric, that I found in the magazine.

the sounds I know, should depend upon any other existence than that of the mind of a hearing being. (160)

Huxley had good reason, of course, to assume that readers would regard the piano as a familiar and homely object whose workings they understood well.[32] But authors in the magazine were apparently able to take for granted their readers' knowledge of a considerable amount of music history as well, and their interest in acquiring a good deal more. An essentially hymnological essay by Alexander Schwartz on the history of the "Dies Irae" (September 1874) concludes with a brief section on musical settings of the sequence. Himself no musicologist, Schwartz asks speculatively "was it sung at first to one of those Gregorian melodies which seem to breathe melancholy mingled with defiance?" (462); but he goes on to mention with easy familiarity settings by Palestrina, Astorga, Pergolesi, Durante, and Jomelli, in addition to the obvious contenders Cherubini and Mozart. Similar literary articles on *Faust* (July 1876 and March 1877) and on contemporary Italian theater (in four installments from August 1876 through July 1877) do much the same.

Despite what thus appears to be a high level of musical literacy among the magazine's readers, not everything was rosy about the picture of Victorian Britain as a musical nation. It is not unusual to find complaints, like H. Sutherland Edwards's in the issue for April 1876, that "in England no disgrace is attached to total ignorance of music and everything connected therewith" (555). Rosalind Orme Masson's two-part article on "Mrs. Thrale (Piozzi): The Friend of Dr. Johnson" (April and June 1876) is telling for the way in which it weighs nationality and musicality, juxtaposing Johnson, the quintessential Englishman—literary, talkative, and as unmusical as can be imagined—against Mrs. Thrale's eventual husband-to-be, the Italian singer Piozzi, introduced to the group as the "lion" of Dr. Burney: "Now, Dr. Johnson did not know a fugue of Bach from a street cry, nor were some others present much wiser. When, therefore, Piozzi took his place at the piano and sang them one *scena* after another, it was for most of them simply a monopoly of noise on his part, and, for them, a condemnation to silence" (535). Masson is evidently sympathetic to the musician, or means to be, and she offers here a tableau of the stolid John Bull that is familiar from dozens of such scenes, fictional and otherwise.

The truth was, certainly, a mixed picture.[33] Britons had throughout the

32. See chapters 3 and 4 on the roles of the piano in bourgeois domestic life.
33. In his magisterial summary view, "English Music During the Queen's Reign," for the *Fortnightly Review* in 1887, Francis Hueffer stresses this ambiva-

century been confessing themselves guilty of a certain musical uncreativity and unoriginality, a dependence on foreign imports that made them worry about their musicality in general. Giving the lie to such a wholesale cultural anxiety, though, *Macmillan's* lets us see music's actual ubiquity, its iconic centrality in this reading culture, which was, as Hoppen tells us, "awash" with it. Music is invoked as a signifying system at every level from probing exploration to the most casual of metaphoric references. To consider just the fiction: of the twenty-five full-length novels that appeared in *Macmillan's* during the fifteen years of Grove's editorship, only one (Dinah Mulock's *A Brave Lady*) contains no references to music, music making, or musical instruments. In the others, music most often serves certain conventional purposes, drawing on similarly conventional associations and social meanings. Unsurprisingly, parlor music appears very frequently as a marker of the domestic circle or as part of a courtship story; courting couples make music together, and an occasional married couple may claim to do so to their social acquaintances, portraying a cozier and more refined domestic atmosphere than they actually enjoy. In the most interesting of these scenes, characters (usually female) may go to the piano to remove themselves from embarrassing situations, to escape a conversation that has taken a disturbing turn, or to mask emotion.

A number of the novels include the opera scenes beloved of novelists throughout the period.[34] Invocations of particular pieces of music are not infrequent—*Don Giovanni*, "Vedrai carino," Handel's *Rinaldo* and *Armida*, Mendelssohn's "Songs without Words"—suggesting their status as familiar icons of bourgeois culture, and the very few historical novels that appear here, like Charlotte Yonge's *The Chaplet of Pearls*, are careful to include an appropriate musical vignette such as singing to the lute. There are also pianos as furniture; the acquisition, exchange, loss, and relocation of these expensive investments tell us a good deal about the fortunes of their owners, as when Henry James's Pansy is banished to a convent and takes

---

lent state of affairs. On the one hand, Hueffer reports, excepting only science "there is no branch of human knowledge, or of human art, in which the change that the half-century of the Queen's reign has wrought, is so marked as it is in love of music." On the other, he dourly observes, "there are still gentlemen of the old school who have a certain pride in confessing their inability to distinguish *God Save the Queen* from *Yankee Doodle*," and at the first planning meeting for the establishment of the Royal College of Music "such men as Mr. Gladstone, the late Lord Iddesleigh, Lord Rosebery, and the Archbishop of Canterbury, almost without exception prefaced their remarks upon music by saying that they knew nothing whatever about music" (899).

34. See chapter 6.

her piano with her in apparent acknowledgement of a long-term exile. (*Portrait of a Lady* is famous, of course, for the scene in which Madame Merle is introduced at the keyboard, insinuating herself into Isabel Archer's confidence by her playing—of Beethoven, here, but of Schubert in James's later revision.)

Music is routinely deployed by novelists to depict character (a young man destined for sanctity composes "a chant"; a rigid and unsympathetic woman is revealed as a "most correct" pianist), health (a beloved singing voice has faded), social status (a "fast" and untrustworthy character gives "matinees musicales"; street children sing tawdry ballads; in a factory tale, the pub fiddle is opposed to the parlor piano), or—markedly—ethnicity, a trait in whose description music comes in very handy indeed. Characters who find themselves in Italian or French countryside are atmospherically located with the help of a village festival or religious procession. In Annie Keary's *Castle Daly,* the story of an Irish colonial family bitterly divided between English and Irish loyalties, strains of "Roisín Dhubh" and other folksongs regularly waft through the text to alert readers to the sympathies of one character or another; in William Black's *Madcap Violet* the eponymous heroine counts the loud singing of "Dixie" among the exploits that get her expelled from school. Julian Hawthorne (son of Nathaniel) uses a banjo in *Fortune's Fool* as the companion and alter ego of his hero, a hapless English boy who somehow finds himself orphaned in the backwoods of Maine: the instrument raises, and refuses to let us ignore, the question whether or not Jack is an American, part of the mystery upon which the story turns.

In general, a persistent distinction is made between folk or peasant music and music of the cultivated tradition, but the relative valuations of those may vary with the fictional situation. On the one hand, the Victorians were clear about the aesthetic and ethical superiority of the "more highly developed" art music repertoire. Even the optimistic social reformer Henry Leslie wishes that some of his fellow Britons would devote their time to more respectable music: "if the Welsh did but know their musical strength, they would not fritter it away as they do at these Eisteddfods" (247). But on the other hand, an occasional novelist wished to stress the "natural" humanity, genuine and spontaneous, of a local peasantry over the constraint and artificiality of cultivated society; the social-Darwinist hierarchy of comparative cultures was always vulnerable to a kind of nostalgia for the preindustrial and communal life of the "folk." On such occasions an overheard lullaby or a fortuitously occurring village wedding served the purpose admirably.

All of these are routine tropes in nineteenth-century fiction, and conventional enough. But they are to be found just as plentifully, and with more or less the same meanings—familiar and easily legible to readers—throughout the entire contents of the magazine.

Music Connects: Individual and Community Therapy

It is emblematic, surely, that Peter Gay chose "the art of listening" as the prologue chapter—the representative "Bourgeois Experience"—for the fourth volume of his magisterial history by that name.[35] For the fourth volume is the one devoted to, as he tells us, "the great voyage to the interior," and it is precisely its interiority as experience that gave music the spiritual powers, both therapeutic and diagnostic, that Victorians attributed to it. Musicians became, Gay says, "the high priests of a new dispensation that provided its devotees with glimpses of the inner life that no other artist could give, not even a poet," and they officiated at the birth of "a secular religion in the making" (23–24).

Macmillan's Magazine is filled, as I remarked above, with articles concerning the betterment of conditions for the poor, the ill, children, workers, and in general anyone who could be seen not to be sharing in the rich fruits of modern industrialized society as they were experienced by the magazine's readers. Predictably, music bears a role in the majority of these articles, as the "secular religion" offered to the needy along with the approved forms of Christianity to help them along the road to betterment. Musical references do tend to be gendered to some extent, but by no means was music as a prescription restricted to girls and women. It was certainly associated with femininity, for the elementary reason that women were taken to be closer to feeling, emotion, and interiority in general than men; but for the Victorians that was never to say that men could not and did not share in its beneficial effects, and indeed in some contexts men were thought to be in greater need of musical ministration precisely because their constitutions were more resistant to internal exploration.

Most of what passed for social work in this era of governmental nonintervention was in fact volunteer work, organized and performed by people of means and good will, albeit in the midst of ongoing debate as to government's appropriate role; as Asa Briggs has observed, "the moral strength of Victorianism often lay in its reliance on amateurs rather than on professionals to get things done."[36] Octavia Hill was one of the best known of these

35. Peter Gay, *The Naked Heart*, vol. 4 of *The Bourgeois Experience: Victoria to Freud* (New York: W. W. Norton, 1995), 11–35.

36. Asa Briggs, *Victorian Cities* (Berkeley: University of California Press, 1993), 22.

volunteers during the 1860s and 1870s, not only laboring among the poor but inventing new methods for dealing with intractable social problems, and writing numerous essays in which her systems are laid out for others to copy. In "Organized Work Among the Poor: Suggestions Founded on Four Years' Management of a London Court" (July 1869) Hill tells of actually purchasing a building in which many poor families lived, in order to be able to exercise both economic and moral suasion over her tenants. She stresses the need for charitable workers to have individual relationships with the poor in order to provide them moral instruction and discipline, explaining that as part of her own program she had established a singing class for the girls living there, and "a drum and fife band" for the boys (221).

Sophia M. Palmer was another such volunteer worker and organizer. In "Dustyards" (January 1880) she describes a gentlewomen's mission to women employed in the filthy and terrible work of cinder sifting, the sorting of recoverable materials in city dumps. Because "many of the guests belong to the most degraded class of women," she explains, and include those who "sometimes . . . reel in quite drunk," the inclusion of hymn-singing during their mission services is quite important. In a later contribution, "Soap Suds" (August 1881)—Palmer was given to pithy and illustrative titles—she provides a description of a lodging house / coffeehouse for single laundresses in which, on one characteristic occasion, there occurred a contest between the women and "the lady in charge" over what kinds of songs the women would sing while at their needlework class. Eventually "'the lady' opened the harmonium and played valses, and accompanied the *Muffin Man*, and kindred ditties," so conquering their taste for more ribald numbers that by the end of the evening "they begged to sing their favorite hymns" before leaving (301).

Beneficial medical effects are expected from music as well, as for example in Katherine S. Macquoid's account of "The Little Hospital by the River" (May 1877), a fund-raising effort for a hospital for incurable children. Macquoid describes the good nature, long suffering, and cheerfulness of the children, and their unselfish fun-loving community; as part of their treatment, she assures readers, there is a harmonium there—"[the children] told us eagerly"—on which Sister plays for them (45). On an altogether darker topic, D. Hack Tuke, M.D., offers "Broadmoor, and Our Criminal Lunatics" (June 1878), a report on the current state of treatment of the criminally insane, describing both successes and failures. He is liberal-minded, stressing the influence of illness and "the evil of gross ignorance" on the poor unfortunates, but despite the many amenities provided in Broadmoor, among them "a band which includes seventeen patients, as well as some attendants, and enlivens the inmates twice in the course of a week," he is forced to come to the conclusion that there is a more aggravated level of "depravity and unhappiness" here than in other places he has experienced.

For the most part, as can be seen, these are not systematic or thought-through discussions of the role and influences of music; on the contrary, their evidentiary value lies precisely in their offhandedness and ready application. But once in a while a writer does offer us a glimpse of the "theory" behind the therapeutic application of musical activity. Frances Martin describes "A College for Working Women" (October 1879), another project undertaken by lady volunteers who came in to teach the women in various subjects, including singing classes. The college, Martin tells us,

> seeks to promote culture, to teach habits of prudence and forethought; it gives thoughtful women an opportunity of meeting each other and forming valuable friendships, and it offers healthy and rational entertainment as a recreation to the older, and a means of guiding and forming the tastes of its younger members. (485)
>
> Beautiful objects should greet the tired eyes and weary brain, and refresh them. The knowledge that this beauty has been provided by the loving service of others will revive many a drooping heart and spirit. (487)

And many are the volunteer social work projects conducted precisely according to this understanding of music's role in the constitution of a good life.

If music played such a significant role in social and medical healing, and the experts appeared to be near consensus on the point, it is no surprise that it could be expected to play a role in education as well. The provision of elementary education was a hot political topic of the moment, given sensitivities to government "intervention," as was the curriculum that elementary schools ought to cover. An anonymous author (identified as Arthur Helps) offered characteristic "Thoughts upon Government" (July 1872, the second part of a longer multipart essay). What is the role of government, Helps asks, in public recreations?

> There is another mode in which the Government may indirectly favour and further one of the best and safest means of recreation. This is by making music one of the subjects for education in all Elementary Schools. It is almost impossible to overrate the effect upon the manners, the morals, and the enjoyments of the people, which may be produced by the encouragement of an art which especially lends itself to the best kind of social recreation. (220)

Anxious articles by progressive educators reported on elementary education in countries that had mandatory, state-supported schools. They suspected—

indeed, feared—that those schools were better than what England provided, and they virtually always mentioned music among the elements of curriculum that were available in these fortunate, though unfortunately foreign, schools. Among these articles can be counted Ann Jemima Clough's "Suggestions on Primary Education" (August 1868); Margaret Sanford's "A Visit to a German Girls' School"(May 1874); Walter C. Perry's "German Schools" (June 1877); Fanny Heath on "Needlework in the German Schools"(September 1879); and an unsigned piece on "Elementary Education in Italy" by "a Member of an English School Board" who very naturally preferred to preserve anonymity.

Music was thought appropriate in the curricula for all classes of society and for all ages. "Music-making, always before the nineteen-sixties understood to be a peculiarly virtuous form of recreation, flourished among the lower as well as the superior strata."[37] E. Carleton Tufnell's "Education of Pauper Children" (August 1875) joins in the standing controversy over whether poor children should be boarded out to families or mainstreamed—as we would say—into district schools; Tufnell believes the latter practice is more conducive to the primary goal, to provide them with a trade and thus "dispose of" them.

[A]s respects boys, how except in institutions of this description could they be taught to play in military bands, and thus fitted for what is found to be the best method of disposing of them—sending them as musicians to the army and navy? . . .
One advantage of sending boys to the army or navy is that they can always be traced, and thus the most favourable reports have been constantly received of their characters and musical capacity. (352)

But similarly Miss [Elizabeth] Sewell, reporting on "An Experiment in Middle-Class Education" (January 1872), offers details of a school she founded for bourgeois daughters. Such a school, she discovered, needed a broader curriculum than national schools offered, for "French and music would be expected." The Rev. J. Llewelyn Davies supports "A New College for Women" (June 1868) according to a proposal for an independent college, not part of Oxford or Cambridge, which would teach the same curriculum. Davies predicts the gendered assumptions that would mark public opinion about the college, and by which "the students should be prepared for such an examination as the University of Cambridge puts before its ordinary Degree, but that Modern Languages, Music, and Drawing should also be regularly taught" (169).

37. Best, *Mid-Victorian Britain,* 233 (see note 18).

Indeed, contemporary authorities and educational historians since are agreed that music in the mid-Victorian period was seen as a progressive educational feature, associated with various upstart ventures rather than with the established practices of the public school. In "More Diversions of a Pedagogue" (January 1882), the second of a pair of articles, J. H. Raven indicates that drawing and music are "modern" parts of the curriculum, not studied by everyone: "Boys on the 'modern sides' of our schools are in a minority of something like one to five; and on the 'classical sides' classics and mathematics still occupy far more time than any others" (223). (The "modern side" would also have included modern languages, natural science "at least on its trial" (223), and larger doses of history and geography than the classical track provided.)

The healing effects of music were most often seen as applied to large groups within the social structure—or, indeed, sometimes for the betterment of society as a whole. Nonetheless, the Victorian rhetoric of betterment was not by any means devoid of individual opportunities for self-development. (Percy Young quotes an article written for the *Musical Times* in 1882 by Sir Frederic Leighton, describing music as "an awakening influence, an ethos of its own, a power of intensification, and a suggestiveness through association which aid those higher moods of contemplation that are as edifying in their way as direct moral teaching.")[38] The word "edifying" is perhaps the one that most governed general conversation about music—which is not necessarily to say that music had yet become a respectable occupation for English gentlemen, as many a nineteenth-century British composer found to his misery.

The distinguished historian and philosopher J. R. Seeley published his major work *Natural Religion* in installments in the magazine, where it ran from February 1875 until October 1976 before Macmillan published the whole in book form. Seeley's is a complex and difficult—if ultimately romantic—argument about the desirability of rescuing religion from supernaturalism and returning it to a more basic and awe-struck recognition of the oneness of nature. His occasional references to music and the other arts leave us in no doubt that Seeley shares the general Victorian sense:

> By means of the Oratorio a really fruitful alliance between religion and music was long since concluded. But it is not precisely such an alliance as this that is here contemplated. The question is not how Christianity may draw the Arts as captives in her triumphal procession, but of setting up the Arts in perfect independence to co-operate with Christian-

38. Young, *George Grove,* 161.

ity in that work in which, whatever may be their quarrel with Christianity, they are her natural allies, namely, the work of stemming worldliness and fostering the higher life. (187)

This higher life could be fostered in fictional characters or historical characters just as well as in seamstresses or pauper children, and Mandell Creighton's biographical essay on Vittorino da Feltre (October 1875) even reports on the successful deployment of music as a weight-loss strategy! Again, the mechanism of healing seems always to have to do with that "voyage to the interior" described by Peter Gay, the conviction that music tells emotional truth. The poem "A Sequence of Analogies" (May 1875), authored by C. H. H. P.—none other than the later composer Hubert Parry—invokes the "Spirit of Music" which keeps the skylark's song (wasted, unheard) among her treasures, as the angels preserve unrequited love.

In *Macmillan's Magazine* for these fifteen years, there is less trace than we might expect of the true British panegyric, the oratorio, which Howard Smither calls "the quintessentially Victorian socio-musical event"; the readers of this magazine were apparently more interested in opera.[39] Nonetheless, they are left in no doubt that music could and did create and define communities. A report on international affairs by Arthur J. Evans, "The Austrians in Bosnia" (October 1878) speaks uncannily to more recent headlines. Evans is obviously pro-Serb and is arguing that the spirit of the Bosnian people and their national traits will prove a force that the Habsburgs cannot manage to defeat. He uses as his most striking icon a Bosnian Serb refugee child, who has become known in the camp as "the little minstrel" for his ability to sing national songs and accompany himself on the "ghuzla or Serbian lyre," enacting Serbian defiance and strength of character. "He sang with a clear, fine voice and singular expression, his pretty boyish face completely wrapped in the lay he sang, his keen eyes gazing beyond the listeners into another world . . . and as he rehearsed the mighty deeds of Serbian forefathers against the Turks his small face flushed with suppressed excitement, and his eyes, bright as those of a young falcon, flashed with all the pride of a great ancestry" (504).

There is no need here to detail the most familiar of all musical forms of togetherness, those used to limn domestic scenes or what Briggs has referred

---

39. On the force of oratorio as a social ritual—so great as to be almost impossible to exaggerate—see any of the standard histories of English music in the nineteenth century, and most recently Howard Smither, *The Oratorio in the Nineteenth and Twentieth Centuries,* vol. 4 of *A History of the Oratorio* (Chapel Hill: University of North Carolina Press, 2000), 249.

to as the "game of happy families."[40] One instance will suffice, the anonymous poem "The House Beautiful" (July 1876), in which, as convention required, "music and song would the hours beguile" in the happy family home
of memory. But our sample fifteen years' worth of *Macmillan's* do turn up
a few interesting variations on the theme, ones that tend on the whole to
confirm our understanding of the ways in which conventional domesticity
devolved to restrictive roles defined by gender. Courtenay Boyle, writing in
"English Autumns" (November 1973) about upper-class mores and particularly the customary decorum of country-house visiting, acknowledges the
common understanding:

> Of course there are men who do not shoot, and cannot ride, men whose
> *forte* lies in a tenor voice, a capacity for playing waltzes on the piano, or
> making small talk on every occasion. But as a rule such men are not the
> most valuable components of society, and the women know it. (84)

Goldwin Smith, as so many others before and after him, takes advantage of
the conventional division of musical labor to make his case against "Female
Suffrage" (June 1874). It is an old story:

> That the comparative absence of works of creative genius among
> women is due entirely to the social tyranny which has excluded, or
> is supposed to have excluded, them from literary and scientific careers,
> cannot be said to be self-evident. The case of music, often cited, seems
> to suggest that there is another cause, and that the career of intellectual
> ambition is in most cases not likely to be happier than that of domestic
> affection. (143)

Music Divides: Social and Racial Diagnosis

Just as Julian Marshall argued that the character of a composer placed an
indelible stamp on his work, so writers used musical practices and sensibilities as diagnostic tools to assess the makeup and moral status of fictional
characters, classes of society, and especially different "races" and ethnic
groups. The panegyric, the force that bound a community ever more ec-
statically close together, had a dark side, the necessary opposite dynamic that
kept others outside, effectively distinguishing "us" from "them." The power
of these reciprocal energies was almost overwhelming in an era when evolutionary theory, anthropological research, mass tourism, and ever-widening
global empire continually brought into focus a multiplicity of cultural prac-

40. Briggs, *Social History of England*, 240. I discuss music's role in the constitution of bourgeois domesticity in chapters 3 and 4.

tices and value systems alien to bourgeois Victorians. In marking and polic-
ing these important boundaries music played its role, precisely because musical activity was so deeply naturalized in contemporary discourse, its products seen as an unmediated—indeed, unthinking—link to the inner life and
"true" character.

In a relatively benign form, casual musical characterization occurs as a
regular component of the magazine's articles on tourism and local color—
which is not to say, of course, that the Briton's familiar jealousies and suspicions do not make their presence felt. In these decades both increasing
prosperity and developments in transportation had combined to produce a
vast increase in the amount of traveling British citizens engaged in,[41] and
there was always intense interest among middle-class readers in reports of
the travels of others. Sometimes the accounts were of musical irritations,
or of dire musical revelations of what the British already knew about their
neighbors. John Hullah (here signing only J.H.), traveling from Nevers to
Dijon to write mostly about landscape and architecture in "Ten Days in the
Nivernais" (July 1868), was disturbed at one point by a nearby building
"many of the inhabitants of which, it was obvious to the dullest ear, devoted
themselves unremittingly to the study and practice of the drum." He spins
out a comical riff on the splendors of the drum when used correctly as "a
very worthy member of the orchestral family," but not by "a succession of
tyros, inexhaustible in number and equal in maladroitness, who from sunrise to sunset drew from it one unintermittent ra-ta-ta-too" (218). Hullah
was a musician, though—and, perhaps more importantly, a music educator—
and he did not lose the opportunity to tell more seriously, and with more
appreciation, of hearing a *cornemuse* and requesting to meet and talk with
the player (223–24).

But the French usually had a difficult time of it in the court of British
opinion, as evidenced by an anonymous travel sketch, "A Morning in the
Tuileries: The Bud—The Blossom" (December 1871), which reports on the
odd and immoral child-rearing practices of the French, resulting in the cyn-
icism and hypersophistication of little French girls. The writer, evidently female, observes a nurse singing to a baby a song with words so shocking that
"it seemed the confirmation of all I had heard and read on the subject of
French mothers, who suffer impure ideas to be imbibed with the very milk
their babies suck" (105)—this after the nurse has placidly suckled the baby
and then rearranged her clothing in full view of the public in the park.

41. See, among others, Lynne Withey, *Grand Tours and Cook's Tours: A History
of Leisure Travel, 1750 to 1915* (New York: William Morrow, 1997).

Musical vignettes do not always bear or need much interpretation, though; often they are simply mentioned, as though each travel venue were to be precisely identified by its musical icon. In Honor Brooke's "A Day at Como" (December 1871) a band of guitars play on board the steamship to Como and "a lovely strain of music" is sung by a peasant girl at the ruins of a tower (135)—guitars, girl, song, and tower all parts of the scenery. "Spanish Life and Character" (April 1874), by an anonymous author identified as Hugh James Rose, is part of a long series of travel letters published over many months reporting on the situation in newly Republican Spain. Rose describes the Spanish folk instruments played at Christmastime: guitar, tambourine, and particularly the zambomba, which the author describes in detail in a footnote, adding the comment "this is called a *musical* instrument, although why, except on the *lucus a non lucendo* principle, I cannot understand" (550). Janet Ross's "Vintaging in Tuscany" (September 1875) and "Oil-Making in Tuscany" (March 1876) both present appreciative and charming accounts of the peasant songs and dances that accompany these ritual activities. Throughout William Black's traveling novel, *The Strange Adventures of a Phaeton* (January–November 1872), national and regional differences are marked by explicit, though usually jocular, descriptions of music in a continually changing panorama.

Americans have a very particular niche in the discourse of Victorian travel. They were a special object of curiosity because, as David Newsome points out, "for the most part, Americans had once been ourselves."[42] Although there was the lingering sense of the United States as an escaped colony, and a growing awareness of its potential as an economic rival, during the late decades of the century it was becoming the destination not only of British tourists but of increasing numbers of British emigrants: first of the thousands of "redundant" women who became a much-discussed social problem around midcentury, and later—more problematically, from the home viewpoint—of men, especially the second sons of the gentry, whose already precarious social niche at home was increasingly eroded by the tides of democratization and the gradual professional gains of women.[43]

For many writers, that Americans are natural objects of satire is self-

---

42. Newsome, *Victorian World Picture*, 99.

43. From time to time *Macmillan's Magazine*, like others of its kind, published articles focusing on the theoretical advantages—and conversely, the more brutal realities—of settlement in North America. For an excellent exploration of this topic and its reverberation in the literary magazines of the late century, see Anne M. Windholz, "An Emigrant and a Gentleman: Imperial Masculinity, British Magazines, and the Colony That Got Away," *Victorian Studies* 42 (1999–2000): 631–58.

evident. An anonymous author (identified as Charles A. Cole) tells of the primitive state of things in "Vermont" (June 1873), populated by rubes among whom "art is utterly unknown, and they are indifferent to it," and "accomplishments are not much practised even by the wife and daughters" (178). In a sequel, "More about Vermont" (May 1874), he continues his screed with complaints about the confused state of commerce: "You may purchase stationery at a chemist's, bed-furniture at a watch-maker's, blinds and paper-hangings and musical instruments at the stationer's, whips and dog-collars at a tailor's, and butter and milk of the ironmonger" (76).[44] Cole does not identify the musical instruments available, but the odds are good that they were banjos—one item, along with ranches and Niagara Falls, that became absolutely iconic in Victorian writing about the United States, occurring in innumerable contexts in the magazine.

If travel accounts provided a certain fascination, as of imagining "ourselves" in different circumstances, the fascination was often colored by all sorts of ill-informed assumptions.[45] American writers sometimes defended themselves, as did Alma Strettell in her celebration of Colorado Springs on its tenth anniversary in "A Little Western Town" (December 1881). Strettell emphasizes the cultural accomplishments of her community even within only ten years.

> Some old citizens who went into mining at Leadville, and "struck pay-ore," have invested their gains in an opera-house, a charmingly pretty little theatre, and the pride of Colorado Springs. At present the house is superior to the artistes who appear there, as the dramatic and operatic troupes who visit Denver and come on here, are never *more* than second-rate. The citizens fondly hope, however, that the fame of the opera-house and of the appreciative public that fills it, will soon entice hither some brighter stars. (121)

And sometimes British writers celebrated the American scene as well. An appreciative essay on "Social New York" (June 1872) was contributed by one J. W. C.—Johnnie Cross, the young banker who would later marry George Eliot shortly before her death. He stoutly defends Americans against British

44. Cole partially redeems himself, in my view at least, by passing along a report he has read that in nearby Northampton, Massachusetts, "there will ere long be opened ... a *Woman's College of the highest and most liberal grade*, founded on the noble bequest of the late Sophia Smith, of Hatfield" (May 1874, 76).

45. In 1890 a fed-up American produced an amusing but pointed protest in *Lippincott's Magazine* against English attitudes, accusing them of ignorance about American culture, institutions, and geography, and complaining as well about "their entire self-satisfaction in such ignorance" (Anne H. Wharton, "British Side-Glances at America," *Lippincott's Magazine* 46 [1890]: 709–12).

charges of barbarity by citing, among other things, "forty millions of the best educated, the best fed, the best clothed, and the most contented people in the world" (118). Cross makes the interesting observation that in America the sexes are together much more, at every kind of recreation, not gender-segregated as in Britain, and reports with appreciation that one especially "pleasant innovation" is the giving of theater or opera parties by "any unmarried young lady or gentleman" with supper following at Delmonico's. "The opera," he comments, "is a much cheaper amusement in New York than in London," though unfortunately "inferior in fully equal proportion" (124).

American blacks were always a special case in Victorian travel writing, treated more consistently with Africans and other "natives"—as I will discuss below—than as Americans.[46] Arthur Stanley, the dean of Westminster, was a close personal friend of Grove's and (symptomatic of the extraordinary currency of religious subject matter in the British press) wrote for the magazine in nearly every issue. In one essay of June 1879, "The Historical Aspect of the American Churches," he attempts to come to grips with this singularly alien aspect of American culture, and on the whole—despite his curious idea that the refusal of the United States to establish a single church had to do with states' rights each to establish its own—he does a creditable job of tracing the history and the regional presence of each one. Considering why so many African-Americans are Methodists, Stanley supposes that "the hymns, originating in the first instance from the pens of John Wesley and his brother Charles, and multiplied by the fertility of American fancy, have an attraction for the coloured population corresponding to that for ceremonial charm which I have already described as furnished to them by the Baptists through the rite of immersion" (103–4). Musical taste is apparently racial, as is ceremony and so much else in the Victorian cosmos.

Perhaps the most offensive piece in this fifteen-year run of the magazine is "A Peep at the Southern Negro" (November 1878) by Arthur Granville Bradley, a British emigrant to America and the nephew of Grove's brother-in-law, so perhaps an unavoidable contributor.[47] The essay marks

46. See Windholz, "An Emigrant and a Gentleman," around 640, on this point, and 645–47 on the various construals of race, racial degeneration, and racial patriotism thought relevant to the American situation.

47. Bradley was also the author, under the pen name "Shebauticon," of "Virginia and the Gentleman Emigrant" (June 1875), an essay drumming up the kind of British emigration I describe above. Such advertisements were frequent in the shilling monthly press during the last third of the century, but Bradley's description here of the ruination wrought on honest white farmers by shiftless and fun-loving negroes could not have provided much encouragement.

the genuine interest the British public had in the fortunes of American blacks after emancipation, but Bradley gives an unusually loathsome account of the "dusky race," concentrating not only on those ubiquitous American banjos but on the "whoopin' and hollerin'" they accompanied; "whisky and candy, dancing and banjo-playing reign triumphant" at Christmastime among "this extraordinary race" (67).

As Bradley's writing indicates, music could also be a diagnostic tool in venues less benign than simple travelogues. It is routinely used in *Macmillan's* during these years to help in delineating class and religious differences—which were, to the Victorians, so intertwined as features of identity as to be almost the same thing, so that churches might be assessed and characterized by their musical tastes and practices. M. A. Lewis's article in September 1882 on "The Salvation Army" announces itself just as the marching army does, with a "sound of distant music" (403). Although Lewis offers a sympathetic and somewhat admiring account of the career of General William Booth, the army's founder, it is clear from the author's description of Salvation Army services that among the possible worship communities in the British Isles this particular group represents alienness itself: "[The service] commences with a hymn sung standing, at a pace that would frighten a good old Wesleyan or Baptist out of his senses, and there is a roaring chorus, which is repeated over and over again with the greatest enthusiasm" (406). This congregation may not be so far removed, in readers' imaginations, from those black American Methodists whose enthusiastic singing Stanley described.

Characteristically, English protestants—especially Evangelicals—distrusted the sensual pleasures of religious accoutrement, particularly those that they associated with the Roman church. In the issue for January 1882 Edmund Ffoulkes, a former convert to Catholicism who had subsequently thought better of it, hastens to assure readers that "it was not the gorgeous or the musical accompaniments of High Mass" that appealed to him (205) but serious matters of doctrine and ecclesiastical procedure; his account has more than a whiff of the narrow escape. In a long poem about the Shaker community entitled "The Children of Lebanon: An American Idyll" (January 1873) a Boston poet identified only as "A. G." uses music as a signaling system throughout, playing the chaste communal hymns of the group against the dangerously private singing of two young people who are falling in (forbidden) love.

But most striking of all musical diagnoses to a modern reader are the confident racial characterizations that accompanied the early stages of anthropological investigation, in dangerous conjunction with the global expansion of the British empire. At this particular intellectual moment, after the publication of the *Origin of Species,* most major scientists accepted both evolution and its mechanism, natural selection (or, as Herbert Spencer complacently insisted on calling it instead, "the survival of the fittest"), and the mainstream magazines carried the news both in essays contributed by the scientists themselves and in less responsible, more casual, amateur writing. "Unfortunately," James Secord says, "this widespread acceptance of evolutionary science tended, largely because of Darwin's insistence on competition and struggle as the mechanisms of evolution, to underwrite unsavory attitudes in social arenas ranging from the management of empire and foreign policy to class and gender relationships at home."[48] The evolutionary metaphor—though too seldom recognized as such—fills *Macmillan's* as it did other publications. William Barry, in a quite sympathetic account of Irish street ballads (January 1872), remarks that "it is curious enough that the taste for these odd effusions still survives amongst a people who are becoming thoroughly Anglicized in most of their habits and customs" (190).[49] Were it not for the evidence of their ballads, that is, the Irish might almost appear to be moving upward on the evolutionary scale. As I commented above, insults to the Irish—sometimes, as in Barry's case, couched as left-handed compliments—are so frequent and so casual as to be both beneath and beyond scrutiny in a context like this; but from the ethnographic perspective, it may be worth noting the extent to which it is taken for granted that Ireland is "many years behind" England's "more advanced civilization" (Hugh Montgomery, "The Present Aspect of the Irish Land Question" [May 1975]). William Gifford Palgrave's orientalist novel, *Alkamah's Cave: A Story of Nejd* (March 1875), begins just so: "It has been remarked, and, I believe, correctly so, that the music of semi-barbarous, or, to put it more courteously, semi-civilized races, is more often sad than cheerful in its character: Welsh and Irish melodies are sometimes cited in proof" (448).

Victorian prose is notable for its preoccupation with and reification of the notion of "race," although it is important to recognize that the word itself served very general purposes indeed, often appearing as a simple synonym

48. Secord, *Victorian Sensation,* 512, 529. David Newsome suggests the "pecking order within the various races and nations of the world" as seen by mid-Victorian English who understood themselves to stand at the pinnacle: Europeans next (headed by Germany, Switzerland, and the Low Countries, with Latin nations last); Jews next; then all Asians—even those known to have the oldest civilizations; and blacks or "natives" at the bottom (*Victorian World Picture,* 93–94).

49. Barry was later the author of an essay on "Wagner and the Bayreuth Idea," *Quarterly Review* 187 (January 1898).

for "category" or "group." Nationalities are spoken of as races, as are ethnic groups, but one is just as likely to come upon references to "the race of women" or "the race of journalists"; in such instances it is much like the equally frequent word "species," a symptom of the era's taxonomic obsession. Nonetheless, where lines of heredity and descent were concerned Victorians believed absolutely in the reality of "racial" categories and in various inborn and apparently ineradicable differences among them. For instance, articles on the history of England are careful to distinguish alien peoples (Celts and Romans) from the original Britons, though we might think that such distinctions of the blood had long since vanished into history, and they dispute whether the ancestors of modern Englishmen were the Britons or the Teutons who conquered them. Similarly, discussions of the endemic and apparently intractable political problems in the Middle East were often thought to hang upon the ability to figure out who was genuinely an Arab.[50]

Although there is nothing in *Macmillan's* during these years that we would recognize as an ethnomusicological perspective, there is plenty of casual ethnographic writing, symptomatic of a fascination with otherness that always wanted to be reassured that the others did not hold within their cultural purview any lasting values to compete with Victorian certainties. Racial essentialism combined readily with the understanding of music as the most direct expression of interiority and true character, to yield a vocabulary that construed music as an easy synecdoche. Charles Clermont-Ganneau, in "The Arabs in Palestine" (August 1875), uses women's songs, among other artifacts and forms of expression, to demonstrate that "they are indeed behind their husbands by several centuries" and provide "what artistic traces yet remain of a people who never really possessed any art but of the most rudimentary kind" (372).

Sometimes authors ruminated on the odd situations brought about by the juxtaposition of the uneven evolution of cultures against the increasing globalization of human interaction and, of course, the experience of empire. An anonymous correspondent (identified as Marwood Tucker) report-

50. Charles Kingsley's article "The Natural Theology of the Future" (March 1871) is especially enlightening on the popular understanding of evolutionary science, which supported a general (and usually intellectually progressive) belief in racial difference. Kingsley allows that "some persons have a nervous fear of [the] word" but insists that "physical science is proving more and more the immense importance of Race; the importance of hereditary powers, hereditary organs, hereditary habits, in all organized beings, from the lowest plant to the highest animal" (373).

ing in "Constantinople: A Sketch during the Conference" (March 1877) encountered this curious phenomenon.

> In this city of contrasts civilisation and barbarism go hand in hand,
> and a line of tramway-cars, which have a special compartment to
> shield veiled women from the profaning eye of man, carries a quantity
> of passengers during the day at Stamboul through streets that are lit
> at night by only the paper lanterns of the few-and-far-between passers-
> by. It is strange, as at one of the brilliant balls at the Austrian palace, to
> dance to the exquisitely civilised music of Vienna, while an Egyptian
> Princess holds mysterious court—to which of course only ladies are
> admitted—behind the gauze curtains of a gallery above. (402)

As is easily predictable, responses to non-Western music were very strong and most often characterized by complete incomprehension, an incomprehension readily—even proudly, perhaps—shared with the reader. Thus Harold Littledale, in "Cymbeline in a Hindoo Playhouse" (May 1880): "the choric music, an excruciating performance, to my profane ears sounding most like an unavailing attempt to smother the squeals of two babies with the din of a bagpipe and a tin kettle" (66). Or Palgrave again, in "Phra-Bat" (November 1881) describing a festival at a Buddhist shrine in Siam: "of all Asiatic music the Siamese is generally held the best—a moderate praise, as those who have attended Persian, Arabian, Hindoo, or Malay, not to say Chinese performances, will testify" (29). Or our Colorado Springs friend, Alma Strettell, reporting on a visit to Taos pueblo in "An Indian Festival" (November 1882): "the runners advanced in two lines, facing each other, and performing a sort of quick hopping step. This was called a dance, but looked like a simple jump. All the while they waved boughs of cottonwood over their heads, and uttered a weird, quavering cry, or whoop" (27). But it should never be forgotten, however gaping the voids of cultural difference, that the frequent appearance of cross-cultural articles like these responded to intense Victorian curiosity about the rest of the world.

And there were also enthusiasts, most notably the knowledgeable and eager Charles G. Leland, an American writer and folklorist who contributed a substantial essay on "The Russian Gipsies" to the issue for November 1879. He is interested in the Gypsies as a cosmopolitan "world civilization" whose anthropological origins are to be found in music and dancing, still the strongest markers of their culture no matter where found in the world. Leland speaks so admiringly of the "weird witchery" of their singing that I would like to offer an extended quote illustrative of the dynamics of this particular set of progressive attitudes:

I have in my time been deeply moved by the choruses of Nubian boatmen; I have listened with great pleasure to Chinese and Japanese music—Ole Bull once told me he had done the same—and I have delighted by the hour in Arab songs; and I have felt the charm of our Red Indian music. If this seem absurd to those who characterise all such sound and song as "caterwauling," let me remind the reader, that in all Europe there is not one man fonder of music than an average Arab, a Chinese, or a Red Indian, for any of these people as I have seen and know, will sit twelve or fifteen hours, without the least weariness, listening to what cultivated Europeans all consider as a mere charivari. When London gladly endures fifteen-hour concerts, composed of *morceaux* by Wagner, Chopin, and Liszt, I will believe that Art can charm as much as nature. . . .

I do not know that I can explain the fact why the more "barbarous" music is, the more it is beloved of man; but I think that the principle of the *refrain*, or repetition in music . . . acts as a sort of animal magnetism or abstraction, ending in an *extase*. . . . The most enraptured audience I ever saw in my life was at a Coptic wedding in Cairo, where one hundred and fifty guests listened, from 7 P.M. till 3 A.M. . . . to what a European would call absolute jangling, yelping, and howling. (50)

He goes on to explain that the Gypsies alone, of all the world's people, "have succeeded in all their songs in combining the mysterious and maddening charm of the true wild Eastern music, with that of regular and simple melody, intelligible to every Western ear."

The message is certainly mixed. We cannot for a moment doubt Leland's wide sympathetic experience of musics around the world, or his genuine passion for Gypsy music (elaborated at considerable length in the course of the essay); we recognize his desire to educate readers as to the self-imposed limits to musical experience that Europeans inflict upon themselves. And yet there is that curious assumption that these instances of world music are "nature" as opposed to "Art"—capitalized, of course—and that the rapture of the Egyptian wedding guests was some sort of aberrant psychic event rather than an aesthetic experience. Leland does not loosen his grip on the evolutionary imperatives of cultural development, and it is surely too much to ask of him that he should. His is, by late Victorian standards, a progressive and educated stance, and characteristic in general of the field of scholarship loosely referred to as "orientalism." It is an enlightened fascination with otherness.[51]

51. A historical exoticism exactly analogous to orientalist enthusiasm governs Sebastian Evans's alliterative and somewhat Hopkinsesque poem "Arthur's Knight-

Just on the eve of the Zulu wars (March 1878), a Christianized Zulu contributed a report to the magazine in which he defended the Zulu king, Ketshwayo, against widely circulated charges that he routinely put to death those who had been converted. The author, Magema Magwaza, establishes his bona fides among English readers by reporting his midjourney halt at a missionary's station: "He then took me and my brother, and showed us a very pretty chapel and its beautiful decorations; he opened the harmonium and played it, and I too played it" (423). A footnote in the text, probably provided by the bishop of Natal, J. W. Colenso (who wrote a foreword to Magwaza's article), assures readers that "Magema can play the chants, &c., for service," and the claim is bolstered by others in the text: Magwaza writes letters home, and he is happy to receive gifts of snuff and trousers from the missionary. By such means both Colenso and Magwaza attempt to interrupt the otherwise inevitable course of their readers' assessment of a converted African "native," a course that would surely render his defense of Ketshwayo incredible back in London.

CONCLUSION: "FRAMED IN MAN"

The poem by Eliza Keary called "The Goose-Girl: A Tale of the Year 2099" (September 1869) responds to a certain strain of Victorian anxiety by hypothesizing a harsh Gradgrindian future of hyperrationalized living, all work and godlessness, measured in "one terrible sort of school-hour all the year through" (425), in which it will, the narrator fears, be impossible any longer to sing. It is well beyond my scope here to discuss the fears of industrialization and of the democratization of literacy and information that this poem hints at, but I do want to note that the image of the singing goose girl, a truth-teller both in her character as peasant and in her music, is an evident and eloquent claim upon the need for a more right-brained future.

As an alignment of ideas this is oddly, and certainly inadvertently, con-

---

ing" (August 1869), which indulges for a stanza or so in the abstruse names of medieval musical instruments—

With citole, sackbut, sawtrey, and sweet stop
Of clariner and cornet, and the clang
Of timbrels and of tabors—pipe and lute
With their wild warble thrilling through the twang
Of harps and wail of melancholy flute.

—as other stanzas play with the assonance of medieval vocabularies of apparel, cooking, and gadgetry.

sonant with Lionel Tollemache's memoir, "Recollections of Mr. Grote and Mr. Babbage" (April 1873), which retells an anecdote the Victorians knew well, the one about Charles Babbage's running battle with organ-grinders. As he aged, Babbage felt himself beginning to lose his mental powers, the author tells us. "Indeed, he gave this as one reason for the vehement war which he waged against street-organs. It was not merely that he hated music—though he did this thoroughly—but also because it often happened that, when his mind was big with some weighty idea, an organ-grinder began, and the idea vanished" (494). A brain with a big idea, in the Victorian cosmos, could be easily overmastered by music.[52]

But George Eliot, along with the goose girl, would have gently suggested to Babbage that he had drawn the wrong conclusion, failing to see the connection of music to truth itself. Her long poem, "A College Breakfast-Party" (July 1878), imagines an undergraduate conversation on art and the aesthetic, at "our English Wittenberg," among a group of young men named for the characters in *Hamlet*. It's Guildenstern who espouses something close to Eliot's own belief in the seriousness of those depths whence music arises, the interior in which music is so closely held. Arguing against a more abstract, aestheticist position—art for art's sake, with absolute rules of its own—he says,

> All sacred rules, imagined or revealed,
> Can have no form or potency apart
> From the percipient and emotive mind.
> God, duty, love, submission, fellowship,
> Must first be framed in man, as music is,
> Before they live outside him as a law.

Such an understanding places music at the center of the internal universe, not only as experience but as law and moral arbiter as well; Babbage's big ideas could not even be framed except in its company.

I want to end with a discussion of a story that may be the strangest to appear in these fifteen years of *Macmillan's Magazine*, or at least the one that most sharply reminds us of the immense gulf of alienness that sepa-

---

52. Such an outraged reaction to street music in London was not Babbage's alone. During the 1860s many prominent writers and intellectuals sought governmental assistance in doing away with what Dickens called persecution by "brazen performers on brazen instruments, beaters of drums, grinders of organs, bangers of banjos, clashers of cymbals, worriers of fiddles, and bellowers of ballads" (quoted in Karen Chase and Michael Levenson, *The Spectacle of Intimacy: A Public Life for the Victorian Family* [Princeton: Princeton University Press, 2000], 151–52).

rates us from the Victorians despite their occasional surface familiarity. The story comes in two parts, "A Little Pilgrim: In the Unseen (*For Easter*)," appearing in May 1882 and "The Little Pilgrim Goes Up Higher" in the following September (suggesting among other things that the first had been well received by the magazine's readers), and its anonymous author has been identified as the very popular novelist and frequent contributor to the magazine, Margaret Oliphant. It is a curiously mawkish tale—in other circumstances Oliphant was a realist with a sharp tongue—and perhaps that is her reason for adopting anonymity in this case.

The "little pilgrim" is a woman who dies and gradually discovers the truth about the afterlife, and the description of her experience and increasing enlightenment is taken absolutely seriously, without a hint of the cynical or the tongue-in-cheek. The tale is theologically liberal and scientifically forward-looking; the author specifies that there are people in heaven from other worlds, although one of the lessons of the story is that those from earth are the chosen race. Even hell, we learn, is not quite so irredeemably unpleasant as we might have thought. Everywhere there is music.

> She wanted to sing, she was so happy, but remembered that she was old and had lost her voice, and then remembered again that she was no longer old, and perhaps had found it again. (6)

Everything in these heavenly, or preheavenly, spaces is musical, from voices to laughter to the sound of angels' language, even to the motion of celestial walking. Of course, there are silver trumpets played by "angels of the musicians' order." As the protagonist and some new friends explore,

> they met with bands of singers who sang so sweetly that the heart seemed to leap out of the Pilgrim's breast to meet with them, for above all things this was what she had loved most. And out of one of the palaces there came such glorious music, that everything she had seen and heard before seemed as nothing in comparison. (348)

Even in what seems to be purgatory (Oliphant does not use the conventional names), those who are waiting there, apparently playing the role of the peasantry in this ultimate travel documentary, have their songs.

> [O]thers arranged themselves in choirs, and sang to her delightful songs of the fields, and accompanied her out upon her way, singing and answering to each other. (352)

As she rushes to welcome some newcomers, fresh from an earthly disaster, she finds that she has learned to sing even more sweetly than in the other life:

the little Pilgrim's voice, though it was so small, echoed away through the great firmament . . . for it was said among the stars that when such a little sound could reach so far, it was a token that the Lord has chosen aright, and that His method must be the best. (355)

It is an ultimate lesson, eccentrically framed but not otherwise out of line with the rest of what we have encountered: music is close enough to the core of being that, when it is present—as an earlier Victorian said—"all's right with the world."

3 "Girling" at the Parlor Piano

La femme n'est pas une *action*, elle est une *influence*.
MARIE DE SAVERNY, La Femme chez elle et dans le monde (1876)

The type-writer is especially adapted to feminine fingers. They seem to be made for type-writing. The type-writing involves no hard labor, and no more skill than playing the piano.
JOHN HARRISON, A Manual of the Type-Writer (1888)

In an excruciating climactic scene in the American girls' novel *Elsie Dinsmore*, the pious eight-year-old heroine finds herself seated on a piano bench facing an irresolvable moral dilemma. Her father has asked her to play and sing for a gathering of his friends, and Elsie would be more than happy to comply, generous and tractable as always, but for the fact that it is Sunday. She protests that "this is the holy Sabbath day," but he is determined to test her obedience, insisting that she has no right to oppose his moral judgment with her own.

> Elsie sat with her little hands folded in her lap, the tears streaming from her downcast eyes over her pale cheeks. She was trembling, but though there was no stubbornness in her countenance, the expression meek and humble, she made no movement toward obeying her father's order.
> There was a moment of silent waiting: then he said in his severest tone, "Elsie, you shall sit there till you obey me, though it should be until to-morrow morning."
> "Yes, papa," she replied in a scarcely audible voice, and they all turned away and left her.[1]

Elsie sits on the bench for several hours, missing her dinner, until she faints. Elsie's predicament is hardly subtle. As a good daughter, she has two

---

Thanks to Elizabeth Harries, Jeffrey Kallberg, Benjamin Korstvedt, Richard Leppert, James Parakilas, Marc Perlman, and Elizabeth Wood, all of whom either generously read earlier versions of this essay or conversed thoughtfully with me after hearing me talk on this topic.
1. Martha Finley, *Elsie Dinsmore* (1868; New York: Dodd, Mead, 1893), 240–41. I am grateful to my colleague Ann Arnett Ferguson for reminding me of the relevance of this novel to my argument.

obligations—to her father and to her God—and they are momentarily at odds; she cannot fulfill both. But that the author situates her moment of moral crisis on a piano bench is far from arbitrary and in 1868 was equally obvious: a daughter spends her time at the piano.

My subject here is a myth, a system of representations: nineteenth-century girls at the keyboard.[2] The myth's relationship to empirical reality—to the actual female piano playing that went on—is not evidentiary but symbolic, offering a rich ground for understanding the values and preoccupations of Victorian culture and something as well about the sacred aura around family domesticity, the myth's most cherished breeding-ground. For myth-making is, as Alessandra Comini says, "civilization's autobiography."[3] The myth is perhaps also, and more interestingly, causal: that is, it affected the actual lives of girls and women, and the more certainly as it gathered strength and definition in the course of the century.

I borrow the term "girling" from Judith Butler, who coined it to describe a two-way process that marks girls' lived experience of their culture's values. On the one hand, girling is the social process that forms girls appropriate to the needs of the society they live in; on the other, it is their own enactment—or, in Butlerian terms, their performance—of girlhood, both to satisfy familial and social demands on them and, as we shall see, to satisfy needs of their own either to resist those demands or to reassure themselves about their own capacity to fulfill them.[4] In pursuit of both sides of this cultural thoroughfare, I want to survey not only the social prescriptions that seated the girls before those keyboards, but also and especially their reactions to finding themselves there.[5]

2. The chapter epigraphs' sources are Marie de Saverny [pseud. Marie d'Ajac], *La Femme chez elle et dans le monde*, 2d. ed. (Paris: Aux bureaux du journal *La Revue de la mode*, 1876), 119; and John Harrison's manual (London, 1888), quoted in Christopher Keep, "The Cultural Work of the Type-Writer Girl," *Victorian Studies* 40 (1997): 405.

3. Alessandra Comini, *The Changing Image of Beethoven: A Study in Myth-making* (New York: Rizzoli, 1987), 415.

4. Butler used the term in a talk at Smith College in January 1994.

5. The rich musicological literature on the social meaning of female piano playing includes most notably Richard Leppert's *Music and Image: Domesticity, Ideology and Socio-cultural Formation in Eighteenth-Century England* (Cambridge: Cambridge University Press, 1988) and *The Sight of Sound: Music, Representation, and the History of the Body* (Berkeley: University of California Press, 1993); and Judith Tick's "'Passed Away Is the Piano Girl': Changes in American Musical Life, 1870–1900," in *Women Making Music: The Western Art Tradition, 1150–1950*, ed. Jane Bowers and Judith Tick (Urbana: University of Illinois Press, 1986), 325–

I believe that a project like this, both gender-specific and music-specific, can help flesh out much of the cultural theorizing that has been so interesting to musicology as well as to other disciplines in recent years; it adds specificity to our understanding of the bourgeois family as the real engine of larger-scale cultural developments, a nexus of relationships that has played a considerable role in much of that theory. For example, Habermas's work on the complex and reciprocal interactions of public and private spheres suggests, among other things, that in such a culture as that of modern Europe it is within these newly construed family groups—hierarchical, blood-related, and emotionally charged—that individuals developed their manner of relating to others and their sense of what behaviors were appropriate to the public arena and what kinds of compensatory satisfaction were to be expected from the private.[6] Norbert Elias's argument about the sociology of manners and of civilized or "respectable" behavior rests crucially on the development of a sensibility of "private things" and of personal, intimate behaviors. Similarly the team of French historians who have been involved in the large-scale exploration of the history of private life demonstrated conclusively that in modern Western culture "private" has not, for better or worse, meant "individual" but always "nuclear family."[7] Friedrich Kittler's "discourse networks" include a mechanism of maternal transmission of literacy—of "natural" acculturation—that speaks directly to this intimate sense of familial interaction.[8] And no one, I think, has taught us more than Peter Gay about the perhaps surprising role of the most inti-

---

348. Leppert's work focuses particularly on iconography, Tick's on women's passage beyond the "piano-girl" stage into professional musicianship. For broader explorations of the implications of domestic music making see Thomas Christensen, "Four-Hand Piano Transcription and Geographies of Nineteenth-Century Musical Reception," *Journal of the American Musicological Society* 52 (1999): 254–98; and James Parakilas, "The Power of Domestication in the Lives of Musical Canons," *repercussions* 4 (1995): 5–25.

6. Jürgen Habermas, *The Structural Transformation of the Public Sphere: An Inquiry into a Category of Bourgeois Society,* trans. Thomas Burger with Frederick Lawrence (Cambridge, Mass.: MIT Press, 1989). On musical ramifications of the increasingly rigid divide between public and private, see Derek B. Scott, "Music and Social Class," in *The Cambridge History of Nineteenth-Century Music,* ed. Jim Samson (Cambridge: Cambridge University Press, 2001), 544–67.

7. Norbert Elias, *The Civilizing Process,* vol. 1 of *History of Manners,* trans. Edmund Jephcott (1939; New York: Pantheon, 1982); Michelle Perrot, ed., *The Fires of Revolution to the Great War,* vol. 4 of *A History of Private Life,* trans. Arthur Goldhammer (Cambridge, Mass.: Belknap, 1990).

8. See Friedrich A. Kittler, "The Mother's Mouth," in *Discourse Networks 1800/1900,* trans. Michael Metteer with Chris Cullens (Stanford: Stanford University Press, 1990).

mate aspects of emotional life in shaping civilization even on the grandest scale.[9] Such lines of research suggest eloquently, I think, that more needs to be understood about the particular behaviors and practices that marked and formed bourgeois families at home, and without doubt music was a predominant one of those practices.

Perhaps it goes without saying that none of the Victorian authors I cite had a particularly strong interest in teenage girls. But I believe that I can make a case for their central importance in this historical process, taking girls seriously enough to consider their real role in the development of societal forces and structures very much larger than what they themselves usually imagined—although some of them, in the privacy of their diaries, did sometimes speculate on their role in the great scheme of things, as teenagers with diaries will do.

I

Victorian texts are rife with observations about girls and pianos, some regarding the phenomenon as part of the natural order of things, but others rather less enchanted by what they saw as an artificial and inadvisable practice.

> How frequently in the present state of narrow feeling do we witness the sad spectacle of a girl, entirely devoid of all musical ability, compelled to drudge away for hours daily at the piano because forsooth, every young lady ought to be able to play. The result is, that for a few seasons the patience of friends is exhausted, and their ears are tortured by the girl's wretched performances.[10]

Thomas Carlyle, admittedly never very musical, complained about the incessant noise of pianos in hotel rooms.

> This miserable young woman that now in the next house to me spends all her young, bright days, not in learning to darn stockings, sew shirts, bake pastry, or any art, mystery, or business that will profit herself or others; not even in amusing herself or skipping on the grassplots with laughter of her mates; but simply and solely raging from dawn to dusk, to night and midnight, on a hapless piano which it is evident she will never in this world learn to render more musical than a pair of barn-fanners!

9. Peter Gay, *The Bourgeois Experience: Victoria to Freud*, 5 vols. (New York: Oxford University Press [vols. 1–2], W. W. Norton [vols. 3–5], 1984–98).
10. M. A. E. L., "The Girl of the Future," *Victoria Magazine* 15 (1870): 495.

Carlyle expressed the irritable hope that "the Devil some good night should take his hammer and smite in shivers all and every piano of our European world!"[11]

In his moralizing volume entitled *Social Pressure*, Arthur Helps uses the same phenomenon as a horrific example of the fate awaiting the sensitive soul living in a large city:

> If he is a father of a family, he learns to bear with something like fortitude the practising of his own daughters on the piano; but it seems hard that he should have to hear the practising of his neighbours' daughters on that formidable instrument; and when, for the sixth time, he hears C flat instead of C sharp played in an adjacent house, he is very apt to be distracted from his work, and very much inclined to utter unbecoming language.[12]

However it came about, and with whatever variation in pace and thoroughness from country to country, there is no doubt that domestic music making, and especially piano playing, had become thoroughly associated with young women by the middle of the nineteenth century; for better or worse, the piano-girl was ubiquitous. Any doubts we might have on that point would be set aside by a perusal of the dauntingly enormous iconographic tradition—a primary repository of cultural myth—and by a glance at the flood of piano music published with explicit inscriptions "to the ladies," "to the fair sex," "to Vienna's beauties," and so forth. In step with this fashion and its associated market, Carl Czerny published *Letters to a Young Lady, on the Art of Playing the Pianoforte* in Vienna around 1840, as a supplement to his more general method book. In it Czerny addresses a fictional pupil he calls, appropriately enough, Cecilia, describing her as "a talented and well-educated girl of about twelve years old." He exhorts her to attend to her posture and to her appearance at the keyboard, he reminds her of her duty as a good daughter to play for the pleasure of her family and their friends, and he reinforces the point that piano playing, while of course suitable for everyone, is "yet more particularly one of the most charming and honorable accomplishments for young ladies, and, indeed, for the female sex in general."[13]

---

11. *Carlyle: An Anthology*, ed. G. M. Trevelyan (London: Longmans, Green, 1953), 182.

12. Arthur Helps, *Social Pressure* (Boston: Roberts Bros., 1875), 46.

13. Carl Czerny, *Letters to a Young Lady, on the Art of Playing the Pianoforte*, trans. J. A. Hamilton (New York, n.d.), 1–2. Matthew Head discusses an earlier stage of this social transaction in "'If the Pretty Little Hand Won't Stretch': Music for the Fair Sex in Eighteenth-Century Germany," *Journal of the American Musicological Society* 52 (1999): 203–54.

In the sixty-two published volumes of the *Girl's Own Paper* more than 250 items on music appeared,[14] including exhortations by leading lights of the aristocracy like Lady Lindsay's "Thoughts on Practising" (1882) or Lady Macfarren's "Music in Social Life" (1895). The iconographic record, already mentioned, furnishes indisputable evidence of the ubiquity of the association. One striking but also typical example is a well-known drawing by Dominique Ingres (opposite page), a family portrait dating from 1818, similar in type to many such portraits both by the same and by other artists. This picture is reproduced in the nineteenth-century volume of *The History of Private Life,* with the following caption:

> The Stamaty Family is a classic of the genre. Each person strikes a pose: the father with his Napoleonic gesture, the mother in her finery, the slender young woman at the piano, the adolescent with his unruly hair, the young child, whose sex is revealed by his toys.[15]

In other words, this placement of the girl at the keyboard was, precisely, emblematic. When a nineteenth-century artist, working in a conventional and commercial genre, needed to represent "daughterhood," he did it with a girl at a keyboard.

An anonymous correspondent to the *Allgemeine Musikalische Zeitung* in 1800 partially explains the tradition:

> Every well-bred girl, whether she has talent or not, must learn to play the piano or sing; first of all it's fashionable; secondly, it's the most convenient way for her to put herself forward in society and thereby, if she is lucky, make an advantageous matrimonial alliance, particularly a moneyed one.[16]

To be sure, the writer goes on immediately to say that sons ought to learn music too. But, like most contemporary observers, this one is remarkably forthright about the purposes that were served by all this piano playing, and why in every advice book the girls were mentioned and addressed first. A young woman in 1800 in Vienna, just like most young women in most places before very recently, had but one job in life: to find a spouse; she soon found that music was highly effective as bait. Popular newspapers and magazines of the period are filled with jokes about escaping the little seductress at the keyboard.

14. A complete index by topic of the *Girl's Own Paper,* compiled by Honor Ward, is available at www.mth.uea.ac.uk/~h720/GOP.

15. Perrot, *From the Fires of Revolution,* 98.

16. Quoted in Alice M. Hanson, *Musical Life in Biedermeier Vienna* (Cambridge: Cambridge University Press, 1985), 118.

Dominique Ingres, *La famille Stamaty* (1818). Musée du Louvre, Département des Arts Graphiques. © Photo R.M.N., reproduced by permission.

Digging a layer deeper into this social phenomenon, we can find a more profound reason why music, and gradually all of the arts, were increasingly associated with women in bourgeois society—always bearing in mind that my discussion here is of amateur, not professional, musicians. It has something to do with the spread of a popularized, or perhaps I should say vulgarized, form of romanticism that idealized and sentimentalized women at the same time that it idealized and sentimentalized the aesthetic experience, creating a natural link between them.[17] As the businessman or the bureau-

17. See chapter 4 for a more detailed exploration of this cultural phenomenon.

crat, practical-minded and uniformed in that nineteenth-century innovation, the business suit, became the Everyman figure of middle-class consciousness, those aspects of his personality and imagination that had to be repressed in competitive professional life gradually formed into the image of a counterpart, an Everywoman who was conceptualized as his opposite: she was intuitive where he was reasonable, artistic where he was pragmatic, nurturing where he was aggressive, delicate where he was robust, domestic and shy where he was public and gregarious, and so forth. The historian of philosophy Geneviève Fraisse says, for instance, that "nineteenth-century metaphysics thrived on concepts of duality, relation, and the unity of opposites, for which sexual difference was one representation and perhaps even a fundamental metaphor."[18] Boys and girls were educated differently, and during the course of the nineteenth century educational "reforms" produced curricula that became in fact *more* sharply differentiated toward the rational/ scientific for boys and the emotional/aesthetic for girls. Despite the fact that women were slowly gaining political and economic equality, the curricula were addressed to their increasingly absolute role differentiation later in life.[19]

There is little need to rehearse here this by now familiar ideology; in place of an extended discussion I offer an emblematic quotation from Florence Hartley's *Ladies' Book of Etiquette and Manual of Politeness*, published in Boston in 1873:

> All circumstances well examined, there can be no doubt Providence has willed that man should be the head of the human race, even as woman is its heart; that he should be its strength, as she is its solace; that he should be its wisdom, as she is its grace; that he should be its mind, its impetus, and its courage, as she is its sentiment, its charm, and its consolation. (294)

Hartley's exposition of the providential facts of life leaves little doubt which gender will take up the piano, and her comments, clichés that they are, are

18. Geneviève Fraisse, "A Philosophical History of Sexual Difference," in *Emerging Feminism from Revolution to World War*, vol. 4 of *A History of Women in the West*, ed. Geneviève Fraisse and Michelle Perrot (Cambridge, Mass.: Harvard University Press, 1993), 53.

19. See, among others, James Albisetti, *Schooling German Girls and Women: Secondary and Higher Education in the Nineteenth Century* (Princeton: Princeton University Press, 1988), which contains numerous quotations from contemporary sources; Linda L. Clark, *Schooling the Daughters of Marianne: Textbooks and the Socialization of Girls in Modern French Primary Schools* (Albany: SUNY Press, 1984); and Françoise Mayeur, "The Secular Model of Girls' Education," in *Emerging Feminism*, ed. Fraisse and Perrot, 229–30.

especially interesting in light of their occurrence in an etiquette book: this is not a sermon, but a source of authority that girls and women might consult on a daily basis for practical advice, and very far from an unusual example of its genre in including such moral speculation. Furthermore, Hartley describes these aspects of the essential nature of men and women in the form of contributions to the "human race," not merely as attributes or potentials for individual development. Another version elaborates even more lavishly the "opposite poles" theory of gender:

> Man is bold—woman is beautiful. Man is courageous—woman is timid. Man labors in the field—woman at home. Man talks to persuade— woman to please. Man has a daring heart—woman a tender, loving one. Man has power—woman taste. Man has justice—woman mercy. Man has strength—woman love; while man combats with the enemy, struggles with the world, woman is waiting to prepare his repast and sweeten his existence. . . . [H]is day may be sad and troubled, but in the chaste arms of his wife he finds comfort and repose.[20]

The last few phrases here underline the particular ways in which the daughter is learning her job by practicing the piano. It was her specific task, as we read in many another etiquette and child-rearing manual, to offset her father's alienated experience of the daily work grind and to provide sufficiently attractive entertainment at home to keep her brothers out of oyster bars and saloons—indeed, the rescue of brothers from the world's temptations became a major issue and was much discussed by the moralists. In 1848 *Punch* defined the ideal daughter as one who "does not invent excuses for not reading to her father of an evening," or, as Judith Rowbotham puts it, "it was woman's first duty in life . . . to become as professional in her sphere as a man in his; to cultivate her feminine talents in the emotional realm so as to maximize their usefulness within the domestic orbit."[21]

H. R. Haweis, a contemporary British clergyman who wrote a lot about the relationship of music and moral life, explains something about the implications of this role differentiation (although I believe that he did not quite fully understand the nature of the transaction involved): "As a woman's life is often a life of feeling rather than of action, and if society, while it limits

20. Thomas L. Haines and Levi W. Yaggy, *The Royal Path of Life* (Cincinnati, 1876), quoted in Judy Hilkey, *Character Is Capital: Success Manuals and Manhood in Gilded Age America* (Chapel Hill: University of North Carolina Press, 1997), 159.

21. Quoted in Joan N. Burstyn, *Victorian Education and the Ideal of Womanhood* (London: Croom, Helm, 1980), 38; Judith Rowbotham, *Good Girls Make Good Wives: Guidance for Girls in Victorian Fiction* (Oxford: Basil Blackwell, 1989), 21. On music's firm assignment to the emotional realm, see chapter 2.

her sphere of action, frequently calls upon her to repress her feelings, we should not deny her the high, the recreative, the healthy outlet for emotion which music supplies. . . . A good play on the piano has not unfrequently taken the place of a good cry up stairs."[22] While Haweis is surely right about the piano's role in female emotional life, my own interpretation of the testimony of memoirs and diaries, as well as countless scenes in nineteenth-century novels, is that the young woman was expected not, indeed, to repress her feelings but rather to enact the graceful and sensitive expression of feeling on behalf of society as a whole: some etiquette books actually taught young women how to weep effectively. The girl's job would surely have included *both* the good play on the piano *and* the good cry upstairs.

Family history can help us understand the kind of intimate situation that provided the context for girls' piano playing and—more to my immediate point—for the mythic system of representation that enfolded the piano-girls. One of the many enormous social changes produced by industrialization, everywhere in the Western world though at varying paces in different countries, was the shift from the relatively large "household" of the eighteenth century and earlier—which might contain several generations, relatives of various types, and a number of retainers and employees—to what the Germans called the *Kleinfamilie,* the nuclear family.[23] As always, an ideology came along with the new formation for, as Justin Lewis writes, "cultural forms do not drift through history aimlessly: they are grounded in an ideological context that gives them their historical significance."[24] The members of the new family were expected to share highly charged emotional bonds and to live in considerable intimacy; this was the era in which arranged marriage was disappearing in favor of affectional choice, and when middle-class mothers were giving up wet nurses and nannies to care for their children themselves.

At the same time, status in the new kind of society was increasingly based on wealth rather than birth, so that "upward mobility" took root as one of the family's goals. Many scholars have detailed the process by which the bourgeois wife gradually became the symbolic representative, first of the leisure her husband's economic success could buy for the family (a leisure

22. H. R. Haweis, *Music and Morals* (1871; New York: Harper and Bros., 1904), 437.

23. Chapter 4 continues the discussion of this transformation.

24. Justin Lewis, "The Meaning of Things: Audiences, Ambiguity, and Power," in *Viewing, Reading, Listening: Audiences and Cultural Reception,* ed. Jon Cruz and Justin Lewis (Boulder: Westview Press, 1994), 20.

more apparent than real in most cases), and then of the family's purchasing power through increasingly elaborated consumer practices. Thus the woman inexorably comes to be associated with—and, according to some historians, confined to—the home, facilitating the century-long process of establishing "an ideal that removed women from all productive labour but childbearing, that separated the men and women of a family during their working hours, and that channeled women's energies, and only women's, into arranging for the consumption of goods and services."[25] This ideal, I would argue, produces piano playing under two guises, both as an expression of leisure and as a form of moral and emotional labor within the family. The cultural reasoning might proceed as follows: music was necessary to society, not as mere entertainment but (in the well-regulated and enlightened nineteenth-century home) as a sort of combination spiritual therapy and mental hygiene. The family, laden with symbolic responsibility in its newly intimate configuration, was the natural and proper locus for this *Herzensbildung* along with other kinds of education and socialization. The father's job was to provide for the family's material sustenance, which he now ordinarily did outside the home; the emotional or spiritual wellbeing of the family, inside the home, was the responsibility of the women. And the adolescent daughter was ideally suited to take over the musical portion of this responsibility; in keeping with the customary ways in which Victorian children were, as J. S. Bratton pithily puts it, "pressed into instrumentality," she could perform this important service role within her birth family while at the same time practicing for her own wifely and motherly career.[26] From this scenario we understand some of the emotional charge that surrounded her piano lessons. She wasn't only learning music or making herself more marriageable, although she certainly was doing both of those; she was also participating in a system of family discipline and, perhaps most important, absorbing the essence of the larger aesthetic and emotional realm that made her femininity convincing.[27]

25. Burstyn, *Victorian Education*, 19. Frances B. Cogan takes a somewhat different view, at least in the American context (*All-American Girl: The Ideal of Real Womanhood in Mid-Nineteenth-Century America* [Athens: University of Georgia Press, 1989]).

26. J. S. Bratton, *The Impact of Victorian Children's Fiction* (London: Croom Helm, 1981), 29.

27. See Ingrid Otto, *Bürgerliche Töchtererziehung im Spiegel illustrierter Zeitschriften von 1865 bis 1915* (Hildesheim: Verlag August Lax, 1990); and Monika Simmel, *Erziehung zum Weibe: Mädchenbildung im 19. Jahrhundert* (Frankfurt am Main: Campus Verlag, 1980).

On this point there is a nearly inexhaustible supply of pertinent quotations for the choosing—from all over Europe, North America, and their colonial sites—since the nineteenth century saw a floodtide of advice manuals, etiquette books, and treatises on family life, and as far as I have seen they all tell more or less this same tale.[28] For one example, consider Sarah Josepha Hale, arbiter of American mores and editor of *Godey's Lady's Book*: "Music is the art of all arts in its sweet and refining influence on humanity." Instruction in music is therefore necessary in every family, since it "will have abiding effect on the happiness of home-life, and the character of our people." Hale urges that children of both genders be taught music, somewhat against the American grain, but her reason for including the males is especially revealing: "To a man himself, ... the power to play is of use. He may not always have a sister, wife, or daughter, to sing and play to him."[29] Here is another version, from a German source:

> Father comes home in a bad temper, having had a hard day in the hostile world outside; his daughter opens the piano, touches the keys and sings her father his favorite song. Isn't it wonderful to see the sunshine return to his face, and the ugly shadows disappear?[30]

and here a considerably less beatific and sentimental admonition:

> I have no mercy for the young lady who has had time and money lavished on her musical education, who will not take the trouble to play to her brothers in the evening. If she distrusts her powers she need never

28. For the German context, see Dagmar-Renate Eicke, *Teenager zu Kaisers Zeiten: Die "höhere" Tochter in Gesellschafts-, Anstands- und Mädchenbüchern zwischen 1860 und 1900* (Bonn: Habelt, 1980), a collection of exhortations from advice books for young women.
29. Sarah Josepha Hale, *Manners; or, Happy Homes and Good Society* (Boston, 1868), 49, 50, 171. I have found precisely the same words in other advice manuals and cannot tell who originally penned them; e.g., the anonymous "Man in the Club Window," in *The Habits of Good Society: A Handbook of Etiquette for Ladies and Gentlemen* (Philadelphia: J. B. Lippincott, ca. 1875) is clearly a reprint of an English book. Apparently "success writers cribbed, pirated, and plagiarized lavishly and unabashedly" from one another (Hilkey, *Character Is Capital*, 48).
But some etiquette books worried that young women were spending *too much* of their time practicing, at the expense of more pious activities or more fundamental aspects of home management. Hence we must read comments specifically on piano practicing in conjunction with other sections or chapters—usually among the first in the book and underlying everything that follows—concerning "woman's role" or "woman's mission."
30. H. A. Köstlin, quoted in Andreas Ballstaedt and Tobias Widmaier, *Salonmusik: Zur Geschichte und Funktion einer bürgerliche Musikpraxis* (Stuttgart: Steiner-Verlag, 1989), 203.

play to other people who may ask her out of compliment; but when brothers ask their sisters to play, they mean that they want the music, and they should have it.[31]

In the German-speaking world a teenage girl was familiarly known as a *Backfisch*—a baked fish or, perhaps, a fish suitable for baking—in any event, a dish, and one waiting for consumption; similar attitudes prevailed elsewhere, even in the absence of such a colorful epithet. In diaries and memoirs women describe this time as unhappy and tense; some of them bitterly accuse society of treating them like commodities, whose market value would decrease steeply if left on the shelf for too long. Others describe a protracted sense of emotional upheaval, a feeling that life was on hold and an intense reliance upon the intimacy that their pianos offered them as ways of killing time while they waited. Here is the source of a whole flood of parlor pieces written and published especially for them: "Backfisch's Dream," "The Maiden's Prayer," "Elsa's Longing."

This repertory was, as may be imagined, highly successful commercially. Just like the present-day romance novels of which they were surely predecessors, these pieces constitute a functionally and ideologically defined genre quite unlike the formally defined ones music history is used to; they bear individual, albeit stereotyped, titles that are in fact not unlike the titles of romance novels. Their emergence vividly exemplifies Jeffrey Kallberg's notion of a "generic contract" between composer and listener[32]—in this case, the solitary performer is her own audience, and the contract specifies the emotional solace she expects in exchange for the money she pays for the sheet music and her hours of practice. On a larger scale, the implicit contract that binds the genre as a whole promises to produce women who are correctly "girled" according to the needs of the society in which they are destined to take their places.

II

Today I put a hen on thirteen eggs and I hope that all of them will hatch. I have also been out milking twice today, and I have finished the comforter I was making for Mamma and I think that is fairly good, for me that is. Then I practiced the piano for an hour.

31. E. Chester [pseud. Harriet Eliza Paine], *Girls and Women* (Boston: Houghton Mifflin, 1891), 150.
32. Jeffrey Kallberg, "The Rhetoric of Genre: Chopin's Nocturne in G Minor," *19th-Century Music* 11 (1988): 238–61.

This is an entry from the diary of Kena Fries, a fifteen-year-old Swedish immigrant living outside Orlando, Florida.[33] I quote her precisely because there is nothing in the least unusual about her, or about her account of her activities on this March day in 1883. The obverse of the coin of girling as social formation, the girls' response to their own acculturation by piano, is readily and ubiquitously visible in their diaries and letters. Many of them, as we shall see, express dramatic and even melodramatic feelings about the process but others, like Kena, seem to take it simply for granted. I found particularly revealing the memoirs (sometimes also the diaries) of women who became prominent later in other fields—not musicians, but women whose public profile was such that they were led to ruminate on the means and ramifications of their own upbringing. Strikingly, it is almost impossible to open a nineteenth-century woman's diary, correspondence, or memoir without encountering piano lessons or piano practice at some point.

Several themes emerge from these girls' accounts. They let us know all the ways in which their practicing and their playing are part of the family dynamic of the household; they speak volubly of their attitudes toward practicing and the kinds of discipline applied in getting them to do it regularly; many of them confide deep feelings about music and about the role "their" pianos play in their emotional lives—pianos and diaries are frequently coupled as expressive confidants; they are at least as aware as their later historians of the piano's potential as a site for flirtation, courtship, and proto-sexual dalliance.

But it is particularly important to keep in mind the intense doubleness of these girls' experience: they surely are subject to social formation at those keyboards, and they know it. Some internalize the lesson without demur, but many exhibit forms of resistance or manage to co-opt the whole endeavor and turn it to their own ends. For most girls, the girling experience was an ambivalent combination of all these reactions; in real life, there were few Elsie Dinsmores.

Family Discipline and Family Service

As I suggested above in describing the intense nineteenth-century form of family life, teenage girls had enormous responsibility in bourgeois families, especially when they were the oldest or only daughter. It was largely unacknowledged responsibility, because it consisted mostly of emotional work. In these families, especially toward the end of the century as essentialism

33. "Diary of Kena Fries," ed. Jean Yothers and Paul W. Wehr, trans. Margareta Miller, *Florida Historical Quarterly* 62 (1984): 342.

grew more and more absolute, the sense of the individual role of each family member was strongly marked and differentiated. Kena Fries, our friend of the thirteen eggs, makes a very typical remark—typical as well in its offhand brevity:

> Friday, September 7, 1883. . . . Mr. Jimmie Mitchell was here this morning, Mrs. Mitchell is dying, poor people, I played for him.[34]

Such a morning's activity seems to be as much a part of daily life as setting the hens, milking, or quilting.

Even in the unlikeliest of circumstances, on the overland trail in covered wagons, the young women provided the cultural consolation of music, and although they did not usually have their pianos with them in the back of the Conestoga, they made do with more portable instruments. Amelia Hadley wrote in April 1851, somewhere outside Council Bluffs, Iowa:

> We are a merry crowd, while I am journalizeing one of the company is playing the violin which sounds delightful way out here. My accordian is also good, as I carry it in the carrige and play while we travel, had a verry hard rain this evening, and everry thing seems affloat.[35]

Mariett Foster Cummings took a melodeon along. In July 1852, from somewhere on the Humboldt River in Nevada, she tells us: "In camp today with a large mule train. Very warm. Got out my instrument and had some fine music."[36]

In effect, in many of these families the teenage daughters were the home entertainment centers. Young Eliza Ridgely of Baltimore, away from home at Miss Lymann's Academy in Philadelphia in 1816, is repeatedly exhorted by her father in his letters. "I hope you will persevere," he says, "in the determination [to win the music prize], as I need not tell you how much importance to you it would be if you could entertain us all with good musick," and again a year later: "I need not remind you of your music and drawing. I hope and believe you will not neglect them—remember how often you can entertain us by good music."[37]

The eldest of the four daughters of Lord Lyttleton, Meriel, was the fam-

34. Ibid., 349.

35. *Covered Wagon Women: Diaries and Letters from the Western Trails, 1851,* ed. Kenneth L. Holmes (Lincoln: University of Nebraska Press, 1984), 3:59.

36. *Covered Wagon Women: Diaries and Letters from the Western Trails, 1840–1890,* ed. Kenneth L. Holmes (Glendale, Calif.: Arthur H. Clark, 1985), 4:157.

37. Beth L. Miller, "The Ridgelys of Hampton: New Perspectives on Musical Life in Early-Nineteenth-Century Baltimore," *Journal of Musicological Research* 14 (1994): 47.

ily pianist and was expected to provide the music for elaborate family theatricals, never to appear in them. Her sister Lucy wrote in her diary in 1857, "Buried alive behind the Fairies' Grotto . . . this most unfortunate individual saw nothing of the whole concern."[38] The scene is reminiscent of numerous such occasions in Jane Austen's novels, in which the sister who has been identified as the "musical" one is doomed to spend whole festive evenings at the keyboard, never to dance herself.

Female Transmission of Musical Responsibility

> Today has been a sad one. Amelia grieved us both so much. She was reading when she should have been practicing and I feel anything like deceit so much. May the poor child never suffer as we do for her. I wonder how she can be cured. I am so distressed as my Amelia was my pride.

Of course, Amelia's mother wrote this: she was Lucy Ronalds Harris of Toronto, and she made this diary entry in December 1880, when Amelia was twelve.[39] Her excessive distress, for such a small transgression, may have been occasioned more by the child's deliberate deceit than by the lack of practice per se, but surely Lucy was also worried about a potential failure of the transmission process that was part of the piano-playing contract between women and Victorian society. Women's prescribed role as providers of musical—and other emotional—sustenance for family and community entailed as well their responsibility to teach the skill to the next generation. The vast iconography of women at keyboards contains a substantial subset of pictures of this intergenerational transaction: young mothers play with infant daughters on their laps or with preteen daughters hanging over their shoulders, young women play for their aging mothers, and so on in innumerable configurations. Mary Lamb's story "The Changeling" invokes common assumptions in its reliance on the inheritance of musicality from mother to daughter to reveal the truth about a pair of switched-at-birth children.[40]

Lucy Harris was not alone in confiding such sentiments to her diary. In 1863 Josephine Clay Habersham of Savannah worried in a similar way about her daughter Anna, age fourteen: "The child has a fund of energy in her

---

38. Sheila Fletcher, *Victorian Girls: Lord Lyttleton's Daughters* (London: Hambledon Press, 1997), 7.

39. *The Eldon House Diaries: Five Women's Views of the 19th Century,* ed. Robin S. Harris and Terry G. Harris (Toronto: Champlain Society, 1994), 471.

40. Mary Lamb, *Mrs. Leicester's School* (1831; London: Macmillan, 1897).

composition *to do what she wants to do* that must be guided and watched....
And yet, often *if she does not feel like it,* she frets over practicing."[41]
Josephine does not seem to care whether or not Anna evinced any musical
talent or interest. As we would expect, the most common transmitters of
female piano playing were piano teachers themselves, and of those the most
interesting for my own purposes are not the ones who were really professional musicians but women who took up music instruction as a business,
usually out of necessity, and are living testimony to the bottomless piano-
girl market. Perhaps the ideological understanding of that intergenerational
female obligation helped society cope with what in many instances would
otherwise have been an alarming intrusion of women into the world of professional work? Louis Ehlert was not alone in attempting to work through
the social meanings of this difficulty:

> though it cannot be denied in a general way that men have exhibited in
> this field [i.e., music teaching], as in all others, an advantage in the way
> of greater productiveness and a more widespread cultivation, the less
> degree, on an average, of feminine intellect may be balanced by moral
> thoroughness. For teaching exacts two qualities that are more feminine
> in their nature than masculine—patience and love.... Not without
> reason, then, is the female teacher often preferred to the masculine
> in rudimental instruction.

His argument invites an analysis like Friedrich Kittler's parallel observation that mothers' responsibility for teaching literacy at the same time si-
lenced them in the wider world of literature and language.[42]

But female teachers could also be preferred simply because they were
available, just as they frequently undertook the teaching only for want of
more congenial work. Millie Gray, for example, lived in Fredericksburg, Virginia quite comfortably until her husband lost his job; she cast about for
ways to help support the family that would be permissible for a genteel married woman in her midthirties, and she ended up doing "writing" (that is,
copying work), dressmaking, and piano lessons. She records them as business transactions:

> It rained & snowed last night, & we have terrible walking—though the
> weather is mild. It did not prevent some of my scholars from coming—
> amongst them Lucy Taylor—She has taken about 3 lessons p-week for

41. Spencer Bidwell King, Jr., *Ebb Tide: As Seen through the Diary of Josephine
Clay Habersham, 1863* (Athens: University of Georgia Press, 1958), 40.

42. Louis Ehlert, *From the Tone-World,* trans. Helen D. Tretbar (1877; New York:
Charles F. Tretbar, 1885), 125. On Kittler, see note 8 above.

I believe 3 weeks—that is, the 1st week in December, when I gave her a Lesson nearly every day—they were interrupted then by the meazles untill the middle of Jany.—say the 11th—since which she comes regularly—and I calculate 3 lessons p-week making up to this day 9 Lessons.[43]

Millie's diary is rather exciting, because during the family's period of hardship her husband decided to move them west into the then-republic of Texas, and the story of her mental and material preparation for the trip is gripping. Once settled in Houston, however, and having secured Texas citizenship, Millie no longer gives piano lessons: instead, she takes in many of the republic's legislators as boarders.

Another sort of accidental piano teacher was Lucy Maud Montgomery, later herself a beloved friend to teenage girls as the author of the well-known series of books that began with *Anne of Green Gables*. Her journals are not published in full, but even from the available portion it is easy to see that Lucy served her whole community in Cavendish, Prince Edward Island, by playing the piano and organ at events of all kinds. From about the age of eighteen, she earned spending money and began to prepare for her planned career as a schoolteacher by traveling to other towns to give piano lessons.[44]

Training Regimes

Here is Louisa May Alcott at the age of eleven: "I had a music lesson with Miss P. I hate her, she is so fussy. I ran in the wind and played be a horse."[45] Louisa is a child right in the painful midst of being girled. At eleven, she'd rather be a horse than a girl, and indeed, under the circumstances, who would not? An eight-year-old who suffered the regime more cheerfully was Florence Nightingale, who wrote to her mother in 1828:

> I do figures, music (both Piano-forte, & Miss C[hris]tie's new way too,) Latin, making maps of Palestine, (and such like about the Bible) & then we walk, & play, & do my patchwork, & we have such fun.[46]

43. *The Diary of Millie Gray, 1832–1840* (Houston: Fletcher Young Publishing, 1967), 232–33.

44. *The Selected Journals of L. M. Montgomery*, vol. 1: 1889–1910, ed. Mary Rubio and Elizabeth Waterston (Toronto: Oxford University Press, 1985).

45. *The Journals of Louisa May Alcott*, ed. Joel Myerson and Daniel Shealy (Boston: Little, Brown, 1989), 45: diary entry for 14 September 1843.

46. *Ever Yours, Florence Nightingale: Selected Letters*, ed. Martha Vicinus and Bea Nergaard (Cambridge, Mass.: Harvard University Press, 1990), 14.

She does not explain, alas, what "Miss Christie's new way" was. Here is a more neutral account from Charlotte Forten Grimké, later the great abolitionist writer, a rare middle-class African American living in Salem, Massachusetts during the 1850s. At the age of seventeen, a record of the daily round of Charlotte's activities—typically saturated with tasks from hour to hour—appears as the very first entry in her diary:

> May 24, 1854. I stand by the window listening to [the birds'] music, but suddenly remember that I have an Arithmetic lesson which employes me until breakfast; then to school, recited my lessons, and commenced my journal. After dinner practised a music lesson, did some sewing, and then took a pleasant walk by the water.[47]

The regimented nature of practicing, as it is reported in countless girls' diaries, results no doubt from a combination of factors: the repetitious nature of the work that is actually required to learn to play the piano together with the boot-camp quality of ordinary Victorian practices of education and what Margaret Beetham calls "the regular collapse of entertainment into instruction" during the period.[48] Dr. Elizabeth Blackwell worried a good deal about "this ruinous system of education," especially as it was practiced in boarding-schools for girls, for its "long hours of unnatural confinement" and its deleterious effects on physical health,[49] but there seems to have been more widespread attachment to the aphorism about the satanic opportunities offered by idle hands.

Musical regimes were not infrequent targets of contemporary satire—even the Victorians sometimes could poke fun at themselves. The popular writer Augusta Webster included a chapter under the rubric "Pianist and Martyr" in her tell-all book called *A Housewife's Opinions*, published in London in 1878, in which she offers a description of the regime:

> When Music, heavenly maid, was young, did she practise many
> hours a day? Did she train her fingers gymnastically with scales and
> shakes and exercises on five notes; and did she plod through the bars
> of toilsome fantasias, repeating them through weeks, a dozen times
> together, until at last the patient process had achieved the crown of
> success, and she could take the allegros, and for the matter of that

47. *Journals of Charlotte Forten Grimké*, ed. Brenda Stevenson (New York: Oxford University Press, 1988), 59.

48. Margaret Beetham, *A Magazine of Her Own? Domesticity and Desire in the Woman's Magazine, 1800–1914* (London: Routledge, 1996), 24.

49. Elizabeth Blackwell, M.D. *The Laws of Life, with Special Reference to the Physical Education of Girls* (New York: George P. Putnam, 1852), 134, 132.

the andantes too, at a fast prestissimo? And did she have next-door neighbours?

Ruminating on the moral implications of all this drilling, Webster concludes sardonically, "The better the girl the longer she practises."[50]

It does not follow that the girls ensconced in such regimes cared for them, that they had warmer feelings for the piano lessons than they necessarily did for arithmetic problems. A teenager in Anthony Trollope's *Miss Mackenzie* is emphatic:

> "Susanna thinks that going to school at all is rather a nuisance," said Miss Mackenzie.
> "You'd think so too, aunt, if you had to practise every day for an hour in the same room with four other pianos. It's my belief that I shall hate the sound of a piano the longest day that I shall live."
> "I suppose it's the same with all young ladies," said Mr. Rubb.
> "It's the same with them all at Mrs. Crammer's. There isn't one there that does not hate it."[51]

I very typically found comments like the following, failed instances of girling: "Music was always taught me by a sister. I gave a certain time—not very much—to the piano every day, but never showed any talent for it."[52] That particular version comes from Louise Creighton, who as a girl was the tenth of twelve children in a family in which many of the others *were* in fact musical, and one of whose regular daily visitors was George Grove.

Particularly intriguing are the accounts left by young girls whose names we recognize from their later achievements in other arenas. How well some of them understood, like Louisa Alcott and Harriet Martineau, Fanny

50. Augusta Webster, *A Housewife's Opinions* (London: Macmillan, 1879), 21. Many thanks to my colleague Cornelia Pearsall for finding this source for me. Jeffrey Kallberg sent me another such in Thackeray's story "The Ravenswing" (*Men's Wives* [Boston: Estes and Lauriat, 1891], 257).

> It is the condition of the young lady's existence. She breakfasts at eight, she does "Mangnall's Questions" with the governess till ten, she practises till one, she walks in the square with bars round her till two, then she practises again, then she sews or hems, or reads French, or Hume's "History," then she comes down to play to papa, because he likes music whilst he is asleep after dinner, and then it is bedtime, and the morrow is another day with what are called the same "duties" to be got through.

51. (London: Penguin, 1993), 63.
52. Louise Creighton, *Memoir of a Victorian Woman: Reflections of Louise Creighton, 1850–1936*, ed. James Thayne Covert (Bloomington: Indiana University Press, 1994), 27.

Lewald and Florence Nightingale, that the piano lessons were not suited to their talents or their inclinations but were still somehow an inescapable part of their daily round. Beatrice Webb, for instance, described her regimen at around age sixteen, conceding that "I have left off music almost entirely; I practise exercises and scales for half an hour, half because Mother wishes it, and half because I do not want to leave it off entirely. Drawing is what I should like to excel in."[53] Resistance was not infrequent, then, but it was usually unavailing. The French novelist Gyp, Sibylle de Mirabeau as a child, recalled her alarm at her grandfather's announcement that piano lessons were impending.

> Je saute en l'air:
> —Le piano! ... Ah! mais non ... Je ne veux pas apprendre le piano!
> —On ne dit pas: "Je ne veux pas!"—observe Grand-père.[54]

The memoirs of the German novelist Fanny Lewald provide one of the most extreme examples of the training regime that I have seen. After she left school, Fanny's father provided daily schedules for her that detailed every moment of her time from the minute she got up in the morning until bedtime. The schedule for Mondays included piano practice "of new pieces" from 8:00 until 9:00 in the morning and a lesson with her teacher at 5:00 P.M.; on Tuesdays the second hour is filled with "practice of old pieces" in the place of the lesson. Fanny comments from her adult vantage point that "this schedule, with its curt commands, seemed neither unusual nor harsh to me. I had been accustomed to a specific schedule and discipline from childhood on."[55]

Elizabeth Rogers Mason Cabot, a Boston schoolgirl, wrote at the age of fifteen:

> A schoolgirl's life, although a happy one as a general rule, and full of interest, in nevertheless often a *very* weary one. To rise in the morning and hurry down and breakfast and hasten to school at nine o'clock; to study from that time till two, recess and all; and never be allowed to open your lips or move from your seat unless in a recitation; to come home, swallow down a dinner, and seat yourself at the piano for an hour and a half; and then if the weather be too unpleasant to walk, to sit down to write a composition or learn some lesson that must

53. Beatrice Webb, *My Apprenticeship* (London: Longmans, Green, 1926), 73.
54. Gyp [Sibylle Martel de Janville], *Souvenirs d'une petite fille* (Paris: Calmann-Lévy, 1927), 1:119.
55. *The Education of Fanny Lewald: An Autobiography*, trans. and ed. Hanna Ballin Lewis (Albany: SUNY Press, 1992), 75–76.

be done during the week; and then to spend the whole evening in studying for the next day: to do this, I say, is enough to weary most anyone.[56]

Lizzie Mason is particularly interesting because she gives us a long, meditative diary entry during her seventeenth year, in which she muses on the difficulty of balancing all of her family responsibilities. Beginning with "What is life? a conflict of emotions" (76), she goes on to puzzle out all of the opposing demands on her time, and how she could possibly meet them. Lizzie's mother was an invalid and demanded her company much of the time when she was not in school; in addition she was expected to do her homework and her daily practicing conscientiously.

> I feel that, situated as I am, an only daughter, with a mother often sick
> and depressed, never gay, it rests upon one, to make our home bright,
> cheerful and attractive to the boys, and comfortable to Father. When
> I think how much boys are exposed to, how much a happy home may
> keep them from, and how much depends on me for making it happy,
> *I feel almost discouraged by my own responsibility.* (78–79)

As we have seen, such responsibilities were very real indeed for a sixteen-year-old in 1850.

Penitential Practicing

Catherine Pozzi, a French girl who grew to modest fame as a novelist, provides a good model for this very familiar trope. She was thirteen when, in 1896, she decided to reform her life thoroughly. "C'est toute une nouvelle vie que je commence. Je vais étudier 2 heures de piano par jour, me lever bien plus tôt, et faire ma prière régulièrement."[57]

Somewhere in Austria there lived a young girl, calling herself Rita, who published her childhood diary anonymously many years later; the book became famous as the subject of an analysis by Sigmund Freud, and it is known in the literature simply as *A Young Girl's Diary*. Rita, too, understood the sacrifice value of practicing, and when, at the age of eleven, she wanted unusual permission to attend a slightly too-grownup party, she knew perfectly well that family business around music was to be transacted with her mother: "Father really lets me do anything I like, but not Mother. Still, if I practise

56. *More than Common Powers of Perception: The Diary of Elizabeth Rogers Mason Cabot*, ed. P. A.M. Taylor (Boston: Beacon Press, 1991), 64.
57. Catherine Pozzi, *Journal de jeunesse, 1893–1904*, ed. Claire Paulhan (n.p.: Editions Verdier, 1995), 30.

my piano regularly perhaps she'll let me go."[58] For many of these girls whose interest in music was modest at best, practicing served as a currency with which they could purchase desired privileges.

There was another side to this particular self-inflicted penance, as well. Harriet Martineau describes in her autobiography occasions when she was essentially sent to the keyboard as a punishment but recognized and relished its ambiguity in that capacity. That is, she learned to co-opt the essentially disciplinary nature of the experience and turn it to her own gratification. After an especially energetic argument with her mother and her sister Rachel, for example,

> I saw . . . that I had gained some ground; and this was made clearer by my mother sternly desiring me to practise my music. . . . The question now was how I should get through. My hands were clammy and tremulous; my fingers stuck to each other; my eyes were dim, and there was a roaring in my ears. I could easily have fainted; and it might have done no harm if I had. But I made a tremendous effort to appear calm. I opened the piano, lighted a candle with a steady hand, began, and derived strength from the first chords. I believe I never played better in my life.[59]

Others internalized the whole process, combining Martineau's revelation of emotional power with complete acquiescence in the moral lesson being offered:

> What a wonderful bond of sympathy there is between lovers of music! . . . With me, a love and knowledge of the science is a passport to my esteem. I contend that it is the only one of the arts exempt from the trail of the serpent—so its devotees must be noble and pure.[60]

The future educator of women Frances Willard ruminated similarly on musicality:

> Father wishes me to be a musician. I have asked myself, "what is the power, the ability to strike in succession several chords upon the piano, melodeon or organ, worth, if it is merely mechanical?" . . . and I have decided with myself that it is worth comparatively nothing. When I hear *music*, it means something to me. It talks with me and tells me that which I did not know before, and makes me by that much, wiser than I was. It conveys ideas to me. If I were somewhat more spiritual,

58. *A Young Girl's Diary,* ed. Eden and Cedar Paul (London: Allen and Unwin, [1921]), 13.
59. Harriet Martineau, *Autobiography,* 3d ed. (London: Smith, Elder, 1877), 1:87.
60. Laura Nisbet Boykin, *Shinplasters and Homespun,* ed. Mary Wright Stock (Rockville, Md.: Printex, 1975), 15–16.

I know I might translate it into words;—and they would be beautiful ones, and the world would listen to them.[61]

Symbolic Domesticity

The instrument, as well as the piece of furniture that embodied it, was ineradicably associated with domesticity in women's minds and not infrequently marked the moment at which a new dwelling, even a particularly rough or humble one, came to feel like home. Rachel Haskell was in her late thirties when she moved with her husband and family to a mining town in Nevada in 1867. Rachel is cheerful and energetic, facing with considerable equanimity the continual dirt, cultural deprivation, and abundance of rough characters in town, but she is not insensitive to the domestic norms the mining families brought with them from the East:

> Monday 11th. . . . How comfortable and cozy the sitting room did look this evening by twilight. The shelves laden with books, specimens, minerals, shells. The Piano, the Sewing Machine, comfortable sofa and easy chair, with healthy, happy, prattling, chippy, little children all . . . I played on the Piano for Mr. C.[62]

Rachel respectfully capitalizes both Piano and Sewing Machine, those preeminent representatives of female civilization.

There are even more dramatic examples of the highly symbolic significance of these pianos to young women living in remote areas in difficult circumstances. I came upon heart-rending accounts of disasters along the overland trail in the American westward migration, when heavy items of household furniture had to be left behind in the struggle to get animals and wagons over the continental divide, the piano a frequent victim of poor itinerary planning.[63]

But sometimes the instrument successfully made the whole journey. Such a scene is shown in a wonderful photograph in Kenneth Ames's material culture study, *Death in the Dining Room;* a "photograph of Mr. and Mrs. David Hilton and children," taken in Nebraska around 1880, shows the family surrounding an elaborate parlor organ, standing outdoors amidst farm

---

61. *Writing Out My Heart: Selections from the Journal of Frances E. Willard, 1855–1896,* ed. Carolyn DeSwarte Gifford (Urbana: University of Illinois Press, 1995), 37.

62. Christiane Fischer, ed., *Let Them Speak for Themselves; Women in the American West, 1849–1900* (Hamden, Conn.: Archon Books, 1977), 61.

63. For similar stories from Australia's European settlement, see Deborah Crisp, "The Piano in Australia, 1770 to 1900: Some Literary Sources," *Musicology Australia* 18 (1995): 25–38.

animals and wagon parts. Perhaps it has just arrived and has yet to be moved into the house? The family members proudly flank the instrument, the Hiltons' two daughters embracing it closely on either side.[64]

A young army wife, taken by her brand-new husband to Camp Halleck, Nevada in 1868, reported on her first night in camp:

> As I lay in bed that night, feeling decidedly homesick, familiar airs, played upon a very good piano, suddenly sounded in my ears. It seemed impossible that there could be a fine musical instrument such a distance from civilization, particularly when I remembered the roads over which we had come, and the cluster of tents that alone represented human habitation. The piano, which I soon learned belonged to our captain's wife, added greatly to her happiness, and also to the pleasure of us all, though its first strains only intensified my homesick longings.[65]

Often, indeed, pianos were singled out in surprising ways for special effort. Luna Warner was fifteen when her family moved from Massachusetts to Kansas in 1871, homesteading on the Solomon River. The Warners arrived in mid-March, and by mid-June had framed and partially enclosed their new house; but before the walls were even completed Luna tells her diary that her elder brother Alf has gone back to Solomon City "after my piano"— note that "my"! She watches the road eagerly for several days, and finally on August 3 she writes:

> Watched impatiently all day for Alf and the piano but did not see them. About half past 9 after we had gone to bed, he came. Soon after he got here it rained hard,

and on the next day,

> They unloaded the piano and got it into the house. We all worked about all day getting it set up. It was soaking wet and the varnish spoiled but the inside is all right but needs tuning badly. I played all evening.

Indeed, for the next several days the diary repeatedly records "I played most all day on the piano," or "I played a good deal" even though the piano was out of tune. What seems to me the most intriguing line of all is recorded on August 28: "I keep the piano locked when I am not playing." Luna obviously regarded the instrument as her own, and the rest of the family clearly

---

64. Kenneth L. Ames, *Death in the Dining Room, and Other Tales of Victorian Culture* (Philadelphia: Temple University Press, 1992), 178; his fourth chapter, "When the Music Stops," focuses on parlor organs and contains many revealing photographs and advertisements.

65. Mrs. Orsemus Boyd, *Cavalry Life in Tent and Field* (New York: J. Selwin Tait, 1894); excerpted in *Let Them Speak for Themselves*, 111–12.

respected her ownership rights and was willing to endure a good deal of effort and expense to accommodate her. A few days later, though, Luna went
too far. A man who was staying with the family while his own house was
being completed made the mistake of playing the piano himself. "Devil take
Root," she writes. "I locked the piano while he was playing. Papa was mad
and took the key away from me."[66]

The Piano in Emotional Life: Companion and Confidant

It is not without significance that one of the best-known books of that Victorian moralist of female lives, Sarah Stickney Ellis, was entitled *Education
of the Heart: Woman's Best Work* (1869). For there is no doubt that the management of the heart *was* women's work, and that the apprenticeship for
such work required a good deal of emotional training and experience during adolescence. Anne Vincent-Buffault's *History of Tears* traces the development of this particular womanly task from the eighteenth century as
an aspect of the sentiment of family feeling and elaborates the theories of
"redemption" through female tears and the somewhat voluptuous pleasure
those tears could sometimes engender.[67]

It has been suggested by more than one writer that for nineteenth-
century girls and women the piano was closely related to the diary itself in
its status as a confidant and source of emotional rescue. Here I should say
that this particular behavioral trope has a considerable history, one not restricted to nineteenth-century females. Much earlier in the century, and indeed even in the eighteenth, a whole genre of poetry grew up in Europe—
especially in Germany and Austria—consisting of apostrophes to the piano
as friend and companion. Schubart's poem "Serafina an ihr Klavier," set as
a *Lied* by Schubert with the degendered title "An mein Klavier," is a typical
representative of the genre. Originally this little poetic convention seems
to have applied to both sexes and to have represented a sentiment that was

66. "The Diary of Luna E. Warner, a Kansas Teenager of the Early 1870s," ed.
Venola Lewis Bivans, *Kansas Historical Quarterly* 35 (1969): 289 ff.

67. Anne Vincent-Buffault, *The History of Tears: Sensibility and Sentimentality in France*, trans. Teresa Bridgeman (New York: St. Martin's Press, 1991); many
thanks to Mary Hunter for alerting me to this book. Similarly, Peter N. Stearns's
"Girls, Boys, and Emotions: Redefinitions and Historical Change" (*Journal of American History* 80 [1993]: 36–74) discusses gender differentiation in the permitted emotions and manner of expression, primarily in the service of the intimate nuclear family. Finally, see also Sally Mitchell's discussion of the significance of daydreams and
other emotional satisfactions in "Sentiment and Suffering: Women's Recreational
Reading in the 1860s," *Victorian Studies* 21 (1977): 29–45.

conventionally expressed in public situations.[68] By the mid nineteenth century, however, and especially in Anglophone cultures, the tradition had shifted: it became both unpublic and decidedly unmanly. For women, in their private diaries, the tradition went on uninterrupted.

Grace Brown Elmore was in her midtwenties and lived in Columbia, South Carolina when she recorded these very familiar sentiments, in 1864:

> My music is very, very much to me, and my happiest if not my only happy hours are those I spend at the piano. Yet I could not define either the thoughts or the feelings excited by the music, but life, the world, every thing is beautiful and full of poetry. The nature of fact and the real disappear, and I for the time am given up to the Imagination, I am glad I possess this outlet to my restless energetic spirit, that while the hands are tied by conventionalities, nothing ever binds the spirit.[69]

It is notable that Grace, like most young women who actually enjoy the musical aspect of their girling, doesn't think of it as one of those oppressive conventionalities she disdains.

Here is another, and I think quite extraordinary, rumination on music from the diary of Pauline DeCaradeuc of Aiken, South Carolina, who was twenty-one when she wrote it:

> August 28th, 1864. I believe there is nothing that our better nature needs more absolutely than music, no other art of perfection possesses that strange power of gliding into our every emotion and forming a part of it. . . . In happiness our joys are expressed & increased by music from the sweet lullaby, sung by a low voiced mother, to the last sad requiem at the grave, music has been unceasingly the soul's true panacea.[70]

Laura Nisbet Boykin lived in Macon, Georgia, during the Civil War—indeed, these diaries from the American Civil War, of which many have been preserved, are an especially rich source of information about the important emotional support pianos provided in the lives of women who watched helplessly from the sidelines as their brothers, husbands, and sons were slaughtered. Laura wrote in August 1864,

> How grateful to my soul, in these turbulent times, is *music!* It lifts me from the earth and bears me away to regions of ethereal bliss and

---

68. Head gives another example, beginning "Süß ertönendes Clavier! Welche Freuden schaffst du mir!" ("'If the Pretty Little Hand,'" 211).

69. *Heritage of Woe: The Civil War Diary of Grace Brown Elmore, 1861–1868*, ed. Marli F. Weiner (Athens: University of Georgia Press, 1997), 69.

70. *A Confederate Lady Comes of Age: The Journals of Pauline DeCaradeuc Heyward, 1863–1888*, ed. Mary D. Robertson (Columbia: University of South Carolina Press, 1992), 56.

purity! . . . My nerves were so excited by playing [last night], that I was a long time invoking sleep, ere it came.[71]

During the following summer, Laura recounts further music making and asks rhetorically in her diary: "Thus we enjoy ourselves, and forget perhaps for the time that our beloved soldiers are in the trenches, living on corn-bread and bacon, and daily exposed to the death-dealing shells of the enemy. Is it right? Is it not selfish?" (16).

Marie Bashkirtseff was a young Russian woman, although she lived for extensive periods in Italy, who famously died of tuberculosis at twenty-five; "famously" because Marie's diary was published posthumously in 1880, around the time that the Goncourt brothers' even more notorious diary also appeared, and she became widely known primarily as a rather flamboyant diarist. In her diary entry for 16 March 1876, at the age of sixteen, she re-hearses an unwanted proposal.

> About 10 o'clock Pietro came in. The *salon* is very large and very handsome; we have two pianos. I commenced to play softly one of Mendelssohn's songs without words, and [he] commenced to chant to me his own particular song. The more seriousness and warmth he put into his plea, the more I laughed and the colder I became. . . . "You are too young," I said, changing the music, and from Mendelssohn passing to a nocturne, sweeter and strong . . . breathless, with tears in his eyes, he fell at my knees. I recoiled, red with anger. Oh, piano, my protector![72]

This last ejaculation in particular is surprisingly frequent in diaries, including those of girls a lot less self-satisfied and grandiose than Marie Bashkirtseff. Clearly they were in the habit, whether seriously or mischievously, of cast-ing their pianos in the role of protector, confidant, and chaperon. Not for nothing does Laura Boykin refer to her piano as "my darling 'grand'"[73] or does John Bennett warn girls as early as 1789,

> It will enable you to entertain your friends; to confer pleasure upon *others*, must increase your *own* happiness, and it will inspire tranquil-lity, and harmonize your mind and spirits, in many of those *ruffled* or *lonely* hours, which, in almost every situation, will be your lot.[74]

71. Boykin, *Shinplasters and Homespun*, 10.
72. A. D. Hall and G. B. Heckel, trans., *Journal of Marie Bashkirtseff* (Chicago: Rand McNally, 1890), 96.
73. Boykin, *Shinplasters and Homespun*, 12.
74. John Bennett, *Letters to a Young Lady, on a variety of useful and interest-ing subjects, calculated to improve the heart, to form the manners and enlighten the understanding* (Warrington, 1789), 235.

"What new can I say, my dear readers, about a piano, this patient friend to whom you confess alternately a sadness or a joy? It will patiently listen to everything and it can sing everything on its own," promised an anonymous writer in the Polish *Magazine of Fashion and Needlework* in 1865.[75] And the girls took the promise very seriously. Thirteen-year-old Catherine Pozzi found that her music sided with her in battles with her mother.

> Et moi! Jamais Maman dit, "Catha, tu es gentille, tu travailles bien,
> tu me fait honneur ... " Voilà ce que je pensais en jouant du piano.
> Et j'ai pleuré, pauvre bête que je suis! Alors, j'ai déchiffré un air de
> Mozart. Ce qu'il y avait dans cet air, je ne sais ... mais il m'a calmée,
> il était si doux![76]

The story of Princess Alice, third child of Queen Victoria and in married life the grand duchess of Hesse, is especially poignant, because the piano could not console her for a tragedy in which it itself had been implicated. In the spring of 1873, her two young sons came running into her room somewhat too energetically while she was playing, and in the confusion the toddler Frederick fell to his death out a window. Some months later, Alice wrote to her mother:

> You ask if I can play yet? I feel as if I could not, and I have not yet done
> so. In my own house it seems to me, as if I never could play again on
> that piano, where little hands were nearly always thrust when I wanted
> to play. Away from home—in England—much sooner. I had played so
> often lately that splendid, touching funeral march of Chopin's and I
> remember it is the last thing I played, and then the boys were running
> into the room.[77]

Romance and Sexuality

There are always plenty of courtship stories surrounding Victorian girls and their pianos; these, I suspect, are sufficiently familiar to need no further illustration. They show up as perfectly conventional situations, endlessly, in Victorian novels.[78] The diaries I have been reading are replete with them as well, and it is interesting to speculate on the relationship between the girls'

75. Quoted in Benjamin Vogel, "The Piano as a Symbol of Burgher Culture in Nineteenth-Century Warsaw," *Galpin Society Journal* 46 (1993): 141

76. Pozzi, *Journal de jeunesse*, 42.

77. Alice, Grand Duchess of Hesse, Princess of Great Britain and Ireland, *Biographical Sketch and Letters* (London: John Murray, 1889), 310.

78. The best discussion of these fictional conventions is still Mary Burgan's well-known essay, "Heroines at the Piano: Women and Music in Nineteenth-Century Fiction," *Victorian Studies* 30 (1986): 51–76.

own attitudes toward their pianos and what they learned from reading such scenes in those very novels, ranging from the strategic deployment of music, like Marie's of Mendelssohn, to ward off an unwanted suitor, to the use of piano music to mask an amorous conversation from eavesdroppers, to the maternal insistence that reluctant young girls put themselves on display as performers before roomsful of local society.[79] It also becomes clear that many men counted "musicality" as a sine qua non in the choice of a wife, as we know from the quantities of personals ads in European newspapers that mentioned the trait along with good character and literacy. Mary Moragné of antebellum South Carolina, the morning after having been introduced to a gentleman she sourly refers to as "squire Danforth of Georgia," reports in her diary that "I suppose I must have made *an impression* on the brusque looking old gentleman:—this morning before I got out of bed, I heard him in the piazza asking my father where I was educated, & what instruments I played on."[80]

The deployment of music and musicality in the sexual marketplace was not, of course, without its dangers, two sorts of which were widely recognized. One was simply that girls were wasting time at the keyboard, applying themselves to frivolous "accomplishments" rather than to the real work of running a household, or becoming "interested in self-display at the expense of womanly modesty"[81]—the fear, in short, that they were enjoying themselves too much. But far more worrisome was the possibility of oversophistication in the emotional realm, the very susceptibility to which was so central to their gender definition to begin with. Strong feeling—especially sexual feeling—was always a dismaying possibility in the presence of music, and more explicitly so at the end of the century. It was a subversion, indeed, of the very ideology of true womanhood because it celebrated and heightened private experience, not family service.[82] Increasingly unabashed

79. Some must have enjoyed the visibility. Arabella Goddard herself found it necessary to warn girls to "wait till [the music] carries you away with *its* loveliness, but don't try to carry it away before the right moment with *your* loveliness" ("How to Play the Piano," *Girl's Own Paper* 1 [1880]: 166).

80. Mary E. Moragné, *The Neglected Thread: A Journal from the Calhoun Community, 1836–1842*, ed. Della Mullen Craven (Columbia: University of South Carolina Press, 1951), 40.

81. Karen J. Blair, *The Torchbearers: Women and Their Amateur Arts Associations in America, 1890–1930* (Bloomington: University of Indiana Press, 1994), 18.

82. See among others Janet Wolff, "The Culture of Separate Spheres: The Role of Culture in Nineteenth-Century Public and Private Life," in *The Culture of Capital: Art, Power, and the Nineteenth-Century Middle Class*, ed. Janet Wolff and John Seed (Manchester: Manchester University Press, 1988), 117–34.

representations of this state of affairs, and increasing suspicions about women's reasons for spending sometimes incapacitating amounts of time at the keyboard, no doubt prompted Edmond de Goncourt's notorious description of the piano as "the lady's hashish."[83]

The *Musical Times* offered in 1893 the alluring description of a particular kind of piano, fitted into an environment whose decoration was hardly subtle; a sort of late-Victorian Martha Stewart with a lascivious twinkle, this author adds a knowing turn to a powerful subtext of privacy and hidden spaces. Whoever plays this piano is no longer edifying the family.

> Placed near a bay window, it shuts in the cosiest lovers' nest imaginable. Soft-cushioned window seats that have room for just two— intuitive seats they might be called—are hidden thus away completely from the cold, cruel world. Little couches may be hidden in the shadow of such a piano when rich hangings fall from a corner window. Or a delightful tea corner is made with a screen for a doorway, and soft divans and dim lights inside. Or the back of the piano may be hung with a soft shade of yellow, brocaded with dull green leaves and flowers. Against this a little tea-table can be placed, with its dainty belongings, and a low chair beside it. A yellow cushioned divan can extend entirely around this corner, lighted by the soft radiance of a lamp with a pale green shade, and piled high with a baker's dozen of pillows.[84]

It is difficult to elaborate very fully on this subject from these particular sources because even in their diaries—not to mention in their published memoirs—most Victorian women were reticent on the subject. But a good deal is revealed to us in the Reverend H. R. Haweis's extremely influential *Music and Morals,* even as he attempts to elevate his language with a romantic purple haze.

> That poor lonely little sorrower, hardly more than a child, who sits dreaming at her piano, while her fingers, caressing the deliciously cool ivory keys, glide through a weird *nocturno* of Chopin, is playing no mere study or set piece. Ah! what heavy burden seems lifted up, and borne away in the dusk? Her eyes are half closed—her heart is far away; she dreams a dream as the long, yellow light fades in the west, and the wet vine-leaves tremble outside to the nestling birds; the angel

83. Quoted in Alan Corbin, "The Secret of the Individual," in *From the Fires of Revolution,* ed. Perrot, 531.

84. Anonymous writer in *Musical Times* (February 1893), quoted in Percy A. Scholes, *The Mirror of Music 1844–1944: A Century of Musical Life in Britain as Reflected in the Pages of the* Musical Times (London: Novello, 1947), 305.

of music has come down; she has poured into his ear the tale which she will confide to no one else, and the "restless, unsatisfied longing" has passed; for one sweet moment the cup of life seems full—she raises it to her trembling lips.[85]

To unpack this lurid paragraph might require an entire essay, but Haweis nonetheless has the appeal of one who takes these girls and their experiences seriously, and for that I appreciate him. He does not seem to make fun of their troubles or complain that they don't work at their music more seriously or that they aren't good enough daughters, and he clearly understands their relationship to their loving piano friends. To be able to confirm this account from the girls themselves would be very satisfying indeed (although I am absolutely certain that Haweis's thinly veiled discussions of emerging sexuality are precisely right), but, again, we may never have the chance to do so, because Victorian mothers and sisters were very likely to read a diary left in any accessible place, and because Victorian girls, especially the younger ones, simply did not have the vocabulary to tell us what we prurient twenty-first-century readers want to know. Some unusually outspoken ones, like Marie Bashkirtseff, explained:

> Music is a traitress . . . beware of her, she makes you do many things
> you would not do, if your head were cool. She seizes hold of you,
> twines herself around you, makes you lose your senses—and then
> it is terrible.[86]

As the diaries make clear, the piano—as furniture, as discipline, as emotional confidant, and as medium of sexual apprenticeship—played its role in innumerable nineteenth-century female lives. For the girls and young women I have quoted, its meanings are very multiple, as often sinister and manipulative as exalted or comforting. Let me give the last word to Elizabeth Lindsay Lomax, a widowed mother of six living in Washington just before the Civil War. She gives us a glimpse of the finished product, as it were, of the girling process; for her, the piano had come simply to mean "home." As southerners, Elizabeth and her family were not welcome in the capital as it became clear that war was impending; for long weary years they moved from pillar to post, living as refugees with friends or in rented houses. On Christmas 1861, writing in Fredericksburg, Elizabeth puts the best possible face on the situation:

85. Haweis, *Music and Morals*, 103. Thanks to Jeffrey Kallberg for focusing my attention on this particular paragraph.

86. Hall and Heckel, *Bashkirtseff*, 291.

Christmas Day, but it does not seem like Christmas.

We dined at Evergreen and returned to our tiny house which we find very comfortable and cozy after being wanderers for so long.

We have no maid, but the girls have taken hold with great enthusiasm and everything goes on harmoniously.

We have a piano.[87]

87. *Leaves from an Old Washington Diary,* ed. Lindsay Lomax Wood (New York: E. P. Dutton, 1943), 181.

4 Biedermeier Domesticity and the Schubert Circle

A Rereading

Instrumental-music has issued from the heart of German family-life.
RICHARD WAGNER, "On German Music" (1840)

Writing in a French periodical in the summer of 1840, Richard Wagner set out to encourage enthusiasm for German music, in part by enlightening his readers as to the essential musical and spiritual differences that distinguish the Germans, the French, and the Italians. He elaborates his argument around a core rhetorical image:

> Go and listen one winter-night in that little cabin: there sit a father and his three sons, at a small round table; two play the violin, a third the viola, the father the 'cello; what you hear so lovingly and deeply played, is a quartet composed by that little man who is beating time. . . . Hear that author's music played, and you will be dissolved to tears, for it will search your heart, and you will know what German Music is, will feel what is the German spirit.[1]

Domesticity is here invoked as a token or outward sign of genuineness, sincerity, heartfeltness—and, of course, of "real" musicality, although Wag-

This essay originated in papers prepared for three occasions: the Schubertiade of the 92d Street YM-YWHA in New York in March 1993; a conference on Schubert's Piano Music at the Smithsonian Institution in April 1995; and the conference "Austria 996–1996" in Ottawa in January 1996. In addition to audiences at those events, I am also grateful to Jane K. Brown, Marshall Brown, Thomas Christensen, Richard Leppert, James Parakilas, and Gary Tomlinson for their thoughtful comments and suggestions on earlier drafts, and to Walter Frisch, Jonathan Neufeld, Peri Shamsai, Elaine Sisman, and Kate Van Orden for very fruitful conversation following a colloquium at Columbia University.

1. "On German Music," in *Richard Wagner's Prose Works*, trans. William Ashton Ellis, 2d ed. (London: K. Paul, Trench, Trubner, 1898), 7:86–87; the essay originally appeared, in French, in the *Gazette musicale* for July 1840. On music's part in the definition of Germanness, see Celia Applegate and Pamela Potter, eds., *Music and German National Identity* (Chicago: University of Chicago Press, 2002).

ner is perhaps too mindful of his French readers to put it quite so baldly. His evident tactic is to create an *Idealbild* of German music, and of German national character as well, but along the way he does something rather more surprising. He goes on: "the German cannot impart his musical transports to the mass, but only to the most familiar circle of his friends." By suggestion, Wagner constructs someone like the shy and private Franz Schubert, surrounded by his renowned intimate circle, as another *Idealbild:* that of the German instrumental composer, or of the German composer in general.

This feels a somewhat uneasy image; we are more accustomed to the titanic Beethoven in this archetypal role, and we are more used to thinking of Schubert as a song composer in any event.[2] But Wagner's language in this early essay takes us back to a time in the opening decades of the nineteenth century—the Biedermeier decades—before Beethoven's image (not to mention Wagner's own) took on its monumentality, when domesticity and what Adorno later called "the magic aura of the family" played a central role in German culture's dominant representational processes.[3]

But Wagner's domestic image, distilled and iconic as it is, is anomalous in the rather odd gender makeup of its heartwarming scene: where are the women? (Even casual acquaintance with the representational system of domestic music making renders the omission glaringly obvious.) Perhaps the all-male quartet is some kind of bid on Wagner's part for professional status, or simply for a level of aesthetic seriousness? It is certainly true that women's musicianship was not taken very seriously in the domestic context and would have tainted the image with the suggestion of musical clumsiness and social manipulation. Still, the result is paradoxical, because the almost aggressive—certainly polemical—domesticity of the scene would have perversely conjured women players in the mind of even the most compliant contemporary reader. As painted, the scene produces oddly mixed signals.

Perhaps the absence of women results simply from the fact that their instrument, the piano, is not in use? But that absence merely begs the question, prompting us in its turn to ask why the quintessential symbolic vehicle of home music making should be missing from the scene: when did the string quartet become the Ur-Musik of family life? It may be, more eccentrically, that Wagner omitted the family's mother and daughters simply because, for him, the music itself *was* the woman and he needed no other.

2. See chapter 1.
3. Theodor Adorno, *Minima moralia: Reflections from Damaged Life,* trans. E. F. N. Jephcott (London: Verso, 1978), 92.

There is a punch line to this drift of whimsical speculation: as a boy Franz Schubert did indeed play in just such an ensemble, and his father was indeed the cellist; whether there was a "small round table" (about which, more below) is moot.[4]

My intent here is to explore Wagner's image, and other representations of music making among "the home-like circle of the few,"[5] as a manifestation of the reconfiguration of public and private life in the early nineteenth century. Language about music plays a compelling role in this realignment process, both by modeling for the developing bourgeoisie the appropriate forms of family life, and (conversely) by helping constitute domestic music as a satisfying and cherished expressive medium for the members of the new nuclear families gathered together in Biedermeier homes. In short, the language of music is part of the new language of private life.

Schubert's lifetime is a late phase of just this historical change, which came to the German-speaking world some time after it first appeared in England, and the contrast between his career and those of his classical-era predecessors, especially Haydn and Mozart, provides a vivid case in point. The early decades of the nineteenth century saw enormous social and institutional changes that have been of great interest to musicologists as well as to other historians. Most significant for the history of music, of course, were the necessity for composers to locate new sources of financial support as royal and aristocratic patronage declined, in particular by selling music and its performance in the new public marketplace, and the concomitant migration of professional musical activity from private homes into public spaces, vastly increasing its accessibility. Musicological work to date has provided a good deal of information about the development of the musical public sphere itself, but it has tended to ignore the other half of the story, the collateral transformations occurring within the newly configured private sphere. That is, within the disciplinary discourse of music history these changes are ordinarily represented in language that spotlights the emergence of public institutions familiar from a later professional perspective, assuming an evolution *from* private *to* public, and restricts the visibility of other arenas of social history in which the same music is implicated.

The music of Franz Schubert, one of the glories of the canonic repertory, led another life within this bourgeois domestic culture, whose outlines can

4. All the standard biographies of Schubert agree on this story; most recently, see Christopher H. Gibbs, *The Life of Schubert* (Cambridge: Cambridge University Press, 2000), 26.

5. Wagner, "On German Music," 92.

be retrieved by a more fully social history. It seems that disciplinary norms for historical musicology still insist on the primacy of explicating (by whatever innovative and postmodern routes) individual works of music, at the expense of understanding the varieties of musicking or the range of meanings of music as a human experience. Even so, I would suggest at the least that envisioning Schubert within an alternative frame—the site of Biedermeier domesticity—may ultimately lead, in other hands than mine, to differently nuanced and therefore historically richer readings of his works.

PUBLIC AND PRIVATE MUSICAL SPACES

As I suggested, musicologists have contributed to the larger historical effort a considerable amount of extremely important information about the emergence and development of the various forms of public concert life during the first decades of the nineteenth century.[6] In addition, at least three other aspects of the established musicological discourse concerning this development have shaped our dominant "reading" of Schubert.

First, the typical account concentrates on the establishment of a canonic repertory of compositions.[7] One of the more intriguing large-scale facts of the history of Western "classical" music is the transition from a practice wholly or largely concerned with contemporary music to a preservation- or revival-based (that is, canonic) performance culture. As musical scholars have shown, it was only after the middle of the nineteenth century that concert programming began to privilege older works by composers no longer living, and what we now familiarly know as "the standard repertory" began to take shape. This phenomenon, of course, is intimately linked to the emergence of the public concert itself, and thus its foundations are already being lain in the earlier decades, since the economics of public music require that programs appeal to a broad audience whose access to the performance

6. The most important contributions to this understanding to date are Alice M. Hanson, *Musical Life in Biedermeier Vienna* (Cambridge: Cambridge University Press, 1985); Mary Sue Morrow, *Concert Life in Haydn's Vienna: Aspects of a Developing Musical and Social Institution* (Stuyvesant, N.Y.: Pendragon, 1989); and William Weber, *Music and the Middle Class: The Social Structure of Concert Life in London, Paris and Vienna* (New York: Holmes and Meier, 1975).

7. Ernst Hilmar makes a typical observation in noting that Schubert's keyboard waltzes are "charming" but "purely utilitarian" and had no important historical progeny: "the development of the waltz, especially that still called the Viennese waltz, did not involve Schubert" (*Franz Schubert in His Time*, trans. Reinhard G. Pauly [Portland, Oreg.: Amadeus Press, 1988], 86).

is limited only by available spending money—and one that, particularly in the German-speaking world, is increasingly driven by a bourgeois conception of *Bildung* that gradually came to consider familiarity with the symphonies of Beethoven and Mozart to be of more consequence than acquaintance with the latest thing on the musical scene.[8]

Second, the standard musicological account of Schubert focuses on his place within the pantheon of canonic composers. Music history shares with the histories of the other arts a heritage of concentration on the "great names" of its tradition. Fascination with those special talents is perfectly natural, to be sure, but as an exclusive historical practice it is a phenomenon that by now has been so thoroughly critiqued as to need no further comment here. It is worth pointing out, in the present context, that the natural impulse of such a historiography will be to distance Schubert from all contemporary musical activity except that of other recognized canonic names, stressing those aspects of his own music making that portend an "eternalized" future and minimizing those that illuminate his embeddedness in the musical activities of his friends and acquaintances.[9] Given the facts of Schubert's social life, it is hard not to see this view as a misreading. As Sigrid Wiesmann has remarked, Schubert was "by temperament anything but a public figure" and "appealed from the outset to likeminded individuals, circles of friends whose musical world was that of the home."[10]

Third and finally, disciplinary discourse has tended to become somewhat

8. For a recent account of this process, see David Gramit, *Cultivating Music: The Aspirations, Interests, and Limits of German Musical Culture, 1770–1840* (Berkeley: University of California Press, 2002).

9. I coin "eternalize" as a temporal equivalent to the critical notion of "universalizing." Carl Dahlhaus, for instance, characterizes Schubert's "situation" as bounded on one side by Rossini and on the other by Beethoven—a classic statement of a classic view of the early nineteenth century, but an Olympian perspective that ignores the activities of countless Viennese musicians in Schubert's immediate surroundings, several of whom played an intimate role in his life ("Franz Schubert und das 'Zeitalter Beethoven und Rossinis,'" in *Franz Schubert: Jahre der Krise, 1818–1823*, ed. Werner Aderhold, Walther Dürr, and Walburga Litschauer [Kassel: Bärenreiter, 1985], 23). David Gramit comments on the tendency of Schubert scholarship to downplay the significance of his circle of friends ("Schubert and the Biedermeier: The Aesthetics of Johann Mayrhofer's 'Heliopolis,'" *Music and Letters* 14 [1993]: 355–82).

10. Sigrid Wiesmann, "Vienna: Bastion of Conservatism," in *The Early Romantic Era: Between Revolutions 1789 and 1848*, ed. Alexander Ringer (Englewood Cliffs, N.J.: Prentice-Hall, 1991), 95.

tunnel-visioned in its attempt to define the alternative or opposite number to this developing public music, and the confusion seems a direct result of its single-minded determination to locate the historical origins of modern concert life and ignore other music making: origin stories always take their historiographic toll. The customary foil has been the salon, which was moving during these years from aristocratic homes into more modest ones, taking on a distinct bourgeois coloration in the process. As a result, music-historical data contribute perplexity rather than clarity to our account, because in this transitional moment, to put it simply, some salons were more private than others.[11] In most of the respects I consider significant here, the salon does not in fact represent the "private" sphere; most especially it does not represent the particular domestic sphere—the conjugal family—that is invoked in Wagner's essentializing image as well as by Habermas and other historians as crucial in the significant structural transformations taking place in both arenas of human interaction, a point I will elaborate shortly. We note, for example, that in Tia DeNora's study of the material and cultural foundations of Beethoven's reputation the title "Beethoven in the Salons" is given to an early chapter in the life of the composer's professional career, or "what Beethoven was able to achieve during his first decade in Vienna."[12] And Habermas quotes W. H. Riehl to the same effect: "this *salon* does not serve the 'house' but 'society'; and this *salon* society is by no means to be equated with the small intimate circle of friends of the house."[13]

On the one hand, it is not news to musicologists that salons functioned in this way. But on the other, somehow the derogatory usage "salon music" persists as the shorthand name for a specious and presumptively amateurish musicking for "mere" social entertainments, rather as though the hapless piano-playing daughters of the bourgeoisie were somehow respon-

11. See, among many others, Ernst Hilmar, "From Musical Salon to *Schubertiade*," in his *Franz Schubert in His Time;* and Hans Christoph Worbs, "Le tribut à la mode: Die Anfänge der Salonmusik," *Neue Zeitschrift für Musik* 132 (1971): 128–33. Imogen Fellinger makes some interesting distinctions among categories of salon-music recognized by nineteenth-century commentators ("Die Begriffe *Salon und Salonmusik* in der Musikanschauung des 19.Jahrhunderts," in *Studien zur Trivialmusik des 19. Jahrhundert,* ed. Carl Dahlhaus [Regensburg: Gustav Bosse Verlag, 1967], 131–41).

12. Tia De Nora, *Beethoven and the Construction of Genius: Musical Politics in Vienna, 1792–1803* (Berkeley: University of California Press, 1995), 115.

13. Jürgen Habermas, *The Structural Transformation of the Public Sphere: An Inquiry into a Category of Bourgeois Society,* trans. Thomas Burger with Frederick Lawrence (Cambridge, Mass.: MIT Press, 1989), 45.

sible for the nowadays much-decried performative excesses of the flashy and eminently professional virtuoso style.[14] On the contrary, "salon" marks a social and cultural space worlds apart from the true site of domestic music making, the parlor. What we need to see in juxtaposition to public concert life is not the historical remnant—music in the salon—but the phenomenon that is newly ideologically constituted as the public concert's counterpart—music at the domestic hearth, or *Hausmusik*.[15]

To tease apart these tangled historical strands, I borrow some aspects of the by now familiar model detailed in Jürgen Habermas's work on the development of bourgeois society.[16] Habermas is particularly concerned with

14. Dahlhaus consigns both categories to the class *Trivialmusik*. Erich Valentin (*Musica Domestica: Von Geschichte und Wesen der Hausmusik* [Trossingen: Hohner, 1959]) is committed to the notion that the nineteenth-century explosion of amateur music making was an unmitigated disaster. Confusion still runs rampant about the meaning of "salon"; in terms of the social functioning of various rooms in the bourgeois home, its referent changed in the course of the century. One of the fullest and most socially based explorations of the topic is Andreas Ballstaedt and Tobias Widmaier, *Salonmusik: Zur Geschichte und Funktion einer bürgerliche Musikpraxis* (Stuttgart: Franz Steiner Verlag Wiesbaden, 1989).

15. A lengthy essay by C. F. Becker, published over three years (1837–39) in the *Neue Zeitschrift für Musik*, is a red herring and the source of much terminological confusion as well as a classic effort of professional discourse to preempt alternative meanings emerging in nonprofessional circles. Becker entitles his essay "Zur Geschichte der Hausmusik in früheren Jahrhunderts" but ignores the amateur social and familial phenomenon his contemporaries refer to, for he is writing a technical and canonic music history. In the sixteenth- and seventeenth-century context, *Hausmusik* simply meant chamber music—any music not written for the church or the theater (Walter Salmen, *Haus- und Kammermusik: Privates Musizieren im gesellschaftlichen Wandel zwischen 1600 und 1900* [Leipzig: Deutscher Verlag für Musik, (1969)]).

. Anthony Newcomb discusses the *Hausmusik* phenomenon in my intended sense in "Schumann and the Marketplace: From Butterflies to *Hausmusik*" in *Nineteenth-Century Piano Music*, ed. R. Larry Todd (New York: Schirmer Books, 1990), 258–315. See also Thomas Christensen, "Four-Hand Piano Transcription and Geographies of Nineteenth-Century Musical Reception," *Journal of the American Musicological Society* 25 (1999): 254–98; and James Parakilas, "The Power of Domestication in the Lives of Musical Canons," *repercussions* 4 (1995): 5–25 on the fluidity of repertories across the public-private divide, and some implications of that fluidity.

16. William Weber reminds me somewhat urgently that historians have moved well beyond Habermas's model, thoroughly critiquing some aspects of it meanwhile: see, for instance, Craig Calhoun, ed., *Habermas and the Public Sphere* (Cambridge, Mass.: MIT Press, 1992) and the Meehan volume cited in note 41 below. Nonetheless, I have decided to keep my sketchy account (all my references are to *Structural Transformation*), both because Habermas's ideas are familiar to musicologists and because some of his specific turns of phrase are particularly germane to my topic. The distinction between public and private remains an unsolved problem, around which it is necessary to tread carefully.

the appearance, development, and eventual dissolution of a liberal public sphere that enabled the emergence of such phenomena as "public opinion." He first makes a distinction that need not detain us long in the present context, between the public or state sphere and a private sphere that comes into existence with a market economy—the sphere of commodity exchange that we nowadays familiarly call the "private sector." More to my immediate point, Habermas goes on to explore the relations between this larger realm (still "public" in everyday usage, and in the remainder of my discussion) and the "intimate sphere" of the conjugal family at its core. What is especially important is that these two arenas are posited not as opposites or antitheses but as mutually complementary and entailed, the one embedded within and enabling the other.

This public sphere Habermas sees as "above all . . . the sphere of private people coming together as a public" (72). That is, the new form of domestic life—the small nuclear family in place of the older "household" with its servants, retainers, apprentices, and extended relationships—produces the people who then constitute the sphere of "public opinion." In this model the bourgeois property owner is fictively conflated with "the human being," and the conjugal family becomes "humanity's genuine site" (52). The home, then, is the ideological wellspring of the public world.[17] Habermas discusses the development of a concert-going public as a particularly vivid example of the very process he is exploring, calling it "not merely a change in the composition of the public but . . . the very generation of the 'public' as such" (39), and he associates it with the emergence of autonomous music: that is, music become a commodity, and for the first time not tied to a purpose. This new purposeless music is seen to emerge directly from an "inner realm" of absoluteness (47), which is not individual but familial; hence, domestic music is the musical form of "purely human" relations or, to follow another suggestion of Habermas's, experiments in "a specific subjectivity . . . [that] had its home, literally, in the sphere of the patriarchal conjugal family" (43). If so, Wagner is quite right to claim that "absolute music" emerges from this domestic scene.

The ambiguity of the realm of the salon can now be somewhat clarified

17. "As an agency of society [the conjugal family] served especially the task of that difficult mediation through which, in spite of the illusion of freedom, strict conformity with societally necessary requirements was brought about" (47). Yet "the ideas of freedom, love, and cultivation of the person that grew out of the experiences of the conjugal family's private sphere were surely more than just ideology" (48)—that is, they had to have "subjective validity" as well, a requirement that music was central in helping to foster.

as another phenomenon in the midst of historical change, as domestic architecture itself adjusted to the process of privatization. Once a large and essentially public space in an aristocratic home, it gradually became "public" only in the sense that the family received and entertained visitors there—a space distinct from the intimate rooms of family members. "The line between private and public sphere extended right through the home" (45). I take these ideas to suggest an understanding of the Schubert phenomenon—Schubert iconography and descriptions of the Schubert circle and of the Schubertiads (domestic performances of his music)—as not merely a historical shift from one sphere to another, but as playing a role in a larger process of social formation, a reorientation of public and private spheres in relation to each other.

THE CULTURE OF DOMESTICITY

This new domesticity has at its heart the representation of a particular mood or atmosphere suffusing the home, a profound comfort and order to which the appropriate response is a kind of worshipful gratitude, and which is provided in particular for the paterfamilias by the other members of the family. The name for this emotional transaction is "Biedermeier." By and large musicologists have not adopted this as a style term as, for instance, art historians have done; "romanticism" has instead been pressed into service for all the musical styles of the nineteenth century.[18] Nonetheless I wish to appropriate the term here, not to describe any category or style of music but to characterize a coherent system of values associated with domesticity and with the activities, including the music, found in the home.

For all the ink that has been spilled in definitions of romanticism, there has been scant attempt to define it as a term of cultural history, as opposed to the history of ideas. Although the aesthetic ideology of its proponents is

18. There has been considerable argument, especially among German-speaking scholars, about whether it would after all be advisable for musicologists to adopt the term in a style-descriptive capacity, and of what it might mean if we did so. See in particular Carl Dahlhaus, "Romantik und Biedermeier: Zur musikgeschichtlichen Charakteristik der Restaurationszeit," *Archiv für Musikwissenschaft* 31 (1974): 22–41; Heinz Funck, "Musikalisches Biedermeier," *Deutsche Vierteljahrsschrift für Literaturwissenschaft und Geistesgeschichte* 14 (1936): 398–412; Horst Heussner, "Das Biedermeier in der Musik," *Musikforschung* 12 (1959): 422–31; and, more recently, Kenneth DeLong, "The Conventions of Musical Biedermeier," in *Convention in Eighteenth- and Nineteenth-Century Music: Essays in Honor of Leonard G. Ratner*, ed. Wye Jamison Allanbrook, Janet M. Levy, and William P. Mahrt (Stuyvesant, N.Y.: Pendragon Press, 1992), 195–223.

well understood, an encounter with "Biedermeier" as an opposed term quickly surfaces several neglected questions: how far into the social fabric did romantic ideology extend? how well, if at all, does it describe the aesthetic experience of the bulk of music's listeners and players? to whom, and in what circumstances, does the term apply at all?[19] The most thoroughgoing and still the most influential account of the relationship between the two is Virgil Nemoianu's construction of Biedermeier as a "taming" of romanticism.[20] As a literary critic he very naturally sees the former as a later stage—a more "perplexed and disappointed" phase—of high-romantic "fantasies and visions" (1), which is to say a reaction.

"Wherever some kind of high romanticism flourished," Nemoianu says, "it was followed by something resembling Biedermeier discourse and mentality." The descriptive terms he gleans from contemporary writers tell the whole story: "inclination toward morality, a mixture of realism and idealism, peaceful domestic values, idyllic intimacy, lack of passion, coziness, contentedness, innocent drollery, conservatism, resignation." Or, to sum up, "diminutive prettifications".[21]

Any use we might hope to make of Nemoianu's argument would have to take into account the peculiar collapse into simultaneity that occurs in music's history. Perhaps, if we were to think of the two ideologies as occurring in different cultural circles, such a reaction could easily be understood as occurring simultaneously with its provocation, as so familiarly happens in complex societies. This Biedermeier attitude might be the stamp of a forming social class, the locus of what Peter Gay has called "the bourgeois egotistical sublime" and "a very banquet of unintended consequences" of romanticism.[22]

However the situation may best be described, what matters ultimately is the coexistence—in music history, even if not in literary history—of two

19. Recent, and nicely nuanced, musicological accounts of the term are offered by Jim Samson in "Romanticism," *The New Grove Dictionary of Music Online*, ed. L. Macy (accessed 13 March 2003) <http://www.grovemusic.com>, and in his introductory chapter to *The Cambridge History of Nineteenth-Century Music* (Cambridge: Cambridge University Press, 2002).

20. Virgil Nemoianu, *The Taming of Romanticism: European Literature and the Age of Biedermeier* (Cambridge, Mass.: Harvard University Press, 1984).

21. Ibid., 2, 4, 6. Though regularly mentioned as constituents of the Biedermeier mood, these heavily ideological traits should not be taken to describe the true state of affairs in early-nineteenth-century Vienna but instead to represent a self-protective and comforting mythology.

22. Peter Gay, *The Naked Heart*, vol. 4 of *The Bourgeois Experience: Victoria to Freud* (New York: W. W. Norton, 1995), 88.

competing but sometimes surprisingly complementary systems of taste and
value. Both evidence the same focus on personal emotion as the hallmark
of authenticity, and for both there is always a dark side just under the surface. At any rate, to the extent that Biedermeier values can be seen as a shad-
owy counterpart to, or a domesticated version of, romanticism, another representation of Schubert emerges that is distinct from the canonic one and
closer to Wagner's. The matter is of consequence because, despite music history's resistance to the term Biedermeier, it inevitably arises in any discussion of Schubert. It is an only slightly facetious paraphrase of conventional
opinion to say that, if there were such a thing as a Biedermeier composer,
Schubert would be it—meaning, of course, that it is Schubert alone among
the composers of the pantheon whose music played a significant role in Biedermeier life and suited its particular taste.[23] As Maynard Solomon aptly
puts it, "the Schubert and the Biedermeier legends . . . reinforce and support one another."[24]

The following nostalgic portrait perfectly conveys that taste, the flavor
of the Biedermeier domestic atmosphere:

> What charm there is in the intimate sociability of a cultured
> home! No patchouli or musk, and yet a characteristic scent; no
> brilliant chandelier, yet a bright splendor! The orderliness and
> the solicitude spread everywhere a warmth and comfort that stir
> the soul as well as the senses. The women's little worktable by the
> window, the workbasket with its little spools of thread, its blue
> English needle-papers, its little lacquer stars for winding silk, the
> thimbles, the scissors, and the pincushions on the little table, along-
> side the piano with its music, hyacinths in forcing-glasses on the
> windowsill, a bird in a pretty brass cage, a carpet that softens with
> every footstep, engravings on the walls, all merely transient neces-
> sities cleared away into distant rooms, the gatherings of the family
> all together in mutual reverence and contentment—no uproar, no
> running and dashing about—visitors welcomed with composure,
> evenings at the round lamp-lit table, the tea-water bubbling, the
> orderliness of give and take, the need for spiritual communication:

---

23. David Gramit discusses this conventional wisdom, and earlier musicological
confrontations with the term "Biedermeier," most effectively in "The Intellectual
and Aesthetic Tenets of Franz Schubert's Circle: Their Development and Their
Influence on His Music" (Ph.D. diss., Duke University, 1987), and in "Schubert and
the Biedermeier."

24. Maynard Solomon, "Schubert: Some Consequences of Nostalgia," *19th-
Century Music* 17 (1993): 45.

in the consonance of all these chords lies a harmony, something moral, that moves, molds, and ennobles everyone.[25]

This passage, effectively one rhapsodic run-on sentence, seems virtually to have been composed to confound the pernicious forces of romanticism. In place of the heroic individual, we find the "intimate sociability" of the family group—harmonized, we note, in an explicitly musical metaphor. The sublime wilds of nature are supplanted by flower bulbs in glasses, a bird in a cage, and an ardent reverence for the everyday products of industrial manufacture, including a thoroughly domesticated piano. Rather than indulge in that most characteristic romantic yearning for the faraway and the exotic, these people apparently prefer to stay at home.[26] We can vividly imagine how music is thought about, used, and cherished in this domestic space; indeed, Heinz Funck observes that music itself commonly became part of the decor of such homes, as musical notation and pictures of musical instruments were used as design elements.[27]

This Biedermeier domestic oasis is at least partially imaginary, a comforting bulwark of fantasy thrown up against a frightening political atmosphere.[28] Nonetheless such images abound, verbal as well as pictorial, outnumbered only, perhaps, by the ubiquitous representations of girls at pianos; very often the two tropes are combined, creating a seamless ideological display of appropriate furniture, behavior, and gendered inhabitant. The omnipresent "little round tables" in these texts and pictures are freighted with the symbolism of the closed circle of the family and at the same time studiously disguise the rigidly hierarchical nature of family membership.[29] What is rep-

25. Karl Gutzkow, "Aus der Knabenzeit," quoted in Georg Hermann [Borchardt], *Das Biedermeier im Spiegel seiner Zeit* (Berlin: Borg, 1913), 47; my translation, with thanks to Elizabeth Harries and Gertraud Gutzmann. A similar passage by Karl Kobald is quoted in Charles Osborne, *Schubert and His Vienna* (London: Weidenfeld and Nicolson, 1985), 135.

26. Berthold Hoeckner discusses the "distance" trope as a hallmark of romanticism in his "Schumann and Romantic Distance," *Journal of the American Musicological Society* 50 (1997): 55–132.

27. Funck, "Musikalisches Biedermeier," 403.

28. On musical escapes particularly, see William M. Johnston, *Vienna, Vienna: The Golden Age 1815–1914* (New York: Clarkson Potter, 1981) and "Cultivated Gardeners," *American Scholar* 50 (1981): 260–66.

29. Many thanks to Richard Leppert for helping me think through the resonances of this commonplace Biedermeier object, in a personal conversation, 4 March 1995. As Kirsten Belgum points out, "the viability of this household order is, of course, dependent on the absolute obedience of domestics, children and women" (Belgum, *Interior Meaning: Design of the Bourgeois Home in the Realist Novel*

resented in such descriptions and pictures is the *neue bürgerliche Wohnkultur* in which, as Kirsten Belgum says, "the interior, which had been an integral part of the bourgeois family's economic activity [in the eighteenth century], acquired the attributes of a noneconomic, nonpolitical, i.e. a personal, private space."[30] It is the privacy and intimacy of these spaces that produce the socializing effects Habermas describes; they are what Bourdieu calls "the spaces of original possibles" and therefore give us indispensable information about the people who emerged from their comforting ambience.[31]

The development of the "culture of domesticity" is, needless to say, a development particularly significant for the lives of women. Part of its experiential essence is the divorce of the workplace from the dwelling place, and thus a constriction of both activities and opportunities for women. Men, of course, continue to function within both worlds and, indeed, the ideological burden of Biedermeier rhetoric is borne chiefly by the condescending image of Papa comfily at home among his children; he negotiates the divide at will. His wife, on the other hand, is now at least theoretically precluded from public work and confined to the single sphere, although in reality she played a considerable surreptitious part in the other, both through her symbolic role as nurturant moral force and through her purchases.[32] But we are concerned with the emergence of cultural symbols here, and the symbol of domestic life is the wife and mother.[33] Within this domestic economy she

---

[German Life and Civilization] [New York: Peter Lang, 1991], 56). A contemporary prefers us to understand that "dieser Tisch versammelte die Menschen in ganz anderer Weise um sich, brachte all einander näher, in ganz anderer Art, als das die länglichen, eckigen Tische von einst getan hatten" ([Borchardt], *Das Biedermeier*, 10). Borchardt's book presents a collection of memoirs, diaries, and other accounts of Biedermeier life.

30. Belgum, *Interior Meaning*, 17; on *Wohnkultur* see Ingeborg Weber-Kellermann, *Frauenleben im 19. Jahrhundert: Empire und Romantik, Biedermeier, Gründerzeit* (Munich: C. H. Beck, 1983), 57.

31. Pierre Bourdieu, "The Field of Cultural Production, or: The Economic World Reversed," trans. Richard Nice, in *The Field of Cultural Production: Essays on Art and Literature*, ed. Randal Johnson (New York: Columbia University Press, 1993), 31. Particularly interesting with regard to spaces and possibilities are Robert Rotenberg's two "metropolitan ethnographies" of the city, *Time and Order in Metropolitan Vienna* (Washington: Smithsonian Institution Press, 1992) and *Landscape and Power in Vienna* (Baltimore: Johns Hopkins University Press, 1995).

32. In a different geographic context, Ann Douglas persuasively argues that when women are removed from the sphere of production they become primarily consumers (*The Feminization of American Culture* [New York: Alfred A. Knopf, 1977]).

33. The literature relevant to this point is enormous. See Ute Frevert, *Women in German History: From Bourgeois Emancipation to Sexual Liberation*, trans. Stuart McKinnon-Evans (New York: Berg, 1989), especially 66–68; and Kirsten Belgum, "Representation and Respite: The Interior and Women's Domestic Work in the

becomes associated with the home and, by extension, with the culturally formative and nurturing activities that take place there, including music.[34] It seems clear that this closely associated network of economic and social changes, supported by the emergence of appropriate ideologies and systems of representation, stands behind the gradual "feminization" of domestic values and eventually of artistic activity that occurred during the nineteenth century. This symbolic identification in turn has important implications for men who are active within the domestic sphere or otherwise become associated with it.

Here is another aging gentleman remembering Biedermeier family life, describing his ideal of womanhood:

> I never cared for clever women who competed with men. But in her
> I found the noblest qualities of spirit, a quick and clear understanding,
> deep insight, fine moral feelings combined with the loveliest grace,
> softness, and gentleness. She was a true, caring spouse, a good mother,
> a tireless friend of the poor, an unpretentious housewife, and an affable
> and serene hostess. I felt myself to be uplifted, purer in her presence
> than elsewhere.[35]

From a twenty-first-century perspective there could hardly be a more shop-worn bundle of clichés. But since the development of these qualities in women was precisely what called for music in the *Bildung* process in the first place, let us imagine that the passage describes the ideal Biedermeier music. "Noble" qualities, "quick and clear," "fine moral feelings," "grace, softness, and gentleness," "unpretentious," "affable and serene"; even the "tireless friend" finds its resonance. "I felt myself to be uplifted, purer in its [*ihrer* = her?] presence than elsewhere." Surely it is precisely to this identification that the period discourse about music and family life leads us: music is meant to do for you what a truly good woman does.[36]

Nineteenth Century," *Center* 8 (1993): 33–43. Some actual women strenuously resisted their genteel imprisonment but, as is always the case, others found gratification in the exaggerated femininity of their new role.

34. The beginnings of this history are discussed very interestingly by Peter Schleuning in *Das 18. Jahrhundert: Der Bürger erhebt sich* (Reinbek bei Hamburg: Rowohlt, 1984). Further exploration of the point may be found in Donald M. Lowe, *History of Bourgeois Perception* (Chicago: University of Chicago Press, 1982); and Richard Leppert, *The Sight of Sound: Music, Representation, and the History of the Body* (Berkeley: University of California Press, 1993), esp. ch. 4.

35. J. C. Bluntschli, *Denkwürdigen aus meinem Leben* (Nördingen, 1884), quoted in Weber-Kellermann, *Frauenleben im 19. Jahrhundert*, 52; my translation.

36. And vice versa, as chapter 3 argues.

MUSIC MAKING IN THE DOMESTIC SETTING: TWO TEXTS

The so-called new historicist critics have taught us by their exuberant and provocative example the many advantages of looking for historical wisdom beyond the documents we are perusing to a broader system of meaning-making texts and practices.[37] "Literary and non-literary 'texts' circulate inseparably," one such critic offers us as an axiom:[38] canonic and noncanonic works travel together in cultural circulation, as do all kinds of texts whether apparently kindred or not, and cultural values at the level of the myths I am exploring emerge from the resulting ferment. How might Biedermeier readers have been prepared to understand the related ideas of family values and home music making?

Nicolai Petrat has attempted to answer this question, or one like it, with a study of accounts of domestic music from the musical press, focusing on reminiscences and fictional occurrences along with critical responses by professionals, both those who promoted *Hausmusik* and those who deplored what they considered its debilitating amateurishness.[39] I intend to take Petrat's project a step further—and a step nearer to my immediate concern—by examining two exemplary period texts that he provides in an illustrative appendix.

The first (appendix 1) is a polemical address to music teachers, calling them to take up a mission in the service of religion and moral values. Its title explicitly invokes music as the best means to the *Bildung* and the spiritual development of the family.[40] Its author, Johann Gottfried Hientzsch, has evidently observed both the development of public concert life and the emergence of that Habermasian autonomous music and finds them wanting: there is nothing there, he laments, "for the family." Here is a professional musician and pedagogue who is not of the romantic persuasion; rather, he unquestionably sees musical life through Biedermeier spectacles.

<hr/>

37. See, most recently, Catherine Gallagher and Stephen Greenblatt, *Practicing New Historicism* (Chicago: University of Chicago Press, 2000).

38. H. Aram Veeser, introduction to *The New Historicism: A Reader*, ed. H. Aram Veeser (New York: Routledge, 1994), 2.

39. Nicolai Petrat, *Hausmusik des Biedermeier im Blickpunkt der zeitgenössische musikalischen Fachpresse* (Hamburg: Verlag der Musikalienhandlung Karl Dieter Wagner, 1986).

40. Johann Gottfried Hientzsch, "Über die Musik als das herrliche Mittel einer vorzüglichen Bildung, einer geistreichen Unterhaltung und religiösen Erhebung in Familie," *Eutonia* 5 (1831): 152–61, reprinted in Petrat, *Hausmusik*, 153–57. Thanks to Silke Schade for help with the translation of both this and the Teczoni texts; I preserve the boldface emphasis of the originals. There is some discussion of Hientzsche's text in Gramit, *Cultivating Music*, 132.

Hientzsch's text takes as its task one of the ideological roles I identified at the outset: helping constitute domestic music as a satisfying and cherished expressive medium for families. What is remarkable from a music-historical point of view—and amply confirms Habermas's insistence upon the continuity of the two realms—is that Hientzsch has no apparent sense of a distinct repertory of *Hausmusik,* or even of the older, simpler division of music practice into church, chamber, and theater. His well-trained family of amateurs performs selections from all repertories and preserves them apparently at random in their album of family favorites. His concern for the selections' correct moral tone far outweighs considerations of their generic appropriateness for parlor performance, not to mention any putative monumentality. Schubert is represented here, in a dense pack of colleagues, by a most ambiguous list of "songs, duets, trios, and quartets," without further specification.

The family group is large but more or less realistically portrayed; the "females" are vivid presences, listening and singing with knitting in hand. And Hientzsch is careful to include the friends and neighbors who may be invited or may drop in more casually. In this family music making we are witnessing that "privateness oriented to an audience" (43) that Habermas insists upon as characteristic of bourgeois society; that is, the musical family is engaged in explicit self-representation as a harmonious and cultured ensemble, just the portrayal that valorizes their fitness (or their patriarch's fitness, at any rate) for public participation.[41]

Like all "family values" rhetoric, this is a prescriptive text, and through Hientzsch's own lamentations we recognize it as a utopian one; it represents a wished-for situation contrary to fact, and a campaign of family betterment through music that is apparently this pedagogue's personal cause. But it is none the less informative for all that, because the values of Biedermeier domesticity and *Bildung* are precisely its raison d'être: to promote, as he says, "if not a frankly religious tone, certainly an aesthetic-moral one." It bears a considerable atmospheric resemblance to Friedrich Schleiermacher's much-discussed "Christmas Eve narrative" of 1805, in which just such an intimate group of family and friends gathers to tell tales of Christmas and to reflect on theological themes appropriate to the birth of Christ. Music mak-

41. For helpful commentary on this "audience-oriented subjectivity," see in particular two essays contained in Johanna Meehan, ed., *Feminists Read Habermas: Gendering the Subject of Discourse* (New York: Routledge, 1995): Joan B. Landes, "The Public and the Private Sphere: A Feminist Reconsideration" (91–116); and Marie Fleming, "Women and the 'Public Use of Reason'" (117–37).

ing is deeply implicated in—indeed crucial to—the moral effectiveness of the event, for, as the father and host of the party explains, "every fine feeling comes completely to the fore only when we have found the right musical expression for it. Not the spoken word, for this can never be anything but indirect."[42]

The second text from Petrat that I want to explore, a pseudonymous fable by one Techo di Teczoni (appendix 2), illustrates particularly well the other of the ideological roles I assigned to representations of music making: modeling appropriate forms of family life for the developing bourgeoisie.[43] "The Concert of Domestic Life" is a bizarre text compared with Hientzsch's: no mere prescription for social betterment, it is a comic allegory whose factual inaccuracies are surely deliberate—this group includes the wrong participants playing the wrong music upon the wrong instruments.[44] No doubt read primarily as an extended joke, its puns and buffoonery elbow us in the ribs, conveying an earthy and unsubtle humor; it warns, for example, that the cello (the husband's secretary) must not play "forbidden octaves" with the first violin (the wife), and that the contrabass husband should take care not to let horns "spring up" above him. It is a humor, we note, that relies upon a considerable degree of musical knowledge to carry home its point. But its message is deadly serious: members of the family ensemble have specific and scripted roles to play, and they must be arduously trained for them.

Although we cannot hope to glean real information about domestic music making from Teczoni's text, it is a revelation as to the ease with which domestic musical performance is metaphorically called into service to exemplify the ideal family life—how musical discourse and domestic discourse, slyly but with plenty of overt ideological force, reinforce each other in an

42. Friedrich Schleiermacher, *Christmas Eve: Dialogue on the Incarnation,* trans. Terrence N. Tice (Richmond: John Knox Press, 1967), 46. I am grateful to Katherine A. Sonderegger for recommending this very pertinent text to me.

43. Techo di Teczoni (pseud.), "Das Konzert des häuslichen Lebens," *Berliner Allgemeine Musikalische Zeitung* 7 (1830): 13–16, reprinted in Petrat, *Hausmusik,* 298–302.

44. Note that this text portrays the "wrong" family for 1830s ideology, the older *ganze Haus* rather than the nuclear family, with an instrumentation more like the disarrayed remnant of an orchestra than a credible domestic ensemble. Kirsten Belgum remarks on the fairly frequent literary occurrence (e.g., in the novels of Adalbert Stifter or in a popular book on family life by Wilhelm Heinrich Riehl) of such conservative efforts to reinstate the older form, in defense against the development of a newly explicit class sense that many conservative thinkers found distasteful and potentially socially disruptive (Belgum, *Interior Meanings,* esp. ch. 2; and "Representation and Respite," esp. 37).

exhortation entirely legible to the music-buying bourgeoisie. It exhibits with perfect clarity the hierarchy of roles within the ideal family, in which age, gender, and class interact. Not only are mother and father rhetorically opposed, as the gender system requires, but also chambermaid and secretary, cook and coachman; the whole text unravels without gender difference, as indeed does the Biedermeier family.[45] This concert, unlike many more public musical events occurring at the time in the real world, is an entirely corporate endeavor; even the paterfamilias is granted no opportunity for individual display. Furthermore, it is an enforced stable grouping, the "permanent intimacy"[46] of a fixed family unit with no chance to opt out or temporarily prefer a different activity. Because it is by definition a "family" discipline, the concert is aggressively private; the "family friend" who might perhaps play the military serpent is clearly portrayed as a dangerous interloper and a challenge to the husband's authority. This event is not an occasion is to be shared with friends acting as a quasi-family, as in Hientzsch, but a performance of family harmony for the edification of the family members themselves.

Finally, we note how much space in this allegory is devoted to the mother and the description of her role; she is the centerpiece, the linchpin, of the ideology, as the first violin is of the ensemble. This does not mean, of course, that she is in control or "calling the tune," as would be the case in such a musical ensemble in the real world, but only that within the domestic grouping her performance of her assigned role is the most conspicuous, the one to which, as the text tells us, "all the other parts orient themselves." For just this reason, we notice that she can cause considerably more trouble than anyone else in this ensemble if she is allowed out of control, and nearly half of the text is devoted to her containment and correction by other members of the group. This text makes clear that only the observance of the approved rules and regulations of family life will guarantee musical success—as Teczoni assures his readers—"whether the wild storm of a Beethoven Allegro, or the gentle peace of a Haiden Andante, or the endless intricacy of a Mozart fugue is set upon the music stand of life."

45. However, and no doubt inadvertently, the author initiates a grotesque confusion of genders when his metaphor becomes overstrained by the problematic identification of instrument with player. The first violin is the wife, but are we to assume that the husband is the *player* of that violin? Not exactly, because the husband is busy being the contrabass. Still, the player of the instrument—and, more strikingly, the one advised to examine it thoroughly before purchase—is consistently represented in the text as masculine.

46. Habermas, *Structural Transformation*, 44.

THE SCHUBERT CIRCLE AS "TEXT"

Just as Hientzsch's text tells us literally in what musical company Schubert's work may have circulated in the domestic sphere, both texts tell us, in their disparate ways, about the circulation of musical meaning in the new realignment of public and intimate spheres. Imagine now a third text, traveling and acquiring its meanings in company with the two we have investigated. I want to invent, somewhat fancifully to be sure, a "text" about Schubert's circle and the musical evenings they held at which his music was played.[47] These were organized but relatively informal gatherings of friends and acquaintances, in the intimate space of a private home, to hear, play, and dance to Schubert's music—avatars of Wagner's primal scene.[48] My text is frankly cobbled together from bits and pieces of verbal and visual material: it is meant to approximate a "received belief" and to investigate the placement of these familiar musical activities within the public/domestic field we have been surveying. What I hope will result is a complicated and ambiguous picture that resists reduction into simple judgments about public and private spheres.

Lawrence Kramer's recent study of Schubert associates his music with a polarized sense of the nature of romanticism that casts it into opposition with Beethoven's as versions of romantic subjectivity.[49] I do not at all wish to dispute this argument but rather to augment it, since my concern here is rather different: Kramer's account works toward his typically sophisticated and provocative critical readings, of Schubert's songs in this case, mine toward a nuanced (even frankly confused) decipherment of the meanings of cultural representation. The Beethoven/Schubert dualism, along with the gendered language of masculine and feminine that so often accompanied or illustrated it in the nineteenth century, can also be read as a symptom of the cultural struggle between romanticism and Biedermeier (or whatever name the reader prefers for romanticism's ever-present tamed or domesticated other). Nothing makes this clearer than the way in which Schubert's

47. "Unter 'Schubertiaden' verstanden die 'Schubertianer'—der sich um Schubert bildende Freundeskreis—jene geselligen Zusammenkünfte, bei denen Werke Franz Schuberts aufgeführt wurden" (Rudolf Klein, "Begriff und Geschichte der Schubertiaden," *Österreichisches Musikzeitschrift* 33 [1978]: 209.

48. In fact, Schubertiads seem to have straddled the social divide: some took place in the salons of ducal palaces and some in the parlors of considerably more humble homes. Here is the very fault line Habermas described, the line between public and private that runs right through the house.

49. Lawrence Kramer, *Franz Schubert: Sexuality, Subjectivity, Song* (Cambridge: Cambridge University Press, 1998), 3.

dance music threatens to contaminate his romantic status—music that did not, as his songs did, rise to "the status of a work of art"[50]—and consequently has little or no place in most accounts. Kramer adumbrates this point in observing how easily the music was taken as anodyne for present misery rather than a bid for some future-oriented "aesthetic" greatness (35).

We have a great deal of information about the Schubert circle and its musical activities, mostly from participants and eyewitnesses, as well as another equally rich layer of commentary upon these source documents by later scholars; I use all of this material in my reading of this fictive text. The participant descriptions that we have are mostly transmitted through scholarly collections, especially Otto Erich Deutsch's monumental *Franz Schubert: Die Dokumente seines Lebens*.[51] The scrupulous reverence with which Deutsch collected and annotated the material (sometimes no more than single-phrase scraps) and, of course, the very fact of their collection, by themselves create and transmit a "text" representing the social locus *from which* Schubert's music has subsequently moved into the public world—that is, into the world of artistic posterity, than which no arena is more public.

If we wish to read this text as associating Schubert with "the history of great composers," or perhaps with "all great romantic artists," there is plenty of evidence to support our interpretation of a musical genius living and working in a typical artists' bohemia. Arthur Hutchings does so, explicitly calling the group "bohemian," as does John Reed: "[Schubert] seems to live on the Bohemian fringes of Biedermeier society, in it but not of it."[52] Indeed, from the perspective of prevailing bourgeois values, the perennial forming and re-forming of this group, its wanderings and dislocations, its hapless, artistically driven but often unemployed young men, take on a bittersweet flavor that frequently echoes in the private correspondence of Schubert and his friends.[53] Otto Biba observes that Schubert was the first Viennese com-

50. Ibid., 10, following a very Dahlhausian line; and see note 7.

51. Of the book's several English versions, the best known is probably *Schubert: A Documentary Biography*, trans. Eric Blom (London: J. M. Dent, 1946).

52. Arthur Hutchings, "Bohemian Days," in *Schubert* (London: J. M. Dent, 1973); John Reed, *Schubert: The Final Years* (London: Faber and Faber, 1972), 114.

53. Schubert to Bauernfeld, September 1825: "As to setting up house together, I should be pleased enough to do so, but I know these bachelor- and student-plans only too well, and do not want in the end to fall between two stools" (Otto Erich Deutsch, ed., *Franz Schubert's Letters and Other Writings*, trans. Venetia Savile [New York: Knopf, 1928], 109). Deutsch reports that Schubert lived at seventeen different addresses during his thirty-one years—and repeated three of them, making a total of twenty moves. Both Mozart and Beethoven moved even more frequently during their years in Vienna (Deutsch, *Biography*, 932). Schubert had a shifting series of roommates from among the intimate circle, including Josef von

poser to live solely from his compositions and adds the provocative comment that "to some of his contemporaries this [may have been] viewed as anti-bourgeois and irresponsible."[54]

In keeping with this assessment, Schubert's contemporaries (and presumably the composer himself) clearly regarded these gatherings—despite the intimate *Geselligkeit* of their ambience—as settings for the display and enjoyment of Schubert's talent as an exceptional individual and artist, much as musicologists and other Schubert-lovers think of him now. They identify themselves as a community of artists and unquestionably see Schubert as a professional composer. The participants represent an affinity group: people who come together because they enjoy the same pursuits, and not because their presence is required willy-nilly, like the players in Hientzsch's or Teczoni's households.

But this Parnassian or canonic view has not been sufficiently stable to displace entirely the shadow of its "tamed" or domesticated counterpart. The ethos of the Schubert circle itself is such that a number of scholars have noticed—and sometimes worried about—a certain slippage between the two systems of taste and value. The art of Moritz von Schwind, an intimate of Schubert, has especially drawn this kind of attention. His painting *Eine Symphonie* (1852) has been characterized by Wolfgang Dömling as "a Biedermeier idyll by a late Romantic."[55] More anxious is Carl Dahlhaus's comment on the drawing *Ständchen* (1862), which shows four members of the intimate group—Schubert, Vogl, Lachner, and Schwind himself—performing in serenade, presumably singing one of Schubert's choruses for male voices. Dahlhaus notes that the picture "[reveals], with a touch of self-irony, how close the romanticism of the 1820s stood to *Biedermeier* the moment its esoteric music culture took on convivial trappings."[56] But those "convivial trappings" are just what created the public market for Schubert's music as

Spaun, Franz Schober (sometimes living as a guest of Schober's family), Johann Mayrhofer, Josef Huber, Moritz von Schwind, and finally his brother Ferdinand (ibid., 929–31).

54. Otto Biba, "Schubert's Position in Viennese Musical Life," *19th-Century Music* 3 (1979): 107.

55. Dömling offers this painting as evidence of "the utopian content that painters attributed to the idea of music from the early nineteenth century on" (Wolfgang Dömling, "Reuniting the Arts: Notes on the History of an Idea," trans. Juliane Brand and Christopher Hailey, *19th-Century Music* 18 [1994]: 6). I suggest that the idea of "utopian content" was widespread, accounting at least in part for music's prominence as a model for happy domestic life.

56. Carl Dahlhaus, *Nineteenth-Century Music*, trans. J. Bradford Robinson (Berkeley: University of California Press, 1989), 177 (picture caption).

well as the *gemütlich* vision of the composer so central to the subsequent self-construction of Old Vienna.[57]

For our "text" is susceptible of another reading as well, one that supports the complementary development of the intimate private sphere: it can be read as a text about a family. For one thing, the group *is* strangely fixed, after all; despite the variability of personnel, all seem to understand who "belongs." Absent members are often commemorated and their health drunk; afterward they are written to with reports of the event, like family members, and told how much they were missed.[58] Most of the Schubertiads, furthermore, are not very professional in atmosphere; after the music and the dinner there are dancing and games—some with intellectual pretensions (charades, *Worteln* [making poems of given words]) but others simply puerile, like the "tossing in a blanket" that Hartmann reports in his diary, or his report after a breakfast gathering that "Enderes juggles beautifully with sticks, rods and the like."[59] Such details render the gatherings less artistic and serious—we can hardly imagine Beethoven in such a setting, despite his looming presence in the same city—and more like what might conceivably go on in Hientzsch's musical family when his pious back is turned. Less salonlike, we might say, and more parlorlike.

One description in particular, from Hartmann's diary, is almost comical in its insistence upon detailing the familial relationships of those in attendance: "The Arnoth, Witteczek, Kurzrock and Pompe couples, the mother-in-law of the Court and State Chancellory probationer Witteczek; Dr. Watteroth's widow, Betty Wanderer, and the painter Kupelwieser with his

57. Ilsa Barea describes the mythology of Alt-Wien as compounded of "the mental climate, the domestic interiors, and certain types of music ranging from Schubert's easier melodies to the waltzes of Lanner and the elder Johann Strauss" (*Vienna* [New York: Knopf, 1966], 111).

58. "[W]e sorely miss our original members and the more intimate ones often remember past times *sub rosa*. It was the same at the Schubertiad where it was secretly felt that we are no longer as sound at the core as before" (Bruchmann to L. Kupelwieser, 2 December 1823 [Deutsch, *Biography*, 303]). A letter from Schubert to Schober just two days earlier makes the same point (ibid., 300); see also another dated 21 September 1824 (374). The rhetoric of these private letters is pure Biedermeier in sensibility.

59. Hartmann's diary, 12 January 1827 (Deutsch, *Biography*, 591) and 14 January 1827 (ibid., 593). There is an entertaining description of such games in a contemporary traveler's account: Richard Bright, M.D., *Travels from Vienna through Lower Hungary; with Some Remarks on the State of Vienna during the Congress* (Edinburgh: Archibald Constable, 1818), 22–23. Not yet assimilated into the interpretive frame around Schubert is Rita Steblin's discovery of the "Nonsense Society" to which at least some of the Schubertians belonged (*Die Unsinngesellschaft: Franz Schubert, Leopold Kupelwieser und ihr Frendeskreis* [Vienna: Böhlau, 1998]).

wife."[60] Johann Vogl, who sang so many lieder at these gatherings with Schubert at the piano, is clearly the prima donna of the family; he has moods, he has to be cajoled: "V. was much pleased with himself and sang gloriously"; "Vogl will sing only in agreeable and respectable society"; Vogl "happened to be in an exceptionally good mood."[61]

Pursuing this interpretive line, we also notice that the personal relationships of the Schubert circle—above and beyond the conduct of the Schubertiads—seem frequently to be described or invoked in familial terms, as when Schubert writes a group letter to Schober, Spaun, Mayrhofer, and Senn from his summer position in Zseliz on 3 August 1818, or when Schober describes his stay with Schubert at St. Polten in 1821: "Our room at St.P. was particularly snug: the twin beds, a sofa next to the warm stove, and a fortepiano made it all very domestic and cosy."[62] To round out this domestic and affectionate picture, we have the tradition from Anselm Hütten-brenner that members of the group tended to wander off with manuscripts of Schubert's compositions that they especially liked, and that eventually Hüttenbrenner's brother Josef made a project of collecting them all from hither and yon, for safekeeping.[63] Finally, because the group had several artists among its number, we have pictures galore of the Schubertians at play—riding in hay wagons, frolicking in the countryside, drinking wine in Grinzing, singing serenades under balconies—in short, a family album.

And the women, the mothers and daughters of the family, were present, too. In contemporary documents, the insistence upon the presence of women at Schubertiads is remarkable, and quite at odds with the image that Wagner offers. They are persistently mentioned in the letters and diary entries that describe the events, often indeed as the hosts, and they are represented in every picture of one that I have seen, not to mention in the pictures of the games and recreations of the group. Present-day writers, in keeping with their preference for the "bohemian" or "romantic" reading, tend to erase them from the scene, either by literally cropping the images or by simply leaving the women nameless—except for the indefatigably meticulous

60. Diary entry, 15 December 1826 (Deutsch, *Biography*, 571).

61. Bruchmann to L. Kupelwieser, 2 December 1823 (Deutsch, *Biography*, 302); Doblhoff to Schober, 2 April 1824 (ibid., 342); Hartmann's diary, 12 January 1827 (ibid., 591).

62. Ibid., 93, 195.

63. The story is told in Anselm Hüttenbrenner's "Fragments from the Life of the Song Composer Franz Schubert" (1854), reprinted in *Schubert: Memoirs by his Friends*, ed. Otto Erich Deutsch, trans. Rosamond Ley and John Nowell (London: Adam and Charles Black, 1958), 183.

Deutsch, who reproduces the best-known, albeit mythic, representation, Schwind's "A Schubert Evening at Josef von Spaun's," with every figure identified.[64] Discussing the same painting, an idealized or imaginary Schubertiad that includes participants who could not possibly have attended at one and the same time, Maurice Brown offers a more typical response:

> If one considers what, as well as who, these people were, it is amusing to find that he has placed not necessarily kindred minds, but kindred arts or interests together. This hardly applies to the five ladies on the right of the piano: the only factor in common there is that all were wives of various Schubertians, but their group enshrines the grace and charm of the occasion.[65]

Surely Brown underestimates the representational importance of the presence of the women, not to mention the probability that their passionate attachment to the music was every bit as strong as their husbands' was.

Despite all this, there is no gainsaying that the musical organization of the Schubertiads is anomalous in gender terms, and probably just because of Schubert's own presence at the center of attention. Women do not seem to participate in the music making except on rare occasions,[66] even at the piano (that instrument most associated with women, and just the one whose music is particularly celebrated at these events, in keeping with their domestic setting), for the good reason that it is Schubert's instrument.[67] There is a representational difficulty here, a kind of dislocation of established tropes and images that would have been easily recognizable to contemporaries: at the center of that closed, adoring circle of listeners, the spotlighted figure at the keyboard "ought" by iconographic tradition to be female. Responses to the problem are various and sufficiently interesting to confirm contempo-

64. Deutsch, *Biography*, plate 31, between 784–85.

65. Maurice J. E. Brown, "Schwind's 'Schubert-Abend bei Josef von Spaun,'" *Essays on Schubert* (New York: St. Martin's Press, 1966), 165. Karl Kobald contributed greatly to this decorative and dimwitted image of the women at the Schubertiads, explaining that "the fair listeners" sat "quiet and grateful" while "lost in a dream of love, in a circle round the genius" (*Franz Schubert and His Times*, trans. Beatrice Marshall [New York: Knopf, 1928], 203).

66. Vera Schwarz names three women pianists who she says played at these events—Irene von Kiesewetter, Marie Pachler, and Henriette von Spaun—but they have disappeared from the best-known accounts of the Schubertiads ("Die Ersten Interpreten Schubertscher Klaviermusik," in *Zur Aufführungspraxis der Werke Franz Schuberts*, ed. Vera Schwarz [Munich: Emil Katzbichler, 1981], 107).

67. Other genres were included—most especially the lieder for which Schubert was then and is now best known—and a good deal of dancing took place. But as far as we know, everything performed at the Schubertiads involved the piano in some role. Pictorially, it is virtually always at the center of activity.

rary awareness of it. Of course, we are familiar with many representations of male composers performing at keyboard instruments: ordinarily, the point is precisely that they are well known "great" composers and not anonymous male figures—in which case they would not be sitting there.

In Schubert's case, the abundantly domestic and *gemütlich* atmosphere in which he plays creates a short circuit of representation that threatens to feminize him at every moment. The danger began to arise early, as is well known.[68] Schubert is also—perhaps most forcefully—feminized by his very association with domesticity, as well as by the century's sheer love of oppositional categories. Anthropologically, Traian Stoianovich tells us, the essentializing issue is a matter of "heads and tails: virilization, domesticity."[69] Kreissle von Hellborn, Schubert's earliest biographer, works hard to dispute some of the womanlike attributes that had already begun to accrue to his reputation—foremost among them "naturalness" and "spontaneity"[70]—yet Kreissle relays the notorious observation that when Schubert's skull was exhumed after death, "the doctors and hospital attendants who were present were astonished at its delicate, almost womanly organisation."[71] This is, of course, a perception saturated with the essentialist preconceptions of nineteenth-century science but, again, it is exactly the sort of observation the circulation of these representations would have paved the way for.[72]

To point the moral of my story, I hope not too heavy-handedly: Heinz Funck wrote of the Biedermeier period that it "was a heyday of German do-

68. Kramer discusses the "persistent feminization" of Schubert in reception history (*Franz Schubert*, 80), and his chs. 3 and 4 explore different ramifications of this trope.

69. Traian Stoianovich, "Gender and Family: Myths, Models and Ideologies," *History Teacher* 15 (1981): 70.

70. See Christopher H. Gibbs, "'Poor Schubert': Images and Legends of the Composer," in *The Cambridge Companion to Schubert*, ed. Christopher H. Gibbs (Cambridge: Cambridge University Press, 1997), 36–55, for a discussion of these and other familiar elements of the Schubert myth.

71. Heinrich Kreissle von Hellborn, *The Life of Schubert*, trans. Arthur Duke Coleridge (London: Longmans, Green, 1869), 2:152.

72. Given the current scholarly dialogue on Schubert's sexual orientation, a comment on it seems necessary. I see little relationship between his possible homosexuality and his "domestication" in Biedermeier culture beyond the obvious: the strange but apparently irresistible link that Western culture has subsequently made between gay sexuality and femininity. Within a system of representations that could not have openly acknowledged the possibility of alternative sexualities, Schubert's feminization—which seems not to have troubled his contemporaries overmuch—offers no evidence one way or the other about his own proclivities.

mestic music."[73] Whimsically, I'll reverse that, observing that German domestic music was a heyday of the Biedermeier, a locus classicus of its values and meanings and a ground of its ideological force, just as Wagner suggested. Schubert and his piano—as is clear from both their verbal and visual representations—were central icons of those values, as well as of the romantic values of the canonic music history with which we are more familiar.

In sum, while the question of a "Biedermeier Schubert" has certainly been repeatedly addressed, it has usually been done in ways that I find unsatisfying, with a grim determination to disallow or discount the influence upon him of the infamously cozy values associated with that term, and to realign him firmly with musical romanticism, which is to say with music history proper.[74] Yet surely this effort turns its back not only on whatever germ of truth there is in Wagner's propaganda but also on a cultural moment that was particularly deeply attached to music and to the values it found there. Perhaps instead we should think at greater length about the complex relation of public and private: maybe, as Mary Hunter has done in a subtle and splendid essay on Haydn's chamber music, searching critically for what she calls "signs of privateness" in music prematurely thrust into a more exclusively public realm and maybe working to account culturally for those very traits.[75]

APPENDIX 1

Johann Gottfried Hientzsch, "Concerning Music as the Marvelous Means of an Excellent Education, of Spiritual Maintenance and Religious Uplift in the Family" (excerpts)

These days, a great deal of music is made, both played and sung, but in a far from correct manner and not toward the right end. Few, very few, carry with them from their music lessons and music making something real, something for life, for the **family**. Unfortunately, vanity and sensuousness appear only too frequently in playing.

. . .

73. Funck, "Musikalisches Biedermeier," 403.
74. An important exception is David Gramit; see notes 8, 9 and 23.
75. Mary Hunter, "Haydn's London Piano Trios and His Salomon String Quartets: Private vs. Public?," in *Haydn and His World,* ed. Elaine Sisman (Princeton: Princeton University Press, 1997), 103–30.

The criterion and goal, in variations, overtures, symphonies, dances, especially those for four hands, ought to be less the achievement of a grand brilliant performance and more the striving for a solid—even if more modestly polished—but intelligent playing.

. . .

[I]t will be good if families regard such teachers as more than mere providers of music lessons, if they befriend them; if in addition to the lessons, they designate one evening in the week to show the gathered family and a few friends (whether they are there of their own accord or are invited) what has been learned through practice during the lessons. The teacher, if not a remarkable singer but just a passable one, will not only perform a nice song himself now and then, but his students will perform them as well; and in addition he should have them sing a few smaller or larger ensemble pieces, depending on the number of family members who are good musicians. He establishes a certain priority and order, without being overanxious about the latter or using coercion. Rather, the whole must seem to happen as if by itself; the thread of his management must be hardly noticeable. And as soon as a member of the musical family becomes more skilled at this, [the teacher] will withdraw more and more and only advise and make aesthetic-critical observations now and then. He can then be satisfied and can say, with a full sense of his own contribution: here in your house you have built an altar to true art and to the education of mankind. It goes without saying that, little by little, he endeavors to bring into play all their heretofore unrecognized musical talents, and so to make life for the whole family group all the more estimable and delightful, and thus to establish the domestic happiness of the family. This should not create any occasion for large and costly celebrations, grand banquets, &c. A glass of beer or a cup of tea with buttered bread would be all that was necessary. The quiet and comfort of the house provide the right setting, and intimate, cultured conversation in between the individual music numbers provides the right seasoning. But I have still explained too little about the actual arrangement of the whole enterprise; I will now endeavor to do so.

If a weighty sonata or a substantial overture, arranged for two or four hands, is well performed to begin with, then the younger and less sure members of the family might present something individually or together—not too quickly one after the other, though, but allowing brief intervals in between for the reading of a nice, generally appealing poem, an interesting story, a portrait or other fragment of a suitable work of **Claudius, Krummacher, Strauß** &c., or from collections of **Pölitz, Heinsius, Heyse** &c. But singing must always remain predominant; it must be the soul of the whole thing.

For each piece that is to be sung, the words are first read clearly and expressively. If someone is there who has some information about the writer, his work, or the connection between the two, then he shares it. If you want an example, for little ones use the *Festbüchlein* of **Krummacher** in three volumes with **Harder's** melodies for them. One of the children reads the excerpt that occasioned the little song. When it is finished, everyone is in the right frame of mind; then the song is begun and heartily sung through. The teacher sits before the piano and the little ones stand around it, each one entrusted beforehand with his part—because everything that is done at such a musical family evening must be rehearsed thoroughly in the lessons beforehand, individually and together, must be as free of mistakes as possible, and must be presented as artistically as possible. One wants to, one should, be delighted and edified by it!

Whoever has gone through **Krummacher's** *Festbüchlein* along with **Harder's** music in this way will have pretty much understood the writer about this point, and will know where more of the same can be had: **Lindner's** *Musikalischer Jugendfreund,* the volumes of **Himmel, Nägeli, Righini, A. P. Schulz, Reichardt, Gläser, Fink,** &c. The collections of **Hientzsch, Stolze, Erk** and many others offer a large selection.

To illustrate the same idea for the **older musical members** of the family, I suggest **Tiedge's** *Urania* with the splendid music of **Himmel.** The poem is read—if not the whole, then chosen passages. If dispositions are thus induced into the proper attitude, the music begins and continues to a satisfactory stopping place. Such a piece must not be gone through in one evening; it can perhaps provide enough material for 4–6 evenings! And if one of the sections is particularly enjoyed, then it can be repeated from time to time, with or without introductory reading. Indeed, if this is rightly carried out, a number of favorite pieces will gradually be assembled—appropriately dubbed treasures of the house—which deserve to be repeated from time to time.

In the works suggested above for small children, one can find a few pieces that will also be suitable either for their collaboration with older family

members or appropriate for the latter alone. But there is incomparably more
material available for the older members of the family than for children.
Here one has the splendid songs, duets, trios, and quartets of **Haydn, Bergt,
Beethoven, Feska, Rink,** Franz **Schubert,** Bernhard **Klein,** Conr. **Kreutzer,
Methfessel, Mühlling, Nägeli** *(Teutonia),* **Neukomm, Riem,** Andr. **Romberg,
Rungenhagen, Schichte,** Fr. **Schneider,** D. **Sörensen, Schnabel,** X. **Schnyder,**
Abt **Stabler, Tomaschek,** Abt **Vogler,** B. A. M. v. und Gottfried **Weber, Zel-
ter, Zumsteeg,** &c.; then music with declamation, like the *Gang nach dem
Eisenhammer* of **Schiller** and B. A. **Weber,** and other similar **melodramas,**
as well as **ballads;** all of them carefully selected for a Christian family. Now
would come the **motets, cantatas, masses,** and **oratorios.** Here in particular
is an arena where the teacher shows his **mastery** both in his knowledge of
them, and in his skill at performing them in such family circles by using all
the means available to him, as correctly and satisfactorily as possible without months of rehearsal. The whole family should be brought to a sufficient
musical level that something like this works after one or two rehearsals. If
the personnel are not sufficient for a complete performance, then individual movements from them can be played.

Among the cantatas, those of **Mozart, Naumann,** Andr. **Romberg, Zumsteeg,
Eberwein, Kunzen, Danzi, Rink, Feska,** &c. would be excellent to consider.
With respect to the oratorios, I will only point out that during Passion time
one would want most especially to do the Passion oratorios with the family. *Der Tod Jesu* by **Graun,** the *Sieben Worte des Erlösers* by **Haydn,** Hesse's
Pilgrimme, **Handel**'s *Messias,* the *Ende des Gerechten* by **Schicht,** Beethoven's *Christus am Ölberge* and many others should eventually become
completely familiar. And if one or the other is well performed in public one
day, what joy, what pleasure!

The author has no objection if one or another piece is selected from serious opera, like *Titus* by **Mozart,** **Righini**'s *Gerusalemme liberata,* the
Schweizer-Familie by **Weigl,** the *Vestalin* by **Spontini,** &c., but [they are]
more [suitable] for the middle than for the end of such a musical family
evening. Here is the reason: since, as the reader has already noticed, the
whole described so far has had, if not a frankly religious tone, certainly an
aesthetic-moral one, so it must, according to [my] opinions and ideals for
such family entertainment, preserve this tone more and more toward the
end of the evening. At the end there must be, to speak frankly, **an evening
service, an evening prayer for the family**—or, where possible, for the whole

household, and for that the hymn must not be absent. Indeed, several verses from a beautiful *Abendliede* of Gellert, &c., with a wonderful familiar old melody, sung if possible in four parts, or a religious aria, then reading of an evening service or contemplation, an evening prayer, the saying of the evening blessing and then perhaps a few more chorale verses—this is the end, the crown of the musical family evening. My musical friends, I think that it must become thus where it is not yet so. Then you are not mere wage earners passing one hour after another; then you are priests of art, you are—if not servants of religion—esteemed fellow promoters of Christian religiosity.

So, gentlemen music teachers in the larger and largest towns, what do you think? If this idea was until now unknown to you, have you the desire and the courage to take it up? Do you want forever to remain for the fingers what dance teachers are for the feet, or do you want to elevate yourselves and be elevated into a higher region, indeed maybe into one of the highest, where you contribute to the noble ideal of the aesthetic-Christian education of mankind? Do you want to become useful instruments of the spiritual happiness of your fellow humans? If you do, then of course you must not be one-sided musicians—at least you must not remain so. It is not enough that you have learned your music no matter how well, that you have the study of harmony and counterpoint so deeply ingrained. You must also have a proper general education. In addition to a deeper understanding of the Christian religion and history, you must have not only several languages and other regular school knowledge, but also knowledge of men, especially psychology (knowledge of the feelings), aesthetics, poetry, and in general a thorough familiarity with the literature of our people, to be able to draw from it whenever and wherever it is useful.

Of course, most people will only be able to have the music teacher at most once or twice a week; should there be no music in the family on the other evenings? Even if singing and playing do not happen on all evenings in such a group, it should still occur several times a week, especially on Sundays and in the winter, even if briefly and without the teacher.

In the evening, when all daily business is finished, when the meal has been eaten, when the very youngest children have been taken to bed (if they are not yet capable of quiet listening), all the members gather by and by around the piano, the females perhaps with knitting in hand. Playing, singing, and reading aloud take turns. The songs that appeal to everyone are noted down and can be repeated from time to time.

If the author has ever hoped that a particularly earnest and deep attention be paid to one of his essays, he wishes it for this one, because it deals with the highest and the holiest interests of mankind, whose enhancement will be most securely undertaken at the family hearth. This essay is, moreover, only the first in a series about this subject; more will follow, and I hope that my esteemed colleagues and friends of the arts will help to realize and fulfill this idea. May it happen! *Vivat, floreat et crescat Musica, imprimis sacra.*

APPENDIX 2

Techo di Teczoni, "The Concert of Domestic Life: An Example of Mutual Instruction by Heads of Families and Musicians"

Perhaps the music-loving public of our city would find it not unwelcome to become acquainted with the principal rules whereby, in the orchestra of domestic life, the parts should be distributed in order to produce effective harmony and pleasant melody. Every husband will know the importance of such a suitable arrangement, every unmarried man will feel it, and both will be grateful to me if I have given good advice.

The woman of the house plays the **first violin** in the concert. She takes the principal melody of the composition, to which all the other parts orient themselves. This part **must** therefore be played well, if the harmonious household is to acquit itself with honor. The instrument itself must have a pure tone, neither shrill nor rasping, and must be able to withstand *forte* playing, when called for, without losing the sweetness of its *piano*. The choice of such an instrument therefore demands the greatest prudence, and one must not be duped by a brilliant exterior. In particular, the instrument must be strung with trustworthy and good strings, and of course with true and not false ones; for otherwise, it will give only discord, no matter with how much art and skill it is played. Even more carefully must one avoid an instrument where one or another of the strings is already half worn. There are also violins on which several strings . . . snap very easily and often. The problem usually lies in the faulty disposition of the instrument itself, which can very seldom be corrected. Some would attempt to render it serviceable by breaking it to pieces and gluing it back together again; however, this treatment is often dangerous—at least the instrument must always be **handled** with strong capable hands if it is to meet expectations. In any case, before one procures an instrument for himself he must examine it and test it thoroughly, because this fault is usually not readily visible; and whoever chooses such an instrument for his first violin very soon experiences the adverse consequences.

But if the instrument is **faultless**, it must be handled with refinement and delicacy, and then every tone will be the expression of pure, natural feeling. But not every first violinist is master of this art. Many lash their way through the notes, ever more fortissimo, and forfeit their salutary effect on the soul. Others sound the strings too faintly and weakly—a mistake of faulty bowing—so that even the most beautiful and pleasing passages become boring. Some, out of musical vanity—in these times, alas! a not infrequent occurrence among young scholars—court brilliance with affected styles and flashy runs and trills, but thereby they easily fall out of the correct meter, and give the whole orchestra a dangerous example. It is even worse when, without warning, the first violinist plays now *forte,* now *piano,* now *allegro,* now *vivace,* according to **caprice**; for such playing is a vexation not only to the orchestra but also to listeners. The first [violin] is a difficult, very demanding part. Even if the violinist avoids all of these mistakes, it is also necessary, not only that he reads notes well and quickly, has a correct understanding of the whole composition so as to be prepared for the difficult passages of the musical household, and does not confuse single or double **sharps**; but also, that he observes the correct naturals, sets the mute at the right time, does not fall into *allegro* when it only goes *andante,* or fool around in major when the piece is in minor. Chiefly, though, he must stay immovably in the right meter no matter how many tails the notes have, and however bright and seductive the figures may be.

But all of these tasks are lightened by the **contrabass** at his side, played by the head of the house and husband. By his nature he has an imposing predominance over all the other parts, which one recognizes so much the more, the more insight and art are in his playing. He **cannot** and **may not** trouble himself about **small matters**, like runs, leaps, and trills, etc.; he would be mixing in the business of the violins and violas, and if he wasted his time that way he could easily depart from the meter himself and neglect his own duties. He has rather to declare, calmly and strongly, the keynote to which all the other instruments must tune, and keep the whole orchestra in time. With Madame *Violino primo* he must always remain in harmony and play no false note; for then the harmony would be interrupted, and one knows of cases where such blunders have ended the whole concert. Hence he must direct his attention more to the **first** than to the **second** violin, for such confusion can bring disaster. If Madame *Primo violino* should go astray, modulating into the wrong key or stumbling into an entirely wrong meter, and through bad example lead the house-orchestra into disorder, straightaway he must return her to her duty with a few distinct and energetic strokes. On the other hand, if he plays too weakly and feebly, he must be careful lest one or another **horn** spring up over him. If he grumbles too strongly, or stays forever on one note, his playing is unpleasant for colleagues and listeners. Finally, if he himself has no meter, he does better to leave it alone: he is not fit for the musical household. The contrabass is a beautiful and worthy instrument, but its player must have knowledge of the whole harmony and rhythm, and must possess dignity and especially a strong and sure stroke. If he has these qualities, any substitute instrument (for instance, the military **serpent**) which might easily be introduced by a **household friend,** will be superfluous.

The **second violin** accompanies the first, is subordinate to her, and must not presume to take the principal melody. It is played by the **chambermaid**—a not unimportant part. For even if the melody and the manner of the first violin are ever so pure and lovely, the chambermaid can enhance these beauties very much while she adds harmony to the melody, and thereby can set off the fine charms of the former, to say nothing of the fact that with an appropriate accompaniment she can improve and adorn a **meager principal voice**—a transaction that demands delicacy. If the **first** violin is very well suited, as she should be, she will hold the **second** to her proper duty and limits, making sure that she pays attention, is not impertinent, and does not play louder than is becoming. If the former plays dully and weakly, the latter must know how to avoid embarrassing her. If Madame *Violino primo* stumbles in the beat [*im Text,* erroneously for *im Takt?*], she must not do the same thing, but must indicate the correct meter lightly but persistently. If this is fruitless, then the contrabass must speak and restore order. If he behaves **passively,** it is his business, and any evident confusion is not to be gossiped about by the chambermaid—presuming that she herself has not contributed to it. One understands that this part as well requires much talent, and there are instances enough where an extraordinary player has risen from **second** to **first** violin.

The **violoncello** sometimes has work in common with the contrabass, and sometimes has special duties of his own in the musical household, which are too petty for the former. The cello does not have the authority to direct the whole; it only **copies**, as it were, the principal tasks of the contrabass, and therefore it is played by the **secretary** of the head of the household. If the contrabass is too weak, or if he plays with too little insight, the violoncello must play especially well, in order to make up the deficiencies with wisdom and adroitness, and if the former plays something wrong, must lead him to the correct note. But he must do it in such a manner that it **appears** as if all of the notes that he supplied, or improved, come from the contrabass itself. The violoncello often plays together with the **second violin** or the **viola**; he must take care not to come into **forbidden octaves with the first violin**.

The **viola** belongs to the **cook**. She is the middle part of the musical economy, but entirely indispensable, because without her the harmony would always remain weak. If this voice is true and mindful of her duty, then much is gained toward full accord; but if she skips notes and in this way **steals** from the musical household, then it is soon wanting now here, now there—especially if the first violin is not paying enough attention. She must especially avoid forbidden **fifths** with the violoncello, for which the opportunity arises all too easily; otherwise she could easily cause a major indiscretion.

The **children** represent the **clarinets, flutes,** and **oboes** in the house orchestra. The more pure and lovely their tone is, and the more temperately they express themselves, the more beautiful the harmony will become. But from time to time they are unfortunately impure, and often even **overblow**—most often, more so than one usually **believes**, this happens in those who sound the sweetest (the flutes); and it becomes hard even for skilled musicians to reteach the overblown instruments the correct tone, especially when they are played over and over by the overblowers. If they **screech** wrong notes loudly and ill-manneredly through the musical house, there is no joy in such a concert, and it would be better to remove them altogether.

The **bassoon** is, so to speak, the **tutor** of this young group. He wields over them the same authority that the double-bass has over the whole orchestra. They seldom appear out of his company, and he has the main part among them. So he must have and **keep** a mild tone, not too weak, but **solid**; but he must also not buzz too much, even though this is necessary at *fortissimo* and gives a **good** effect, although it easily offends **sensitive** ears.

The **horns** are comparable to the **servants** of the house, whose presence is comfortable and pleasant if they are not impertinent, but are satisfied to come in at the right time and take care of their business. At once they give the whole musical household a distinguished appearance. In newer music they are, now and then, used *obligato* to the first voice. The **trumpets** and **drums** are **outriders** and **coachmen,** who only appear when the entire house goes out with full stateliness and pomp. But one must keep an especially tight rein on them and give them no part of their own; for if one allows them too much, they easily make too much noise, and can particularly anger the delicate Lady *Violino primo.* If all the parts of the house orchestra are competent and well-filled, the whole concert of domestic life will always get on well, whether the piece is *adagio* or *presto, moderato* or *pomposo,* whether the wild storm of a Beethoven Allegro, or the gentle peace of a Haiden Andante, or the endless intricacy of a Mozart fugue is set upon the music stand of life; each one will be performed to the honor of the players and the pleasure of the listeners.

5 "Tadpole Pleasures"

Daniel Deronda *as Music Historiography*

We are but "in the morning of the times," and must learn to think
of ourselves as tadpoles unprescient of the future frog. Still the tadpole
is limited to tadpole pleasures; and so, in our state of development, we
are swayed by melody.

GEORGE ELIOT, "Liszt, Wagner, and Weimar" (1855)

Music was a deep love and a strong force in the personal life of George Eliot—
that is, of Marian Evans, whose birthday fell on St. Cecilia's day; it makes
its presence felt in virtually all of her writing.[1] "If Eliot's religion was 'the
religion of humanity,'" writes William Sullivan, "then music was that religion's most efficacious sacrament."[2] But its deployment in her last novel,
Daniel Deronda, is by far the most thorough-going, and is consistently the-
matized within the structure of the plot in such a way as to dramatize the
relationships among the characters, their communities, and their histories.

Much has been written about Eliot's use of music, focusing on its diagnostic role as an index of the sensibility and authenticity of a character, or
on her deft application of its social functions to sketch the strata of society

Many colleagues gave me generous help in the preparation of this essay, reading earlier versions and offering reality-checks against my excessive flights of fancy; I am
grateful to Allan Atlas, Raphael Atlas, Jocelyne Kolb, Cornelia Pearsall, Gary Tomlinson, and Leo Treitler, and especially to Lawrence Kramer for helping me see the
organization of my argument more clearly. I would also like to thank Theresa Muir
for sharing with me her dissertation work on the Victorian reception of Wagner.

1. [George Eliot], "Liszt, Wagner, and Weimar," *Fraser's Magazine* 52 (July
1855), reprinted in *Essays of George Eliot*, ed. Thomas Pinney (New York: Columbia University Press, 1967), 103; the quoted phrase is from Tennyson's "The Day
Dream." A good summary of Eliot's lifetime involvement with music is in Beryl
Gray's *George Eliot and Music* (New York: St. Martin's Press, 1989), ch. 1. And Edward Dannreuther's later insistence that it would be wrong to understand the music of the future as something "that is ugly to us, but may possibly sound all right
to our grandchildren" suggests that evolutionary readings like Eliot's were irresistible to the Victorians (*Richard Wagner: His Tendencies and Theories* [London:
Augener, 1873], 18).

2. William Joseph Sullivan, "George Eliot and the Fine Arts" (Ph.D. diss., University of Wisconsin, 1990), 38.

and trace her characters' movements across them.[3] Although these points are all well taken, such readings do not always suffice to explain Eliot's particular musical choices, especially in this most historiographic of novels. Her wide middle-class readership might have gotten these general messages just as well, as they did in many another novel, from such Victorian mainstays as "The last rose of summer," "I dreamt I dwelt in marble halls," or "Home, sweet home." After all, *Middlemarch*'s Rosamond Vincy sings the latter to an aging uncle who considers it "the suitable garnish for girls," and the scene gives us information enough about both Rosamond and her uncle.[4] But Mirah Lapidoth sings Beethoven, and not without reason.

I propose, rather, that the depictions of music and music making in *Daniel Deronda*—including a somewhat surprising number of specific compositions, both real and imaginary, some lovingly described—carry a subtext about music's history that contributes centrally to the novel's overall engagement with the varieties of history and relationships to the past. My purpose here is not to read *Daniel Deronda* through musicological eyes but, on the contrary, to see what evidence the novel can provide about the understanding of music history in circulation among the Victorian bourgeoisie. A best-selling novelist who also happens to be a leading member of one of the central intellectual circles of mid-Victorian England is one who understands well the cultural issues and conversational topics of the time, a kind of bridge between the intelligentsia and an unusually wide reading public. In the happy phrase of a contemporary critic, Julia Wedgwood, "she had a voice to reach the many and words to arrest the few."[5]

Indeed, it might be argued that the close connection to her public that Eliot had developed with her earlier novels was only enhanced by the serial format in which both *Middlemarch* (1872) and *Daniel Deronda* (1876) first appeared. As they encountered each monthly fascicle, readers became

3. See Alison Byerly, "The Language of the Soul: George Eliot and Music," *Nineteenth-Century Literature* 44 (1989): 1–17; Shirley Frank Levenson, "The Music of *Daniel Deronda*," *Nineteenth-Century Fiction* 24 (1969): 317–34; Phyllis Weliver, "Music as a Sign in *Daniel Deronda*," *The George Eliot Review* 27 (August 1996): 43–48; Sullivan, "Eliot and the Fine Arts"; and Gray, *George Eliot and Music*.

4. George Eliot, *Middlemarch*, ed. David Carroll (Oxford: Clarendon Press, 1986), 113. The first-named tune is an Irish traditional song popularized in Friedrich von Flotow's *Martha* (1847), the second is from Michael Balfe's *The Bohemian Girl* (1843), and the third from Henry Bishop's *Clari* (1823).

5. Julia Wedgwood, "The Moral Influence of George Eliot," in *Nineteenth-Century Teachers and Other Essays* (London: Hodder and Stoughton, 1909), 230; originally published in the *Contemporary Review* for February 1881, shortly after Eliot's death.

engrossed in the plot and developed a certain illusion of coauthorship.[6] *Daniel Deronda* was published in eight monthly installments (autonomously rather than in a periodical) from February to September 1876. In many literary journals of the time, each installment was reviewed as it appeared, heightening the audience's sense of involvement in the fate of the characters and fostering an oddly public set of expectations for the continuance of the story. Underlying the effect was the textured realism of Eliot's prose, empowered by research habits so meticulous that her companion, George Henry Lewes, remarked that "she is as fidgety about minute accuracy as if she were on oath."[7]

Daniel Deronda has customarily—and richly—been read as a novel about the sweep of world history, perhaps about the possibility of a positivist utopian future, and above all about the relation of a community's future to its specific past. The source of the hero's given name is well known: in one of her several research notebooks for the novel Eliot quotes Abraham Kuenen to the effect that the author of the Book of Daniel was "the first who grasped the history of the world, so far as he knew it, as one great whole."[8] Matched to this world-historical time scale, though, is the microcosmic scale on which individuals encounter the passage of time and their own relationship to a larger sense of history. Elizabeth Deeds Ermarth has provocatively characterized the late nineteenth-century novel as the disseminator of a particular historical narrative code she calls "humanist time"—that is, a time not "end-stopped by teleology" or saturated with divine agency.[9] Just so, *Daniel Deronda* explores many varieties and calibrations of humanly experienced history.

THE IMPERATIVES OF HISTORY

When Victorians thought about history, a tangle of scientific and social questions provided the context for their thinking. What they themselves called

6. See Carol A. Martin, *George Eliot's Serial Fiction* (Columbus: Ohio State University Press, 1994), 26.

7. Quoted in Gordon S. Haight, *George Eliot: A Biography* (New York: Oxford University Press, 1968), 320. Haight's is still the definitive study of Eliot's life.

8. Pforzheimer notebook 710, f.14 (Jane Irwin, ed., *George Eliot's* Daniel Deronda *Notebooks* [Cambridge: Cambridge University Press, 1996], 406). Eliot's source here is Abraham Kuenen, *The Religion of Israel to the Fall of the Jewish State*, trans. Alfred Heath May (1875).

9. Elizabeth Deeds Ermarth, *The English Novel in History, 1840–1895* (London: Routledge, 1997), 73 and passim.

the "spirit of the age" was a sense of "living in the stream of history"—a feeling that their lives and their world were governed no longer by divine providence or even by nature, but by history itself.[10] An awareness of evolutionary process (often called "transformation" or "transmutation") had been commonplace since the late eighteenth century, playing a central role in historical writing and in various aspects of social science well before its now best-known scientific promulgators—Lyell, Darwin, and Wallace—began to publish. Patterns of publication and readership in the period meant that the general cultural influence of Victorian science was profound and pervasive, both because of the voracious reading habits of the public and because science writing was still largely done in the ordinary language of current events or arts criticism.

By 1876, then, there was no longer much question in the minds of the educated classes that evolution drove biological development (indeed, the very idea of "evolution" became a craze), although there was still dispute about whose account of its mode of operation was the most accurate. That is, contrary to popular belief nowadays, there was nothing new or shocking about evolution per se when Charles Darwin published the *Origin of Species*—after two decades of hesitation—in 1859. What was scandalous about the *Origin*, rather, was Darwin's insistence that natural selection, his candidate for evolution's sole and unique driving force, was a random process of adaptation neither guided by a benevolent divine hand nor in fact purposive in any sense: natural selection was not driven in any goal-oriented direction and offered no guarantee of the "progress" that had attained an almost sacramental status for the Victorians. Thus in place of the older image of the evolutionary *ladder*, unidirectional and culminating in an evident (human) pinnacle, the newer Darwinian thinking substituted the *tree*, branching in various directions that were unpredictable and potentially infinite in number. By late century the average Victorian reader, though of course unlikely to claim knowledgeable allegiance to any particular model of evolutionary science, was very likely indeed to hold in imagination an array of competing ideas, along with their iconic representations, that could go comfortably under the banner of "evolution," and in this way a confused mélange of evolutionary language was understood as appropriate to the discussion of historical processes of all sorts.[11]

10. See A. Dwight Culler, *The Victorian Mirror of History* (New Haven: Yale University Press, 1985), 41.

11. The literature on the history of evolution, both as scientific theory and as social model, is one of the most voluminous in all of modern scholarship, and not without its controversies. My own thinking has been guided principally by its cur-

In George Eliot's intellectual circle, social applications of evolutionary science were a primary focus of discussion and debate. On the one hand, some argued that evolution enjoined a laissez-faire attitude to the fate of societies, since nature would take its course and the laws of progress and history would have their inexorable way in any event. The best-known apostle of this viewpoint, Herbert Spencer, was a close lifelong friend (and sometime opera companion) of Eliot's; over many years she grappled with and developed her own arguments against his commitment to the "survival of the fittest" in human societies as well as animal species.[12] On the other hand, others preferred to cushion the force of random accident, opting instead for Lamarck's version with its allowance for "purposive adaptation" by individuals and therefore of "directed evolution."[13] Perceiving there an opportunity to help progress along in some beneficial direction, a number of social thinkers designed utopian futures upon evolutionary principles, foremost among them the positivism of Auguste Comte, whose rather chilling historical motto was "savoir pour prévoir et prévoir pour pouvoir."[14] Comte, too, was a fundamental intellectual influence upon George Eliot and her circle.

Above all, the past loomed as the harbinger of some determinate future the discernment of which, it seemed, was a matter of solving one particu-

rent revisionist wing, especially the work of Gillian Beer (in *Open Fields: Science in Cultural Encounter* [Oxford: Clarendon Press, 1996], among others); Peter Bowler (in *The Non-Darwinian Revolution: Reinterpreting a Historical Myth* [Baltimore: Johns Hopkins University Press, 1988] and *The Invention of Progress: The Victorians and the Past* [Oxford: Basil Blackwell, 1989], among others); Adrian Desmond (*The Politics of Evolution: Morphology, Medicine, and Reform in Radical London* [Chicago: University of Chicago Press, 1989]); James A. Secord (*Victorian Sensation: The Extraordinary Publication, Reception, and Secret Authorship of* Vestiges of the Natural History of Creation [Chicago: University of Chicago Press, 2000]); and Stephen G. Alter (*Darwinism and the Linguistic Image: Language, Race, and Natural Theology in the Nineteenth Century* [Baltimore: Johns Hopkins University Press, 1999]).

12. Spencer substituted this term for Darwin's "natural selection," because he found it too metaphysical and suggestive of a supernatural guiding hand at work; Spencer's stress was always on the deterministic aspect of evolutionary progress. His 1857 essay, "Progress: Its Law and Cause," is a concise explanation of Spencer's views, which Eliot knew well and had many occasions to discuss with him over the several decades of their friendship. See note 69.

13. On the relative impact of Lamarck and Darwin on Victorian thought, especially that of George Henry Lewes (GHL), see Peter Allan Dale, *In Pursuit of a Scientific Culture: Science, Art, and Society in the Victorian Age* (Madison: University of Wisconsin Press, 1989).

14. Kenneth Thompson, *Auguste Comte: The Foundation of Sociology* (New York: John Wiley and Sons, 1975), 15.

lar problem: discovering for human history the laws equivalent to those the biologists had discovered for the development of species. And so the Victorians became, wholesale, historiographers. George Eliot in particular always insisted on the importance of knowing history, precisely so that processes of social change could be fathomed.

> For want of such real, minute vision of how changes come about in the past, we fall into ridiculously inconsistent estimates of actual movements, condemning in the present what we belaud in the past, and pronouncing impossible processes that have been repeated again and again in the historical preparation of the very system under which we live.[15]

George Henry Lewes, Eliot's companion from 1854 until his death in 1878 and himself a classic instance of the Victorian polymath, understood the important "laws" to be biologically rather than historically imposed—he was little given to mystification—but like most Victorians he believed in progress. But "progress . . . was the optimistic face of the notion of development which, as Darwin thought, involved much waste and pain, and guaranteed no improvement," and Lewes tended to a more Lamarckian view of evolution.[16] To rehearse only very hastily an account of Eliot's own complex of ideas that has been thoroughly covered by others, it seems important to point out that she did believe in incontrovertible—but ultimately beneficent— laws of development. In an early review of Wilhelm Riehl she identified the central historical problem as protecting the roots of the past while sowing the seeds of the future. She wrote approvingly that Riehl's method "sees in European society *incarnate history*" and went on, "What has grown up historically can only die out historically, by the gradual operation of necessary laws."[17] Always, however, she insisted upon the central significance of the decisions and choices made by individuals, and she worried at the relation-

15. "Historic Imagination," written between 1872 and 1879; later included in *Essays and Leaves from a Notebook,* ed. Charles Lee Lewes (London: W. Blackwood and Sons, 1884), 289.

16. Hock Guan Tjoa, *George Henry Lewes: A Victorian Mind* (Cambridge, Mass.: Harvard University Press, 1977), 41, 42.

17. [George Eliot], "The Natural History of German Life," *Westminster Review* 66 (July 1856), reprinted in Pinney, *Essays,* 287; it reviews new editions of Wilhelm Heinrich von Riehl's *Die bürgerliche Gesellschaft* (1851) and *Land und Leute* (1853). See Rosemarie Bodenheimer, *The Real Life of Mary Ann Evans: George Eliot, Her Letters and Fiction* (Ithaca: Cornell University Press, 1994), on Eliot's concern for preserving the past in the future and its relationship to metaphors of organicism. See also Sally Shuttleworth, *George Eliot and Nineteenth-Century Science: The Make-Believe of a Beginning* (Cambridge: Cambridge University Press, 1984).

ship between these two commitments, to developmental laws and to individual action. For moral reasons Eliot feared determinism, and her fear was symptomatic of a generation in which the apparent waning of religious faith in the face of scientific discovery threatened to leave a vacuum dangerous to social order and well-being as well as to the human psyche.[18] Her early translations of Feuerbach and David Strauss familiarized her with "one of the most crucial aspects of nineteenth-century European thought, namely the attempt to reinterpret the Christian religion and its Jewish ancestry as a purely secular phenomenon—as history of culture or anthropology rather than as theology."[19] Thus Victorian thinkers sought a synthesis of intellect and emotion, an integration of materialism and idealism in whose quest Eliot's own novels played a highly visible role. It was in this connection that Lord Acton said of her: "If ever science or religion reigns alone over an undivided empire, the books of George Eliot might lose their central and unique importance, but as the emblem of a generation distracted between the intense need of believing and the difficulty of belief, they will live to the last syllable of recorded time."[20]

In the course of her research for this last novel, Eliot would have learned from Alexander Macfarren and other authorities she consulted that inexorable laws operated in music history too,[21] but we may surely assume that she probed the assertion as thoughtfully in the musical arena as elsewhere. A law-governed history of art would subvert artistic freedom and creativity; such a deterministic view was radically challenged by the image of the autonomous and free-spirited romantic artist, which thrived into the late nineteenth century and was a favorite literary topos of Eliot's. This strand of meaning also makes its way through *Daniel Deronda*.

To sketch my argument about the novel in prospect: *Daniel Deronda* is, among many other things, a commentary on its author's ambivalence to-

18. Comte's positivism included a quasi-liturgical calendar for "sociolatry, or social worship," specified rituals and priestly duties, and a three-volume catechism. On the general point see, among many others, U. C. Knoepflmacher, *Religious Humanism and the Victorian Novel: George Eliot, Walter Pater, Samuel Butler* (Princeton: Princeton University Press, 1965).

19. Terence Cave, ed., introduction to *Daniel Deronda* (London: Penguin Classics, 1995), xix. See David Carroll, *George Eliot and the Conflict of Interpretations: A Reading of the Novels* (Cambridge: Cambridge University Press, 1992), esp. ch. 1.

20. Lord Acton, review of John Cross's *Life of George Eliot*, in *Nineteenth Century* 17 (March 1885): 464–85, quoted in *George Eliot: The Critical Heritage*, ed. David Carroll (London: Routledge and Kegan Paul, 1971), 463.

21. See Macfarren's *Six Lectures on Harmony* (1867), of which GE and GHL owned a copy (William Baker, *The Libraries of George Eliot and George Henry Lewes* [Victoria, B.C.: University of Victoria Press, 1981], item no. 597).

ward "the music of the future"—which is to say, toward Wagner. It has frequently been observed that the novel offers a movingly even-handed treatment of two alternative ways of being Jewish, drawn in two archetypal characters who receive equally sympathetic treatment: one, the visionary Zionist Mordecai, appeals to specifically national ("racial," in Victorian terms)[22] values, his overriding concern the preservation of Jewish culture as it is and has been in history; the other, the cultivated composer Klesmer, appeals to universal values and looks to an assimilated cosmopolitan future as the best hope for his people.

These two visions of the Jewish future are based on two readings of Jewish history encountered in Eliot's research,[23] and they are accompanied and amplified, I am arguing, by two visions of the future of music. But the relationship between the two is nothing so simple as a struggle between the "music of the future" and that of the past, although on occasion it presents itself discursively in these terms. Rather, it is a balancing act between Wagnerian progressivism and the gradual formation of a musical canon. Like the contemporary debate about Jewish identity, the conversation about music's future imagines a decision to be made between the preservation of a cultural past and the embrace of a cosmopolitan future. The balancing act, with the widespread ambivalence that accompanied it, arose from those very Victorian conversations about progress, development, and evolution. There were both ladderlike and treelike models in play: as far as the history of art is concerned, evolution does not necessarily lead upward on a ladder to the "artwork of the future"; it might just as well branch out abundantly to yield what Matthew Arnold called "the best that has been thought and said in the world."[24]

22. In Victorian usage, "race" and "nationality" were often synonymous; for classic instances in Eliot's writing, see "Three Months in Weimar," "A Word for the Germans," and "Madame de Sablé," all reprinted in Pinney, *Essays*.

23. Eliot did exhaustive research on the history of the Jews and details of Jewish custom, culture, and liturgy; her principal sources were the assimilationists Leopold Zunz (*Die Gottesdienstlichen Vorträge der Juden* [1832] and *Die synagogale Poesie des Mittelalters* [1855]) and Abraham Geiger (*Das Judenthum und seine Geschichte* [1865–71]) and the Zionists Heinrich Graetz (*Geschichte der Juden von den ältesten Zeiten bis auf die Gegenwart*, 11 vols. [1863–76]) and Salomon Munk (*Palestine: description géographique, historique et archéologique* [1845] and *Mélanges de philosophie juive et arabe* [1857]). Her notes are to be found in Irwin, *Notebooks*.

24. This bifurcation can be thought of as the intellectual shift from an evolutionary to a historicist orientation, as for example Glenn Stanley does ("Historiography," in *The New Grove Dictionary of Music Online*, ed. L. Macy [accessed 13 March 2003] <http://www.grovemusic.com>). But it is very important to recognize

Daniel Deronda is itself a dialogic fiction, not least in the large-scale division its contemporary readers perceived, into "the English part" and "the Jewish part." But its author's interest in antitheses and paired alternatives goes far beyond that simple structural matter, taking up the debate I outline and working it quite explicitly into the text. In chapter 42, near the center of the novel, a group of working men ("poor men given to thought," Mordecai calls them) assemble for conversation and debate in the Hand and Banner.[25] It is a company Eliot takes pains to portray as multiethnic, some of its members more so than they themselves are aware. Their conversation veers from the "law of progress" and the causes of social change to the "idea of nationalities" and the fate of nationalist sentiment; the Jewish assimilationist Pash's insistence that in advanced European countries "the sentiment of nationality is destined to die out" (584) is met with Mordecai's passionate commitment to his contrary belief, that "each nation has its own work" (590). The men, who have apparently been conducting the same conversation for years, come to no conclusion.

Imagining a hypothetical scene involving Klesmer in debate with a group of his professional colleagues, we can hear a precisely analogous conversation about the implications of the "music of the future," and one that was surely taking place all over Europe at that very moment.

THE MUSIC OF THE FUTURE

Meetings with two musicians who were at the center of the progressive movement bracketed George Eliot's life with George Henry Lewes, and the visits helped keep the topic of futurist music in the forefront of their attention and of their regular concert-going. In 1854, on their first trip together, they spent three months in Weimar where they made the acquaintance of Franz Liszt and his companion, Princess Carolyne Sayn-Wittgenstein. Liszt was court

---

that both attitudes could be comfortably accommodated to prevailing contemporary understandings of evolutionary theory.

25. George Eliot, *Daniel Deronda*, ed. Barbara Hardy (Harmondsworth: Penguin, 1967), 580–99; all further references in the text are to this edition. Bernard Semmel suggests (*George Eliot and the Politics of National Inheritance* [New York: Oxford University Press, 1994], 125) that this conversation among "four Jews, a Scotsman, an Irishman, and three Englishmen" reflects an understanding of the "law of progress" as popularized in Henry T. Buckle's *History of Civilization in England* (1857), which Eliot had read. Buckle asserts that mental, moral, and physical laws together govern human behavior. GE's and GHL's reading of Buckle is reported in her diary for 3 September 1857 (*The Journals of George Eliot*, ed. Margaret Harris and Judith Johnston [Cambridge: Cambridge University Press, 1998], 70).

kapellmeister at the time, and he was able to introduce the Leweses to Anton Rubinstein and to invite them to musical parties at which they heard performances by, among others, Clara Schumann—"a melancholy, interesting creature," according to Eliot's journal. Most significantly, in Weimar they heard performances of *Lohengrin, Tannhäuser,* and *Der fliegende Holländer* and made the acquaintance of Joachim Raff, author of the recently published *Die Wagnerfrage.*[26]

Thus they found themselves among the most up-to-date of English listeners, saturated with what was regarded as Europe's most progressive music as well as participating in several months' worth of conversation among its principal apologists. Eliot learned much of the movement's rhetoric in detail, translating an essay of Liszt's of which Lewes used parts for his regular column in *The Leader,* with his own commentary interspersed.[27] As always, she read and listened carefully, giving full and thoughtful attention to the new musical ideas as well as to the understanding of historical process that underlay them. From two extended essays of her own, we have a good sense of her train of thought.[28] First and foremost, she was enormously impressed by Liszt, both as musician and as human character: he was, she insisted, far more than "the Napoleon of the *salon*" portrayed in England. In characteristic fashion she assessed the moral nature and the musical genius together and found the combination satisfactory: "in him Nature has not sacrificed the man to the artist" (97). George Lewes kept up correspondence with Princess Carolyne for a while after their sojourn in Weimar, and in general the personal relationship between the couples seems to have left a lasting impression.[29]

Eliot's assessment of progressivism itself, exemplary of advanced Victorian thought, rests on the argument that innovation reveals an unmet need.

26. Haight discusses the Weimar trip (*Biography,* 154–68), as does Alan Walker (*The Weimar Years, 1848–1861,* vol. 2 of *Franz Liszt* [New York: Alfred A. Knopf, 1989], 246–51). Raff's pamphlet is *Die Wagnerfrage kritisch beleuchtet* (Braunschweig, 1854), of which the Leweses owned a copy. For an account of Raff's relationship to Liszt, see Walker, "The Raff Case," in *Weimar Years.*

27. [GHL], "The Romantic School of Music," *Leader* (28 October 1854): 1027–28, based on brief sections of Franz Liszt, "Scribe's und Meyerbeer's *Robert der Teufel,*" *Neue Zeitschrift für Musik* 25 (16 June 1854): 261–69.

28. "Liszt, Wagner, and Weimar" (96–122) includes a capsule history of opera derived from Liszt's *Neue Zeitschrift* essay and concludes with descriptions of the three Weimar productions of Wagner. The other Weimar essay, not quoted here, is "Three Months in Weimar," *Fraser's Magazine* 51 (June 1855), also reprinted in Pinney, *Essays,* 82–95.

29. *The Letters of George Henry Lewes,* ed. William Baker (Victoria, B.C.: University of Victoria Press, 1995), 1:234–38.

Much cheap ridicule has been spent on the "music of the future";
a ridicule excused, perhaps, by the more than ordinary share Herr
Wagner seems to have of a quality which is common to almost all
innovators and heretics, and which their converts baptize as profound
conviction, while the adherents of the old faith brand it as arrogance.
It might be well, however, if the ridicule were arrested by the consid-
eration that there never was an innovating movement which had not
some negative value as a criticism of the prescriptive, if not any pos-
itive value as a lasting creation. The attempt at an innovation reveals
a want that has not hitherto been met. (99)

She entirely accepts the Wagnerian premise that "the drama must not be a
mere pretext for the music; but music, drama, and spectacle must be blended,
like the coloured rays in the sunbeam, so as to produce one undivided impression" (100). She was prepared for this notion by much of her earlier
reading, and particularly by her close acquaintance with the writing of Ludwig Feuerbach, whose *Essence of Christianity* she had translated in 1852;
his argument that the identity of music imagery and feeling imagery "suggests that the complementing of the visual or figural representation with
the musical gives the total image of feeling its fullest scope" sat comfortably with Wagnerian rhetoric, as Feuerbach's emphasis on feeling and his
positing of an infinite human "species being" did with her own view of art
as "a mode of amplifying experience and extending our contact with our
fellow-men beyond the bounds of our personal lot."[30] What she seems especially to value in Wagner's operas is his use of mythic themes, and precisely for the reason that later drove Adorno to warn us of their danger:
their claim to universality.[31] Eliot's early response to revolutionary ideas is
entirely in keeping with her intellectual commitments in general, as is clear
from a much later essay on the role of innovation in history:

> The criticism of radical, revolutionary schemes, that they are a breach
> of continuity, has to be justified by showing that they are made futile

30. Marx W. Wartofsky, *Feuerbach* (Cambridge: Cambridge University Press,
1977), 286; see the discussion of Feuerbach's thoughts on music, and Wagner's response to them in S. Rawidowicz, *Ludwig Feuerbachs Philosophie: Ursprung und
Schicksal,* 2d ed. (Berlin: Walter de Gruyter, 1964), 388–411 (and below in note 57,
Wagner's claim about Feuerbach's influence); [Eliot], "Belles Lettres and Art," *Westminster Review* 66 (July 1856): 54.

31. "Liszt, Wagner, and Weimar," 105; Theodor Adorno, *In Search of Wagner,*
trans. Rodney Livingstone (London: Verso, 1991), ch. 8. Turning the tables ironically, a writer who attended the first Wagner festival at Bayreuth reported on "the
minute development of tone and character painting which makes Wagner the
George Eliot of music" (C. Halford Hawkins, "The Wagner Festival at Bayreuth,"
Macmillan's Magazine 35 [1876]: 63).

by the continuous existence of conditions resulting from the past which either obstinately oppose themselves to the immediate amelioration of things by statute & the high hand & so turn the proposed reform into a fatal condoning & avowal of disregard to the laws & constitution, or else carry in solution previous sentiments & habits of mind which would make it socially pernicious to expunge them.[32]

In 1877, when Richard and Cosima Wagner came to London for a series of performances at the Royal Albert Hall, the Leweses made a particular point of meeting them and coming to know them as well as schedules and circumstances permitted. At a gathering at Edward Dannreuther's home "Wagner read his *Parzival,* which he did with great spirit and like a fine actor."[33] Again George Eliot was most stirred by the personalities of the famous visitors. She asked permission to introduce Cosima to Edward and Georgianna Burne-Jones, "that I may be allowed to bring to you Madame Wagner at a time when you will be personally at liberty. She is, I think, a rare person, worthy to see the best things, having her father's (Liszt's) quickness and breadth of comprehension" and, shortly afterward, told her friend Barbara Bodichon that "we are in love with Mad. Wagner!"[34] In a later letter to Cosima, Lewes too blurted that "altogether the stirrings of the soul which the Meister's music and your personality excited in us will make the May of 77 ever memorable to us."[35]

Despite this sympathy, however, and although they both understood and were not undisposed toward the agenda involved, after repeated attempts they simply could not like the music, and perhaps it was this disappointment that planted the first seed of ambivalence about the Wagnerian reading of music's historical imperative. As the contemporary critic Francis Hueffer cannily remarked of Eliot, "her appreciation of Wagner's music was of a very

32. "Historic Guidance," probably written between 1874 and 1879 (later included in Thomas Pinney, "More Leaves from George Eliot's Notebook," *Huntington Library Quarterly* 29 [1966]: 373).

33. GHL diary, 17 May 1877, quoted in Haight, *Biography,* 502. In that party were also George Grove and George Meredith; of course, the reading was of *Parsifal*'s text only. Alas, GE and GHL's acquaintance with the Wagners began only after the publication of *Daniel Deronda.*

34. Letter to Edward Burne-Jones, 8 May 1877, in *The George Eliot Letters,* ed. Gordon S. Haight (New Haven: Yale University Press, 1954–78), 6:368 (hereafter *GEL*); to Barbara Bodichon, 18 May 1877, in *GEL* 6:374.

35. Quoted in Geoffrey Skelton, "George Eliot and Cosima Wagner: A Newly Discovered Letter from George Henry Lewes," *George Eliot Fellowship Review* 13 (1982): 28.

platonic kind."[36] Their difficulty persisted from first exposure to the end of their lives without noticeably abating, even given their remarkably tenacious efforts at acclimation; letters and diaries continue to reveal periodic attendance at performances of Wagner's operas, both in England and on their frequent trips abroad. Theory and practice simply could not be brought comfortably together. Eliot wrote in "Liszt, Wagner, and Weimar,"

> Without pretending to be a musical critic, one may be allowed to give an opinion as a person with an ear and a mind susceptible to the direct and indirect influences of music. In this character I may say that, though unable to recognize Herr Wagner's compositions as the ideal of the opera, and though, with a few slight exceptions, not deeply affected by his music on a first hearing, it is difficult to me to understand how any one who finds deficiencies in the opera as it has existed hitherto, can give fair attention to Wagner's theory, and his exemplification of it in his operas, without admitting that he has pointed out the direction in which the lyric drama must develope [sic] itself, if it is to be developed at all. (100)

Lewes agreed:

> I do not myself venture to pronounce an opinion on the vexed question whether this music is really destined to be the "music of the future," or whether it is a pretentious and chaotic effort. . . . As far as my ear in its present state of musical education determines what is exquisite for it, the Wagner music wants both form and melody.[37]

It is important to recognize that their displeasure was not principled, as it was or pretended to be with so many other critics. Quite the contrary: as Eliot wrote to a friend, "pity we can't always have fine *Weltgeschichtliche* dramatic motives wedded with fine music, instead of trivialities or hideousness. Perhaps this last is too strong a word for anything except the Traviata."[38] Nonetheless, Lewes confided to his son, "the Mutter and I have come to the conclusion that the Music of the future is not for us—Schubert, Beethoven, Mozart, Gluck or even Verdi—but not Wagner—is what we are made to respond to."[39] Their negative reaction to Wagner was, of course, far from isolated in Victorian England. Despite the influx of German cultural

36. Francis Hueffer, *Half a Century of Music in England, 1837–1887: Essays Toward a History* (London: Chapman and Hall, 1889), 72.

37. GHL, "The Drama in Germany" (1867), in *On Actors and the Art of Acting* (New York: Grove Press, 1957), 195–96.

38. Letter to Sara Hennell, 11 July 1863, in *GEL* 4:92.

39. Letter to Charles Lee Lewes, February 1870, after hearing *Tannhäuser* in Berlin, quoted in Haight, *Biography*, 424.

products during Victoria's reign, at least partly under the influence of her German consort, British audiences often stuck at the Wagnerian idea. True, they had not heard very much of the actual music before the 1877 visit, and they were primarily responding to various arguments put forward in his prose writings.[40] Even so, the "Wagner question" and the catchphrase "of the future" loomed large in Victorian conversation. As late as 1877 a surveyor of the scene reported that "the most opposite views about [Wagner's] works are held by people who ought to know, but there can be no doubt that his influence upon English musicians has been profound."[41]

Wagner's writings are infamous for their saturation with national and racial identity, an exaggerated and tendentious form of what was, however, a nearly universal nineteenth-century belief system. The idea that various nationalities (as the Victorians said, "races") differed from one another in essential character was a commonplace and appeared to be supported by one well-known strand of evolutionary science.[42] Popular Wagnerism focused not on the rich diversity resulting from continual speciation, but on the subsumption of outworn forms by better-adapted ones; it looked forward to a state of "perfection" in which latent tendencies would be realized and needs fulfilled—one prominent Victorian vision of progress, albeit a decidedly non-Darwinian one. As Dannreuther wrote, "it appears to [Wagner] evident that each art, as soon as it has reached its utmost limits, imperatively demands to be joined to a sister art," at which point the old form would be overcome and left behind.[43]

At the same time a strangely diasporic understanding of human nation-

40. See Gisela Argyle, *German Elements in the Fiction of George Eliot, Gissing, and Meredith* (Frankfurt am Main: Peter Lang, 1979); and Anthony McCobb, *George Eliot's Knowledge of German Life and Letters* (Salzburg: Institut für Anglistik und Amerikanistik, Universität Salzburg, 1982). No complete Wagner opera was performed in England until 1870, when *Dutchman* was given in Italian. British audiences heard fragments of orchestral music from *Meistersinger* and *Tannhäuser* and frequently encountered the overture to *Rienzi*.
41. Walter Parratt, "Music," in *The Reign of Queen Victoria: A Survey of Fifty Years of Progress*, ed. Thomas Humphry Ward (London: Smith, Elder, 1887), 2: 618. See also Theresa Muir, "The Reception of Richard Wagner in the Victorian Musical Press (1850–94)" (Ph.D. diss., City University of New York, 1997).
42. For the politics and problematics of this racial idea, see especially Semmel, *Politics of National Inheritance*, although I believe he underestimates Eliot's competing concern for cosmopolitan cultural values and personal freedom. Also of interest are George W. Stocking, Jr., *Victorian Anthropology* (New York: Free Press, 1989); and the contemporary observations of Charles Kingsley in "The Natural Theology of the Future," *Macmillan's Magazine* 23 (1871): 373–74.
43. Dannreuther, *Richard Wagner*, 15.

alities assured that although "the German spirit" would triumph along with the "artwork of the future," this culmination must take place universally and not in Germany alone. In 1850 Wagner had written that "history plainly presents two principal currents in the development of mankind—the *racial-national* and the *unnational-universal*. If we now look forward to the completion of this second developmental process in the future, we have plainly before our eyes the completed course of the first one in the past."[44] And a late essay for American readers, purportedly written by Wagner, observes that the German people had rejected his ideas (even as packaged in nine volumes of his collected writings, recently issued), prompting his turn "toward the land beyond the ocean" where, he felt, "the Germanic spirit, in untrammeled development" flourished more genuinely. Throughout the essay, the strong implication is that the future of music he has in mind will evolve, as he now understands, only in diaspora.[45] A contemporary critic of *Daniel Deronda* catches the point in a manner that sharply augurs Adorno's later horror at the universalizing gesture: "What can be the design of this ostentatious separation from the universal instinct of Christendom, this subsidence into Jewish hopes and aims?"[46] For this writer, the particularity of Jewish culture and history marks a repugnant "subsidence," a reversal of evolutionary progress and a step backward down the ladder.

To the Victorians, Wagner and the music of the future represented above all a modernity marked by the dismissal and disavowal of the past. A contemporary apologist in England recounted jubilantly what he took to be Wagner's own views: "the artist is to be the longed-for Messiah, to deliver

44. Richard Wagner, "The Artwork of the Future," trans. Oliver Strunk, in *Source Readings in Music History* (New York: W. W. Norton, 1998), 6:57. Wagner's attitudes about nationalism and universality changed over time and from one written manifesto to another. For a recent discussion that cites much of the vast earlier literature on this topic, see Thomas S. Grey, "Wagner's *Die Meistersinger* as National Opera (1868–1945)," in *Music and German National Identity*, ed. Celia Applegate and Pamela Potter (Chicago: University of Chicago Press, 2002), 78–104.

45. Richard Wagner, "The Work and Mission of My Life," *North American Review* 273 (August 1879): 107–24 and (September 1879): 238–58. John Deathridge tells me, in a private communication, that this essay was written not by Wagner but by Hans von Wolzogen, though surely in conformity to the master's intentions. See also John Deathridge, "A Brief History of Wagner Research," in *Wagner Handbook*, ed. Ulrich Müller and Peter Watnewski, trans. and ed. John Deathridge (Cambridge, Mass.: Harvard University Press, 1992).

46. Unsigned review in *Saturday Review* 42 (16 September 1876), quoted in Carroll, *Critical Heritage*, 377.

future generations from the fetters of custom and prejudice."[47] George Eliot was not sympathetic to that aspect of the Wagnerian gospel, having a life-long concern for the preservation of the past and its lessons, not to mention custom. But something about the Wagnerian synthesis, along with its re-liance upon deeply rooted myth, appealed. As Dannreuther explained,

> His great problem, then, or rather the problem of the art-work of the future as he calls it, somewhat like the social problem of Comte, is this: how can the scattered elements of modern existence generally, and of modern art in particular, be united and interfused in such wise that their rays, issuing from all and every side, shall be concentrated into one luminous focus so as to form an adequate expression of the vast whole.[48]

To this believer in community and sympathy, that message was attractive.

"WAGNERIAN" CHARACTERS AND ASSIMILATION

In counterpoint with the numerous commentators who have remarked upon its preoccupation with the past, Gillian Beer refers to *Daniel Deronda* as "a novel haunted by the future."[49] Both suggestions are insightful. The novel engages in the contemplation of different futures informed by different un-derstandings of the past, different interpretations of the imperatives of heredity and sympathy. Deronda confronts a difficult but perhaps glorious nationalist future in Palestine; Klesmer already glimpses a cosmopolitan future in the universal aristocracy of art.

Within the novel, it is of course Julius Klesmer who is primarily associ-ated with Wagnerism and the "music of the future." He has a noticeable, if lovable, trace of that "arrogance"—the arrogance of the Messiah-artist—that Eliot had earlier ascribed to innovators in general and to Wagner in particular. Distinctly Jewish, as his name alerts us, Klesmer nonetheless em-

---

47. Franz [elsewhere Francis] Hueffer, *Richard Wagner and the Music of the Fu-ture: History and Aesthetics* (London: Chapman and Hall, 1874), 13. GE and GHL owned a copy of this book (William Baker, *The George Eliot–George Henry Lewes Library: An Annotated Catalogue of Their Books at Dr. Williams's Library*, London [New York: Garland, 1977], lxi n.27).

48. Dannreuther, *Richard Wagner*, 16. There is no concrete evidence that Eliot read this book, although it seems likely given her interests and her up-to-date read-ing habits. Dannreuther was host of the gathering in 1877 at which she and GHL were introduced to the Wagners.

49. Gillian Beer, *Darwin's Plots: Evolutionary Narrative in Darwin, George Eliot, and Nineteenth-Century Fiction* (London: Routledge and Kegan Paul, 1983), 181.

bodies assimilation in his own person, being "a felicitous combination of the German, the Sclave, and the Semite" (77). In devising this particular ethnic heritage, Eliot responds rather slyly to current musical controversy. She would have known, as early as the 1854 Weimar visit, Wagner's scandalous writings about Jewish composers; she would have learned, from her reading of Helmholtz and other period sources, that "in the historical point of view . . . [the tonal system] is wholly the product of modern times, limited nationally to the German, Roman, Celtic, and Sclavonic races."[50] By adding a Semitic strain to Klesmer's mix, she claims modernist musical practice for Jewish composers and refutes one aspect of the Wagnerian polemic that disturbed her. Klesmer further enacts his cosmopolitan, assimilationist position by marrying his pupil Catherine Arrowpoint—the only non-Jewish character in the novel who is represented as a talented performer and composer—much to the dismay of her propertied and hypocritical parents.

In the smallest details, Eliot is careful to link Klesmer to other composers the reading public associated with modernism and the music of the future.[51] In general physical appearance he is almost certainly modeled upon Anton Rubinstein, and Alan Walker believes that Klesmer's words may be ones that Eliot heard from Liszt in 1854.[52] The Arrowpoints, proud of their possession of a "first-rate musician"—at least until he threatens to become their son-in-law—consider him "not yet a Liszt" (280). In an anxious scene between Klesmer and Catherine just before their decision to marry, we see him at the piano, "touching the keys so as to give with the delicacy of an echo in the far distance a melody which he had set to Heine's 'Ich hab' dich

50. Hermann Helmholtz, *On the Sensations of Tone as a Physiological Basis for the Theory of Music,* trans. Alexander J. Ellis, 2d ed. (1875; New York: Dover, 1954), 249.

51. One of the most substantial and intriguing contemporary reviews of *Daniel Deronda* was Henry James's polyvocal "Daniel Deronda: A Conversation" (*Atlantic Monthly* 38 [December 1876]: 684–94). James responded to the welter of opinion about the book, and no doubt to his own ambivalence, by allowing three fictional characters of disparate views to discuss it. James's Pulcheria comments, "you must not forget that you think Herr Klesmer 'Shakespearian.' Wouldn't 'Wagnerian' be high enough praise?" Outspoken anti-Semite that Pulcheria is (reflecting the attitude of many of the book's readers and critics), it is the very highest praise she can muster.

52. *Weimar Years,* 250 n.74. Eliot is known to have modeled many of her characters on real persons, thereby setting off an interminable parlor game. Many suggestions have been put forth for Klesmer's original, including Liszt, Joachim, and the fictional Johannes Kreisler. But Eliot commented in May 1876 about an entertainment at which Anton Rubinstein would play, "we shall so like to see our Klesmer again" (Haight, *Biography,* 490); in addition, Rubinstein has the right general appearance and ethnic background.

geliebet und liebe dich noch'" (286)—a double message to the reader. We learn of Klesmer's feelings toward Catherine, of course, from the text; but we also recognize the poem as one of the *Lyrisches Intermezzo,* the cycle from which Schumann's *Dichterliebe* were taken.[53] Lest this association of Schumann with the futurist school surprise nowadays, note a contemporary critic's recollection of Clara Schumann's appearance at the Monday Popular Concerts in 1865 (the year in which the novel's story commences): "the programme on that occasion was devoted entirely to the works of her husband, which, in those days, were thought to be the abstruse effusions of the modern spirit."[54]

In the end, it is the "abstruse effusions" of Klesmer's own music that inform us of his place within the story of musical progress. To be sure, what we "hear" of it is not opera but instrumental music—perhaps an accommodation to the exigencies of a plot in which music is heard, as Klesmer himself says, "from the drawing-room *standpunkt*" (299)—but always it is associated with text. These unheard texts are carefully chosen to bear meanings to the reader although, as we discover in due course, this very dependence upon text to convey fullness of meaning is an aspect of Wagnerism with which Eliot herself didn't entirely agree.

Klesmer makes his first appearance in *Daniel Deronda* in one of those drawing-room scenes that lulled Eliot's readers into the belief that they were embarking upon a conventional Victorian novel. He is pressed for his reaction to the socially obligatory singing of Gwendolen Harleth—our heroine so far, presented to us as beautiful, spoiled, and self-satisfied—who chooses "a favourite aria of Bellini's, in which she felt quite sure of herself" (78). At the musical outrage that results Klesmer's artistic integrity overwhelms his manners; not only does she produce her notes badly, he tells her, but

> that music which you sing is beneath you. It is a form of melody which
> expresses a puerile state of culture—a dandling, canting, see-saw kind
> of stuff—the passion and thought of people without any breadth of
> horizon. There is a sort of self-satisfied folly about every phrase of such

53. Although some thirty settings of "Ich hab' dich geliebet" are known, none is by a major composer or is still in the repertory (see Gunter Metzner, *Heine in der Musik: Bibliographie der Heine-Vertonungen,* 12 vols. [Tutzing: H. Schneider, 1989–94]). The poem is only one quatrain in length, perhaps too short for a very effective lied.

54. Hueffer, *Half a Century,* 17. An 1852 review by J. W. Davison cites (negatively) the "aesthetic" school of "Richard Wagner, Robert Schumann, &c" (quoted in Howard Smither, *The Oratorio in the Nineteenth and Twentieth Centuries,* vol. 4 of *A History of the Oratorio* [Chapel Hill: University of North Carolina Press, 2000], 294).

melody: no cries of deep, mysterious passion—no conflict—no sense of the universal. It makes men small as they listen to it. (79)[55]

Klesmer's own composition, immediately following, provides a stern corrective; he plays "a fantasia called *Freudvoll, Leidvoll, Gedankenvoll*—an extensive commentary on some melodic ideas not too grossly evident" (80), whose poetic reference for readers familiar with Goethe's *Egmont* supplies full measure of "deep, mysterious passion."[56]

> Freudvoll und leidvoll,
> gedankenvoll sein;
> langen und bangen
> in schwebender Pein . . .

The audience is unconvinced; we get the idea that Gwendolen's "dandling and canting" are on the whole preferred, especially by one of the guests— "young Clintock, the archdeacon's classical son"—who wishes she would sing again because "I never can make anything of this tip-top playing. It is like a jar of leeches, where you can never tell either beginnings or endings. I could listen to your singing all day" (80). From this Philistine's-eye description we understand perfectly that Klesmer's music does not resemble that of Beethoven or Schubert, not to mention Haydn or Mozart, which would be familiar and comfortable for this "classical" young man, but that it is progressive for 1865.

Just in case we should fail to get the point, young Clintock reappears at the end of the scene to hammer it home, commenting in an aside to Gwendolen, "depend upon it croquet is the game of the future. It wants writing up, though" (81): croquet has not yet found its Wagner or its Feuerbach.[57] The same young character seems altogether taken with this modernist trope, assuring Gwendolen in a later scene that he (unlike Klesmer) admires her singing because it is not "addressed to the ears of the future" (137). Philistine though he may be, Clintock is well able to take his tadpole pleasures.

But Klesmer is not the only "Wagnerian" or cosmopolitan figure in *Daniel Deronda;* a more astonishing character, Daniel's mother, belongs with a vengeance to this company. Daniel, raised by a wealthy and kindly aris-

---

55. Just months earlier, Edward Dannreuther had written of "the sugar plums and fireworks of Rossini [and] the moonshine sentimentalities of Bellini," in "The Opera: Its Growth and Decay," *Macmillan's Magazine* 32 (1875): 69.

56. Nicely suggested by Cave, *Daniel Deronda*, 816 n.12.

57. Ludwig Feuerbach's *Grundsätze der Philosophie der Zukuft* (1843), which Wagner later identified as an influence on his thinking, may have been the original source of the craze for identifying various phenomena "of the future."

tocratic "uncle," learns only in adulthood—and only near the end of the novel—that his mother is alive, that she is Jewish, and that she gave him away in infancy both in pursuit of her own operatic career and to spare him "the bondage of having been born a Jew" himself (689). Dying now, she summons him to Genoa to learn his heritage and his family history.

Daniel's mother has many names; we meet her as the Princess Halm-Eberstein, partner in a marriage of convenience entered into after the failure of her voice ends her stage career. Her family name (and that of Daniel's father, a cousin) is Charisi, adapted on the stage as Alcharisi, in keeping with the tradition that attached the article to the names of divas, here Arabic *al* for Italian *la*. "I was the Alcharisi you have heard of: the name had magic wherever it was carried" (697). Her given name, inevitably, is Leonora. (Both Beethoven's and Tasso's Leonoras are invoked within the course of the novel.)[58] Unfortunately, we are not told what roles she sang.

She is a dramatic, even histrionic character, as befits a diva, and her story is operatic and vivid. The daughter of a pious and observant Jew who demanded her absolute submission to Jewish law, Leonora experienced her religion as a virulently misogynistic force bending her to a purpose to which her nature was not suited—"a woman's heart must be of such a size and no larger, else it must be pressed small, like Chinese feet" (694), a chilling assessment that bears a whiff of Klesmer's reaction to Bellini ("it makes men small"). She testifies to the terrible human cost of the commitment to racial identity, one she has thrown over in favor of the superior and universal identity of the artist.

Leonora insists, in what Rosemarie Bodenheimer calls her "confessional coloratura,"[59] upon her absolute right of self-determination, given her along with her musical talent: "I was a great singer, and I acted as well as I sang. All the rest were poor beside me" (688). As a number of feminist critics have observed, George Eliot has told this story before, in her long poem *Armgart* (1870).[60] Like Leonora, Armgart is a celebrated and successful diva

58. Ironically, Leonora seems to have gotten her family name from Judah Alcharizi, composer of thirteenth-century songs of return; Eliot owned a copy of Franz Delitzsch's *Zur Geschichte der Jüdischen Poësie* (1836), where a marginal note highlights the name. See William Baker, *George Eliot and Judaism* (Salzburg: Institut für Englische Sprache und Literatur, 1975), 151.

59. Bodenheimer, *Real Life of Mary Ann Evans*, 185.

60. See Wendy Bashant, "Singing in Greek Drag: Gluck, Berlioz, George Eliot," in *En Travesti: Women, Gender, Subversion, Opera*, ed. Corinne E. Blackmer and Patricia Juliana Smith (New York: Columbia University Press, 1995), 216–41; and Rebecca Pope, "The Diva Doesn't Die: George Eliot's *Armgart*," in *Embodied Voices: Female Vocality in Western Culture*, ed. Leslie C. Dunn and Nancy A. Jones (New

whose voice suddenly fails and who sees her favorite roles given away to younger and newer stage sensations. In her case, the moral of the story is a perplexing one, since Armgart is made to see her own artistic ambition as unworthy and to accept in its place a life of dutiful service to another; she is greatly humbled. Leonora is brought down by fatal illness and under its devastation is less sure of herself than she once was, but she does not seem to regret her rebellious choices. The difference between the two cases may be the matter of Judaism, or rather of a racial identity, which Leonora rejects with violence even as her own son is learning to embrace it: "I was [supposed] to love the long prayers in the ugly synagogue, and the howling, and the gabbling, and the dreadful fasts, and the tiresome feasts, and my father's endless discoursing about Our People, which was a thunder without meaning in my ears. . . . I did not care at all. I cared for the wide world, and all that I could represent in it" (693). On the subject of assimilation, she does not mince words. "Before I married the second time I was baptised. I made myself like the people I lived among. I had a right to do it; I was not like a brute, obliged to go with my own herd" (698). Once again, the commitment to a given national or racial group is backward, brutish, unevolved.

CANON FORMATION AS COUNTERVAILING FORCE

Historiographically speaking, the single most resistant force to the triumph of the "music of the future" in the second half of the nineteenth century was the phenomenon of canon formation, the identification—quite new in the history of music—of a "standard" repertory of musical works that remained in regular performance even as they aged. Not simply a "conservative" force combating progressive music, the canon in itself represented (and was understood to represent) a competing vision of music's future.

The music critic Henry Chorley, an aging pessimist when he issued his *Thirty Years' Musical Recollections* in 1862, was not only anti-Wagnerian but not overfond of most of the forms modern music was taking. Seeing a mixed picture as he surveyed the English scene, he noted that "the years during which singers' music has been stamped into bits as so much trash by the Wagners of New Germany, and bawled into a premature destruction of its voice by the Verdis of infuriate Italy, have been also those in which

York: Cambridge University Press, 1994), 139–51. On another interpretation of Armgart's fate, see my "'Music Their Larger Soul': George Eliot's *The Legend of Jubal* and Victorian Musicality," forthcoming in *The Figure of Music in Nineteenth-Century Poetry*, ed. Phyllis Weliver (Aldershot: Ashgate Press).

the magnificent vocal music of Handel has been more largely circulated and studied, in all its range, than during the time when it was thrown off." Here Chorley takes absolutely for granted the availability of the canonic repertory, and what's more he takes its wide diffusion as a measure of the country's musical progress. Chorley understood the canonizing process by way of an aphorism that he applied to Bach: "those, indeed, who never looked young never will look old."[61]

Similarly, John Hullah argued that Wagnerism showed contempt for the music of the past; while he accepted the idea of a *Gesamtkunstwerk,* a transformation of musical art back to its ancient powers in conjunction with its sister arts (and considered it by no means a new idea), Hullah rebelled against what he saw as its interference with natural evolutionary processes. "Its realization," he wrote, "would involve the calling into existence of a new kind of music; and the interruption of that process of gradual development to which the musical art has submitted for the past five hundred and fifty years."[62] Thomas Pinney comments that "the past in *Deronda* is not a private past, and its authority depends not on affection but on some reasoned principle of inheritance and duty,"[63] and certainly for Eliot the past provided not only a treasure trove of time-proven codes and values, but also the solidity of community through whose traditions both duty and sympathy bound the individual fortunate enough to inherit them. In a much-quoted sentence elsewhere, Eliot observes that "the nature of European men has its roots intertwined with the past, and can only be developed by allowing those roots to remain undisturbed while the process of development is going on, until that perfect ripeness of the seed which carries with it a life independent of the root." She characterizes bruited attempts at the creation of a common language for Europeans as "language which has no uncertainty, no whims of idiom, no cumbrous forms, no fitful shimmer of many-hued significance, no hoary archaisms ... a melancholy 'language of the future!'"[64] Just such a trove of past riches was her copy of Chappell's *Popular Music*

61. Henry F. Chorley, *Modern German Music,* (1854; reprint New York: Da Capo Press, 1973), 48. See Eliot's unsigned review in *The Leader* (29 April 1854), 403–4. Henry F. Chorley, *Thirty Years' Musical Recollections,* ed. Ernest Newman (1862; New York: Alfred A. Knopf, 1926), 398. GE and GHL enjoyed Chorley's writing and owned a copy of *Thirty Years* (Baker, *Libraries,* item no. 168).

62. Hullah, *History of Modern Music,* 206, 205. See also Hullah's review of Meyerbeer's *L'Africaine,* published in the *Fortnightly Review* [2 (1865): 43–50] under GHL's editorship.

63. Thomas Pinney, "The Authority of the Past in George Eliot's Novels," *Nineteenth-Century Fiction* 21 (1966): 143.

64. [Eliot], "Natural History of German Life," 287–88.

of the Olden Time, a gift to her from George Lewes in February 1860; this bounty of good tunes, in which "every air has been re-harmonized upon a simple and consistent plan" by Alexander Macfarren, contained an extensive discussion of the national character of tunes and the origins of national musics. Chappell attributed national differences in music to "first, the character of the musical instruments in common use, and . . . second, the spirit of the songs of the people."[65]

The force of national character is just as present here as it was to Wagner and his followers—it was ubiquitous in nineteenth-century thought—but it takes an importantly different form. By convention, many of the "great moments" of music history involved particular repertories emerging from different corners of Europe and epitomizing different national styles; "in the course of three centuries, music has, so to speak, made the tour of Europe," says John Hullah.[66] A forming canon, for example, might highlight renaissance sacred music of the Netherlands, Italian baroque music, German instrumental music of the eighteenth century, and Italian or perhaps French opera of the nineteenth. Rather than suggesting the obsolescence of national schools of music in favor of its "perfection" in a universalized (albeit German) music-drama, this set of mind preferred to preserve them in an internationalized, dehistoricized basic repertory—"the best that has been thought and said," in Arnold's famous phrase—and revel in their celebration of national difference.[67]

In "Hebraism and Hellenism" Arnold wrote: "Science has now made visible to everybody the great and pregnant elements of difference which lie in race, and in how signal a manner they make the genius and history of an Indo-European people vary from those of a Semitic people" (135), although the continuation of the essay insists upon an underlying "essential unity" of mankind as well. This dialectical view of human nature is possible because, to reiterate, the Victorian understanding of national (or "racial") character is not, in most hands, invidious; in context, it was seen as a self-

65. [William] Chappell, *Popular Music of the Olden Time* (London: Cramer, Beale, and Chappell, [1859]), 1:vi, 2:789. See Baker, *Eliot–Lewes Library*, 225.

66. John Hullah, *The History of Modern Music: A Course of Lectures* (1862; London: Longmans, Green, 1901), 141. A copy is listed in the Eliot-Lewes library (Baker, *Libraries*, item no. 450).

67. There are two slightly different versions of Arnold's aphorism. Eliot copied one of them, reversing the verbs—"culture is: To know the best that has been said & thought in the world"—from his *Literature and Dogma* (1873) into her notebook (Pforzheimer 711, f.14; see Irwin, *Notebooks*, 253). The slightly different formulation, "to make the best that has been thought and known in the world current everywhere," occurs in *Culture and Anarchy*, 79.

evident and progressive notion, sanctioned by the latest in evolutionary science.[68] This principle of specialization was as central to Herbert Spencer's thought as to Darwin's. In "Progress: Its Law and Cause" (1857) he announced that "we propose . . . to show, that this law of organic progress is the law of all progress. Whether it be in the development of the Earth, in the development of Life upon its surface, in the development of Language, Literature, Science, Art, this same evolution of the simple into the complex, through successive differentiations, holds throughout."[69] George Eliot read *The Origin of Species* in 1859, as soon as it appeared, and by all accounts she was already perfectly familiar with earlier versions of evolutionary theory.[70] Darwin's text, unlike many other Victorian versions of development, does not privilege the present moment at the expense of either past or future, but its emphasis on the proliferation of species and increasing specialization as a matter of continual process could be read as a model for a future based on the preservation of what was best in the past. After all, as Gillian Beer reminds us, the "survival and continuance" of some well-adapted species are part and parcel of the evolutionary scenario; they "depend upon an apt conjunction of the individual organism's particular strengths with the particular current demands of the environment."[71] Perhaps the Arnoldian aphorism is simply the cultural translation of this Darwinian scientific insight: what survives from the past—the canon—has proven its evolutionary fitness.

"CANONIC" CHARACTERS AND ZIONISM

One of the two parallel plots in *Daniel Deronda*, the one contemporary readers persisted in calling "the Jewish story," concerns Daniel's gradual acknowledgment of his own Jewish identity through his meeting with a re-

68. In the period, those most likely to demur against notions of national or racial character were biblical fundamentalists who argued on the literal basis of common descent from Adam and Eve. On the general topic, an interesting discussion is in Harriet Ritvo, *The Platypus and the Mermaid, and Other Figments of the Classifying Imagination* (Cambridge: Harvard University Press, 1997), esp. "Barring the Cross."

69. Herbert Spencer, "Progress: Its Law and Cause," collected in his *Essays, Scientific, Political, and Speculative* (New York: D. Appleton, 1907), 1:10.

70. She found the book "not to be well written: though full of interesting matter, it is not impressive, from want of luminous and orderly presentation" (*Journals*, 82).

71. "Anxiety and Interchange: *Daniel Deronda* and the Implications of Darwin's Writing," *Journal of the History of the Behavioral Sciences* 19 (1983): 37.

markable pair: Mirah, whom he rescues from suicide by drowning, and her brother Mordecai (or Ezra), a passionate but terminally ill Zionist who is determined to pass on his mission into Daniel's hands.[72] The interest that all these characters have in racial identity, nationhood, and heritage is reflected in the music they perform. Just as they resist assimilation into the English mainstream, their music resists subsumption into the tidal wave of the "music of the future."

Of George Eliot's last publication, the collection of essays cryptically entitled *Impressions of Theophrastus Such* (1879), Nancy Henry remarks that it "goes beyond even her last novel *Daniel Deronda* in positing the role of collective memory in the future of national cultures."[73] An essay in that collection takes up once more the issues of Jewish separatism and assimilation, sharpening rather than resolving Eliot's own ambivalence on the point. Understanding the difficulty of the choice Jews must make, she observes that they might either "get rapidly merged in the populations around them," or come to "cherish all differences that marked them off from their hated oppressors."[74] In the end, though, the attitude emerges that led Eliot to the intensely sympathetic portrayal of Daniel, Mirah, and Mordecai: "after being subjected to this process, which might have been expected to be in every sense deteriorating and vitiating, they have come out of it (in any estimate which allows for numerical proportion) rivalling the nations of all European countries in healthiness and beauty of *physique*, in practical ability, in scientific and artistic aptitude, and in some forms of ethical value" (157). Her admiration for the Jews, be it noted, entails some commitment to what modern readers experience as racial essentialism but is none the less genuine for that.

In *Daniel Deronda*, the "collective memory" to which Nancy Henry refers is as often as not musical. Mirah remembers her mother, from whom she was taken at an early age, only as a smiling face singing Hebrew hymns to her (250). Daniel gets an early inkling of his own story while visiting a synagogue in Frankfurt: "The chant of the *Chazan's* or Reader's grand wide-

---

72. Nearly all the Jewish characters in the novel have a disconcerting number of names, a point commented on by Alcharisi herself in an aside to Daniel—"the Jews have always been changing their names" (701). Mordecai is also Ezra; he and Mirah may be surnamed Cohen (the name he uses) or perhaps Lapidoth (as she is introduced to us); Daniel is not Deronda after all, but Charisi. Eliot's text is uncharacteristically casual about this oddity.

73. *Impressions of Theophrastus Such*, ed. Nancy Henry (Iowa City: University of Iowa Press, 1994), ix.

74. "The Modern Hep! Hep! Hep!" (ibid., 152).

ranging voice with its passage from monotony to sudden cries, the outburst of sweet boys' voices from the little quire, the devotional swaying of men's bodies backwards and forwards . . . all were blent for him as one expression of a binding history, tragic and yet glorious" (416–17). Daniel's friend Hans Meyrick, flippant and ironical, cynically insists upon the reversal of an old dictum that Eliot wishes thereby to plant in our minds, to the effect that "If a man were permitted to make all the ballads of a nation, he need not care who should make the laws" (773).

The principal and most serious musician of this camp is Mirah, whose stage career travesties Alcharisi's: a devout Jewess, she has been stolen away from home by her dishonest and godless father and exploited for her talent as an actress and singer. Her reaction, pious and dutiful, could not be farther from Leonora's pride and defiant independence; Mirah loathes the vulgarity of the theater and longs only to cultivate her small voice in a respectable career as a teacher and drawing-room singer. Klesmer, for all his futurism, admires Mirah and regards her as a true musician—no small compliment.

Mirah's repertory has three components: the Hebrew melodies she remembers from childhood, a varied collection of European composers who specialize in nationalisms either musical or poetic, and Beethoven. Here George Eliot's sense of music history is accurate and prescient, for it is by now well understood that the whole process of musical canon formation in the mid nineteenth century revolved centrally around the hemisphere-wide apotheosis of Beethoven as the first musical giant and "eternal" composer.[75] In this novel, as in the culture at large and in Eliot's own life, Beethoven remains the iconic figure of The Composer despite Wagner's best efforts.

Eliot's research notebooks contain brief but significant extracts from A. B. Marx's *Ludwig van Beethoven: Leben und Schaffen* (1859), extracts that we can recognize as probing artistic heroism, the special dignity as well as the solitary suffering of the artist: a section of the agonized "Heiligenstadt testament" in which Beethoven reports that despair at his deafness nearly drove him to suicide but—in the portion Eliot transcribed—"only she, Art, held me back. Ah, it seemed to me impossible to leave the world before I had brought forth all that was in me," a sentiment resonant with

75. See, among many recent discussions of this phenomenon, Scott Burnham, *Beethoven Hero* (Princeton: Princeton University Press, 1995); Tia De Nora, *Beethoven and the Construction of Genius: Musical Politics in Vienna, 1792–1803* (Berkeley: University of California Press, 1995); and Lydia Goehr, *The Imaginary Museum of Musical Works: An Essay in the Philosophy of Music* (Oxford: Clarendon Press, 1992), esp. ch. 8.

Mirah's abortive leap into the Thames. In the same entry Eliot notes without comment the nickname "Riesensonate," or "gigantic sonata," as Marx had nicknamed Beethoven's opus 106.[76] Mirah sings Beethoven on several occasions. "Per pietà . . . non dirmi addio" occurs three times and takes on the role of a character in its own right.[77] She sings it for Daniel "with a subdued but searching pathos which had that essential of perfect singing, the making one oblivious of art or manner" (422) and at a moment in the plot where there is no fear whatsoever of Daniel's bidding her *addio*. Nearer the end of the book we understand its message; it is poor musically challenged Gwendolen, in her marital misery dependent upon Daniel's sympathy and affection, who sends him this message (625), as Daniel finally realizes: "Gwendolen had said for the first time that her lot depended on his not forsaking her, and her appeal had seemed to melt into the melodic cry—*Per pietà . . . non dirmi addio*. But the melody had come from Mirah's dear voice" (835). (Like Klesmer, Daniel also embodies his politics in a marriage, choosing Jewish Mirah over gentile Gwendolen.)

On other occasions we hear Mirah either singing or accompanying what the text identifies as "Herz, mein Herz"—that is, Beethoven's setting of Goethe's "Neue Liebe, neues Leben" (op. 75), a wonderfully apt and vivid choice for someone newly rescued from drowning by a handsome young benefactor who offers the possibility of a "neue Liebe" as well. Her non-Beethovenian repertory includes songs of Schubert and Gordigiani—composer of popular songs on Tuscan folk melodies[78]—and a strikingly rendered though purely imaginary concert aria on Leopardi's "Ode to Italy" (540–41). The latter, whose text was no doubt chosen by Eliot because Giuseppe Mazzini and the Italian nationalist movement had become an important inspiration to her in thinking about the Zionist cause, Klesmer recognizes as "Joseph Leo's music." "Yes," Mirah tells him, "he was my last master—at Vienna" (Leo, readers knew, was also the singing master of the

76. The reference occurs in Marx's biography, 2:339. Many thanks to William Meredith of the Ira F. Brilliant Center for Beethoven Studies at San Jose State University for verifying this identification and finding another occurrence of the nickname in Marx's *Anleitung zum Vortrag Beethovenscher Klavierwerke* (Berlin: Otto Janke, 1863), 148–49. The "testament" is available in virtually any biography of Beethoven; a readily accessible version in English is *The Beethoven Compendium: A Guide to Beethoven's Life and Music,* ed. Barry Cooper (London: Thames and Hudson, 1992), 170. Eliot's copy of Marx's biography is listed in Baker, *Libraries,* item no. 623. The notes are in Pforzheimer notebook 711, f.5 (Irwin, *Notebooks,* 241).

77. From the concert aria "Ah, perfido!," Opus 65.

78. Most likely Eliot has in mind Luigi Gordigiani (1806–60), the younger of two composer brothers.

diva Armgart, who suffered the fate of Leonora Alcharisi; apparently Mirah made better use of his teaching).

But a case can be made that Mirah's most important music in this novel—Almirena's aria "Lascia ch'io pianga" from Handel's *Rinaldo*—emerges not from her own story but from the aura of characterization around Daniel. He is not a professional musician like Klesmer, Mirah, or Alcharisi, but the author is at great pains to let us know that Daniel is indeed "musical" in that wider, sympathetic sense that was to her so important a trait of human beings: "Not his vanity, but his keen sympathy made him susceptible to the danger that another's heart might feel larger demands on him than he would be able to fulfil" (835). Indeed, he so continually vibrates with sympathy to whatever others need of him that he even describes himself as a kind of instrument in Mordecai's hands, "like a cunningly wrought musical instrument, never played on, but quivering throughout in uneasy mysterious moanings of its intricate structure that, under the right touch, gives music" (819). Daniel has found Mirah—observed her preparing to leap into the river—through musical sympathy, rowing and singing aloud the gondolier's song from Rossini's *Otello,* a setting of Dante's "Nessun maggior dolore" that could hardly be more fitting to Mirah's desperate situation (ch. 17). It is almost as though he has conjured her up through his own excruciatingly sensitive imagination.

The crisis of the novel, or one of them, is the crisis of Daniel's identity, associated as he has been with English high culture at its most refined. As a child, he sang "Sweet Echo"[79] with "one of those thrilling boy voices which seem to bring an idyllic heaven and earth before our eyes" (207), but he nevertheless reacts with repugnance when his uncle suggests that he might be interested in a musical career. Understanding that the operatic stage is no line of work for an English gentleman, he takes the notion to be a hint at his own illegitimacy. In his new Jewish character and his embrace of the Zionist cause, there is more room for the essential musicality of his nature to manifest itself.

Barry Qualls has made the ingenious argument that the plot of *Daniel Deronda* reenacts that of *Rinaldo,* but for the reversal that in the latter-day case the Jewish characters must come to the rescue of the Christian ones.[80] I am rather inclined to believe, though, that *Rinaldo*'s prominence in this

---

79. From Milton's *Comus,* most probably in the setting by Henry Lawes.
80. Barry Qualls, "Speaking through Parable: *Daniel Deronda,*" in *George Eliot,* ed. Harold Bloom (New Haven: Chelsea Books, 1986), 203–21. *Rinaldo* (1711), with a libretto by Aaron Hill translated into Italian by Giacomo Rossi and based on episodes in *Gerusalemme liberata,* was the first opera Handel wrote for London.

novel reflects its ability to invoke two important associations, the preeminence of Handel as England's adopted canonic giant (if nothing else, Eliot knew that her readers were intimately familiar with his works) and the obvious relevance of its source text, Tasso's *Gerusalemme liberata*, to the topic.[81] For Mirah, the aria "Lascia ch'io pianga" is a musically perfect choice, given the size and character of her voice, and it furthermore echoes appropriately her muted role as female patriot; hers, like Almirena's, is a patriotism of sensibility and helpless faithfulness in contrast to the ferocious intellectuality of her brother's or the prospective heroism of Daniel's. Though the text has nothing immediately to do with Mirah's own situation, the aria allows her to resonate sympathetically with the wish of her whole community for freedom and self-determination.

MELODY AS SIGNIFIER

"Melody," both as idea and as concrete experience, served as a kind of lightning rod in the controversy about Wagnerism. Its centrality had to do primarily with its iconic status as the bearer of musical emotion, which for many Victorians was the measure of music's moral force. But two interrelated aspects of Wagnerian rhetoric seemed to challenge that status directly: first, Wagner's insistence that the "artwork of the future" necessitated the union of several arts within an expressive *Gesamtkunstwerk*, since music alone could no longer adequately serve the necessary expressive function; and second, critical propaganda about the "endless melody" of the progressive style, which many a listener simply did not recognize as "melody" at all—recall Klesmer's critique of the Bellini aria Gwendolen performs, focusing on the triviality of its melody, and the ironic characterization of Klesmer's own music as "melodic ideas not too grossly evident."

By and large, always excepting Catherine Arrowpoint, English characters in *Daniel Deronda* are represented as unmusical, which is to say devoid of sensibility, insight, and self-knowledge (although it is surely important to recall here that "English" characters in this story are also *bourgeois* characters). Poor Gwendolen undertakes her parlor performance with confidence,

81. Eliot makes the point of bringing Tasso into the story very early, in a comic context. Catherine Arrowpoint's mother, a somewhat foolish bluestocking, tells Gwendolen that she is writing a book on Tasso and Leonora [Borgia] (76); she opines that Leonora "was a cold-hearted woman, else she would have married him in spite of her brother"—a remark we recall with amusement when she reacts with fury at Catherine's very warm-hearted decision to marry Klesmer.

because "about her French and music, the two justifying accomplishments of a young lady, she felt no ground for uneasiness"(70), and were it not for the unanticipated and foreign attitudes of Julius Klesmer her triumph would have been quite in line with her own expectations. For Eliot, it may be that those stereotypical female drawing-room musicians (recall also Rosamond Vincy in *Middlemarch*, depicted as rather talented but only at mimicking the performances of others) had a parodic relationship to Darwin's account of music's role in sexual selection. Eliot herself reacted strenuously against the notion, arguing that women's character and inner life enabled them to take music seriously on its own terms, and she offers us both Catherine and Mirah in evidence.[82] But Gwendolen, like Rosamond, is no musician.

Klesmer himself has a farcical run-in with a local peer upon whom the Arrowpoint parents have designs. Poor Mr. Bult, who "had no idea that his insensibility to counterpoint could ever be reckoned against him" (283), unfortunately attempts to compliment Klesmer by graciously acknowledging that he has "too much talent to be a mere musician" (284) and is rewarded with a tirade of Olympian proportions. For Eliot herself, as she makes clear in a good deal of her poetry and particularly in her epigraph for chapter 44 of *Daniel Deronda*, the appreciation of musical sound speaks to sensibility, attunedness to the world:

> Thus all beauty that appears
> Has birth as sound to finer sense
> And lighter-clad intelligence.

Such characterizations, which function efficiently as clues to readers, come about because of established conventions whereby the emotional power of music resides primarily in melody. This idea, too, has its connection to the popular understanding of evolutionary science. Even Spencer's argument with Darwin about the origin of music rested centrally on the idea that "melody is . . . an idealized form of the natural cadences of emotion." Because music originated in the expression of emotion, Spencer thought, still today humans who are capable of "sympathetic pleasure" experience such pleasure in melodies.[83]

---

82. See Paxton, *George Eliot and Herbert Spencer,* 176. Several critics have suggested that *Daniel Deronda* is Eliot's response to Darwin's 1870 book, *The Descent of Man*, which elaborates the theory of sexual selection; see, e.g., K. Theodore Hoppen, *The Mid-Victorian Generation, 1846–1886* (Oxford: Clarendon Press, 1998), 505.

83. Herbert Spencer to Charles Darwin, 16 November 1872, reprinted in Spencer's *Autobiography* (New York: D. Appleton, 1904), 2:279–80. The original debate began with his "The Origin and Function of Music," *Fraser's Magazine* 56

This attitude toward melody was common coin in the period. We might read, in George Eliot's own translation, Feuerbach's apothegm: "Who has not experienced the overwhelming power of melody? And what else is the power of melody but the power of feeling?"[84] In 1869 she was reading Hermann Helmholtz's massive treatise *On the Sensations of Tone,* where again she would have found the underlying premise that "the essential basis of Music is *Melody.*" Perhaps surprisingly from his vantage point as a physical scientist, Helmholtz explicitly sides with the anti-Wagnerian critic Eduard Hanslick, commenting that Hanslick had "triumphantly attacked the false standpoint of exaggerated sentimentality, from which it was fashionable to theorise on music, and referred the critic to the simple elements of melodic movement."[85]

For his part, Wagner insisted that the *Gesamtkunstwerk* of the future— a staged music-drama that would enlist the expressive capabilities of all the arts—"can be effected only through the willing subjugation of music to the formative power of words," in Thomas Grey's formulation.[86] His overwrought demand for the "impregnation" of melody by poetry, most lavishly expounded in *Opera and Drama* (1851), apparently distressed George Eliot, who seems almost to have responded to it directly in more than one passage of her late writings. Into one of her notebooks for *Middlemarch* she has copied out a passage from the apocryphal Ecclesiasticus (32:4) that pointedly advises, "Pour not out words where there is a musician,"[87] and Mirah Lapidoth has taken this lesson to heart in her recollection of her mother's singing. "They were always Hebrew hymns she sang; and because I never knew the meaning of the words they seemed full of nothing but our love and happiness" (250)—Mirah is less concerned with *the* meaning of the hymns than with the meaning they have for her, conveyed by the melodies

(October 1857): 396–408, reissued later in much-expanded versions that take up Darwin's countertheory in detail. See also Ernest Newman's rebuttal, "Herbert Spencer and the Origin of Music," in his *Musical Studies* (London: John Lane, 1905), 189–218, although Newman rather misses the full implications of Spencer's evolutionary point. Darwin's discussion of the topic occurs principally in *The Expression of the Emotions in Men and Animals* (1872).

84. Ludwig Feuerbach, *The Essence of Christianity,* trans. George Eliot (1854; New York: Harper and Bros., 1957), 3.

85. Helmholtz, *On the Sensations of Tone,* vii, 2. Apparently Eliot read the original, published as *Lehre von dem Tonempfindungen* in 1863, because Ellis's translation did not appear until 1875. "I am reading about plants, & Helmholtz on music," she noted on 24 February 1869 (*Journals,* 135).

86. Thomas Grey, *Wagner's Musical Prose: Texts and Contexts* (Cambridge: Cambridge University Press, 1995), 136.

87. Irwin, *Notebooks,* 64.

alone. Later, when asked to sing one of the hymns in company, she confides that she does not sing the "real words" but that "if I were ever to know the real words, I should still go on in my old way." Strikingly, Daniel recalls his experience in the synagogue. Mirah's Beethoven works upon her hearers on the same principle, "with that wonderful, searching quality of subdued song in which the melody seems simply an effect of the emotion" (625).

It was not only theoretical writing, then, but a specific feature of Wagner's music that irritated the English melodic sensibility. Eliot wrote in her 1855 article,

> it is difficult to see why this theory should entail the exclusion of melody to the degree at which he has arrived in *Lohengrin,* unless we accept one of two suppositions: either that Wagner is deficient in melodic inspiration, or that his inspiration has been overridden by his system, which opposition has pushed to exaggeration[88]

and once again Lewes concurred, if this time in a rather eccentric judgment.

> Melody is to opera what poetry is to the drama.... In lieu of a lyric to touch the feelings, [the melodically deficient composer] presents us with a procession of vast splendour. Instead of expressing musical *emotions,* he is ingenious in expressing *meanings:* as if the end and aim of opera were to make musical phrases follow closely the various meanings of the words. The climax of this error is seen in the theory and later operas of Wagner; and it may be lucky that such a *reductio ad absurdum* has so soon been achieved. Let any one hear *Lohengrin* and *La Gazza Ladra* on two consecutive nights, and decide between Meaning and Melody![89]

Of the hero of this novel, Leslie Stephen once wrote, "I have always fancied—though without any evidence—that some touches in Deronda were drawn from one of her friends, Edmund Gurney, a man of remarkable charm of character, and as good-looking as Deronda."[90] Stephen's intuition was better than he knew, for there is, in fact, some evidence for this connection: Oscar Browning claimed that "she wrote to me enthusiastically of the visit [to Cambridge], and in speaking of one young man, who may have been the prototype of Deronda, said that he was so handsome that for some time she thought of nothing else, but that she afterwards discovered that his mind

---

88. "Liszt, Wagner, and Weimar," 102.

89. [GHL], "The Opera in 1833–1863," *Cornhill Magazine* 8 (1863), 301.

90. Leslie Stephen, *George Eliot* (New York: Macmillan, 1902), 191. In a diary entry for 19 May 1873 Eliot reports her first meeting with Gurney during an outing to Cambridge, where he was an undergraduate (*Journals,* 143).

was as beautiful as his face." Eliot herself referred to him as "the handsome young Gurney" in an 1876 letter to her friend Cara Bray.[91]

Gurney's own ideas and writings also support the identification with Daniel, albeit circuitously, at least insofar as his resistance to the "melody of the future" is concerned. Near the beginning of his lengthy treatise he proclaims that "music is first and always melody,"[92] later taking more direct aim:

> It is curious to observe how the metaphysician Wagner and the positivist Comte, who, though on different grounds, agree in considering the germs of song to have preceded speech, have missed in different ways the essentialness of form or order to the ideal of art. (361)

and, in the chapter specifically dedicated to Wagner, offering the coup de grâce: "while melody does not the least want to be infinite, it does very much want to have one bar intelligibly and organically connected with the next" (501). Thus Gurney gives us the crucial clue to the Victorian discomfort with Wagner's melodies: the need for that intelligibility of shape and succession. It seems odd that lovers of melody should react with such bewilderment to something prominently anointed *unendliche Melodie*, until we recognize their complaints as essentially *formal* ones.[93] If "young Clintock" heard a jar of leeches in the new music, no less a personage than Eduard Hanslick heard a "boneless tonal mollusk," and John Ruskin complained of *Die Meistersinger* that "as for the great *Lied* I never made out where it began or where it ended—except by the fellow's coming off the horse block."[94] The critic James W. Davison, reviewing the composition of an English Wagnerian in

---

91. *GEL* 6:321. Oscar Browning, *Life of George Eliot* (London: Walter Scott, 1892), 116. Browning claimed, however, that Eliot's letters to him had all been lost, so the story cannot be substantiated. Eliot was widely said to be "in love" with her own character, Daniel, so her slight infatuation with Edmund Gurney may indeed suggest a connection.

92. Edmund Gurney, *The Power of Sound* (1880; New York: Basic Books, 1966), xi.

93. Grey discusses this problem in *Wagner's Musical Prose*, ch. 5.

94. Hanslick is quoted in ibid., 244; and Ruskin in the unsigned introduction to *Wagnerism in European Culture and Politics*, ed. David Large and William Weber (Ithaca: Cornell University Press, 1984), 20. Invertebrate metaphors seem the runaway favorites to describe the melodies of the future. The Viennese critic Johann Georg Woerz reviews a performance of what he calls Liszt's *Harmonies poétique et reliquieuses* [sic]"where only the palest glimmer of a melody appears, blundering about like a glow-worm in the pitch dark chaos" of the piece (quoted in Sandra McColl, *Music Criticism in Vienna, 1896–1897: Critically Moving Forms* [Oxford: Clarendon Press, 1996], 118).

1852, complained of its "vagueness and incoherency, its subjects made up of a multitude of beginnings without middles or ends," and Chorley had written sourly in 1844 of "Herr Wagner, the young Dresden composer whose operas we have heard rapturously bepraised, because they contain no tunes which anyone can carry away."[95] It now appears that perhaps young Clintock is better-read than we might at first have surmised.

In an essay surveying music in Victoria's reign, Francis Hueffer makes an explicit connection between the myths of the flying Dutchman and the wandering Jew.[96] Strikingly, both images appear in the novel, both tinged with despair. Gwendolen uses the first to describe her imprisonment on a yacht (a "plank island") by her sadistic husband; the second is Klesmer's description of himself to Mr. Bult, whom he fears Catherine will marry. (For Bult's part, he takes Klesmer for "a Pole, or a Czech, or something of that fermenting sort" [284].) Both images represent the cost of cosmopolitanism, the lack of that rootedness in place and memory that Eliot found crucial to human well-being. But there is a cost, too, to confinement within one's own parochial group, as Leonora Charisi knew all too well. It is a historiographic problem that has no solution, but one that the microhistory of each individual human life must negotiate anew.

From her early coupling of unprescient tadpoles and musical pleasure to the end of her life, George Eliot thought about development, evolution, and music together. On 8 September 1879, shortly after George Lewes's death and some sixteen months before her own, she wrote in one of her increasingly telegraphic diary entries:

Darwin. Schubert.[97]

95. Davison is quoted in Anne Dzamba Sessa, *Richard Wagner and the English* (Rutherford: Fairleigh Dickinson University Press, 1978), 17; and Chorley in *The Attentive Listener: Three Centuries of Music Criticism*, ed. Harry Haskell (Princeton: Princeton University Press, 1996), 112.
96. Hueffer, *Half a Century*, 33.
97. *Journals*, 180.

6 Fictions of the Opera Box

In Paris, . . . an Englishman, Howard Tempest, looked in, at the Opéra, on his cousin, Camille de Joyeuse. This lady, connected by birth with Britannia's best, and, through her husband, with the Bourbons, delighted the eye, the ear, and the palate. In appearance, she suggested certain designs of Boucher; in colouring and in manner, the Pompadour. . . .

One evening in May, Tempest entered her box, saluted her, examined the house, and, as, in a crash of the orchestra, the curtain fell, seated himself, in response to a gesture, beside her.

This passage is taken from *The Monster*, a rather fey and histrionic novel by the eccentric (and comma-prone) Edgar Saltus. Within mere paragraphs it contains all the earmarks of a scene utterly familiar in American fiction around the turn of the twentieth century, a scene set in a box at the opera. The opera box is a marker of wealth and social distinction, and it is a place for visiting. It is also a place for seeing and being seen, its primary focus the physical appearance of a female character who is carefully set off against a background that is discovered by "examining the house." Of music, there is only a vanishing trace.[1]

This essay first appeared in *The Work of Opera: Genre, Nationhood, and Sexual Difference*, ed. Richard Dellamora and Daniel Fischlin (New York: Columbia University Press, 1997) and I am grateful to Columbia University Press for permission to include its later version here. I delivered a shorter version of this essay at the conference on Gender and Sexuality in Opera, SUNY at Stony Brook, 14–17 September 1995. I wish to thank the participants at that conference, and also Elizabeth Harries, Daniel Horowitz, Susan Van Dyne, and Elizabeth Wood for the generosity of their many astute comments.

1. Edgar Saltus, *The Monster* (New York: Pulitzer Publishing, 1912), 23, 24.

What is astonishing about this example in particular is that the two characters portrayed have nothing whatever to do with the story. Rather, Saltus employs a trope so thoroughly conventionalized by 1912 that the setting had itself become a picture worth thousands of words, carrying meanings far beyond those spelled out on the page and saving the author a good deal of trouble. I propose in this essay to examine the opera box trope as it is found in novels by American authors between about 1870 and 1920, a period that in literary history covers the genteel tradition and—more importantly—the emergence of realism, and that in political history includes the aptly called Gilded Age and the progressive era.

During the nineteenth century opera gradually became detached from other aspects of the theatrical world, fixated as it was on its most extravagant and gorgeous manifestations in ways that became unfashionable in theater, literature, and the visual arts. At the same time, opera gratified the Victorian taste for theatricality in all its forms from charades to *tableaux vivants*.[2] Its notorious reputation as a specular site marked it as peculiarly adapted to the expression of class difference and—by the century's end, after the Wagner craze was spent—resistant to modernism and social change in just the same ways that its privileged boxholders were. Since the books I discuss are novels of manners, most of them by writers engaged in developing the realist mode in fiction, it is not surprising that they so frequently take up the opportunity that opera affords to study the morals and mores of the era, its social interactions and significations.[3] I want to be clear that I do not intend an act of textual criticism here; still less do I mean to interpret fictional material literally as historical information. Rather, I want to

2. See Karen Haltunnen, *Confidence Men and Painted Women: A Study of Middle-Class Culture in America, 1830–1870* (New Haven: Yale University Press, 1982), ch. 6; and William Leach, *Land of Desire: Merchants, Power, and the Rise of a New American Culture* (New York: Pantheon, 1993), ch. 3.

3. Parallel studies have been done of European novels, for the opera-box setting occurs there no less frequently. But the social meanings of opera attendance are very different in Europe, as are the relations of class and of gender that are so crucial in deciphering these scenes, and so I focus here on the work of American authors—though several of their scenes, like Saltus's, take place in Europe. European novels are briefly studied in Dominique Dubreuil, "Opéra: l'oeil de la fiction," in *Littérature et opéra*, ed. Philippe Berthier and Kurt Ringger (Grenoble: Presses universitaires de Grenoble, 1987), 177–83. English novels are the principal subject of Emily Auerbach, *Maestros, Dilettantes, and Philistines: The Musician in the Victorian Novel* (New York: Peter Lang, 1989). Structural and critical rather than social-historical studies include Alex Aronson, *Music and the Novel: A Study in Twentieth-Century Fiction* (Totowa, N.J.: Rowman and Littlefield, 1980); and Peter Conrad, *Romantic Opera and Literary Form* (Berkeley: University of California Press, 1977).

investigate aspects of the social history of opera in the United States that help illuminate these texts and offer us a glimpse of the assumptions and interpretive strategies their contemporary readers brought to them.

THE PERFORMANCE OF STATUS

> The Opera . . . plays its part as the great vessel of social salvation, the comprehensive substitute for all other conceivable vessels; the *whole* social consciousness thus clambering into it, under stress, as the whole community crams into the other public receptacles, the desperate cars of the Subway or the vast elevators of the tall buildings.
>
> HENRY JAMES, "New York: Social Notes" (1907)

No doubt the most familiar of these opera scenes, and the most frequently discussed, is the opening chapter of Edith Wharton's *The Age of Innocence,* in which we are introduced to the principal characters at a performance of *Faust* in New York's old Academy of Music. Numerous readings of the text have been offered, focusing especially on the interplay between the novel's story and that told in the opera, or on the interactions between Ellen Olenska and Newland Archer, fatefully meeting here for the first time.[4] But working outward, so to speak, from the details of Wharton's narrative, we can also learn much from the surrounding nimbus of social import that the setting itself would have conveyed to a contemporary reader.

Although *The Age of Innocence* was written in 1920, at the very end of the period I am concerned with, its narrative is set in the early 1870s. Just as important as the particular interactions that occur in the opening scene is the simple fact that it takes place at the opera, the quintessential site of privilege and social display. Like the original "royal box" in European court theaters, opera boxes are designed to facilitate lines of sight in all directions. That ubiquitous accessory, the opera glass, adds its iconic force as well as its optical power to an already saturated visual environment. Fictional characters use boxes just as their real-life counterparts did, both to see and to be seen. Ellen Olenska's presence in the box is, precisely, her grandmother Mingott's nose-thumbing challenge to Society to view Ellen as one of its number. Boxes are also their own advertisement: those who are seen sitting in them can afford to, and in the elaborate social geography of the house they

---

4. See especially Herbert Lindenberger, *Opera: The Extravagant Art* (Ithaca: Cornell University Press, 1984), 174–75.

visibly do not mix with the hoi polloi in the orchestra seats.[5] Even more, "going to the opera" is a social ritual crucial to the maintenance of the urban patrician class. Etiquette books of the day include elaborate instructions for each phase of the activity: wardrobe, the manner of entering the box, the promenade between acts, and the recognition or not of acquaintances as the occasion demands.[6]

Opera is taken for granted in the world of *The Age of Innocence*; it is a common enough feature of daily life, and references to it and to the rhythms of its season are scattered almost negligently through the book. Henry James's characterization is apt: "the great vessel of social salvation" is just the one in which Ellen Olenska's reputation must ride if it is to float at all.[7] But, in truth, James's concern was less with persons of Ellen's class than with the despised parvenus, the "new rich" whose money was flowing in almost uncountably fast in the sudden postwar industrial expansion and who, old society felt, were ill equipped to spend it with appropriate dignity and taste. (As Bourdieu says, "the manner in which culture has been acquired lives on in the manner of using it." Or, modified for the American situation: "Boston is the only place in America where wealth and knowledge of how to use it are apt to coincide.")[8] The contest between the two groups was felt everywhere in urban America, but nowhere more than in New York's old Knickerbocker society, proud, correct, and by this time scarcely able any

5. "Some place in the house there was a dividing line between those who looked down on each other and those who looked at the stage, but I have not, in fifteen years of research, been able to determine just where it began" (Irving Kolodin, *The Story of the Metropolitan Opera, 1883–1950* [New York: Knopf, 1953], 58). On this "geography," see also Lois W. Banner, *American Beauty* (New York: Knopf, 1983), 67–68; and John Frederick Cone, *First Rival of the Metropolitan Opera* (New York: Columbia University Press, 1983).

6. See, for one example among many, Florence Hartley, *The Ladies' Book of Etiquette and Manual of Politeness: Complete Handbook for the Use of the Lady in Polite Society* (Boston: J. S. Locke, 1873), 174–77. On opera as ritual mystification, see Bruce A. McConachie, "New York Operagoing, 1825–50: Creating an Elite Social Ritual," *American Music* 6 (1988): 181–92. For an analysis of the 1849 "Astor Place riot" as a lens into urban culture and social relations, see Peter George Buckley, "To the Opera House: Culture and Society in New York City, 1820–1860" (Ph.D. diss., SUNY at Stony Brook, 1984). This pre-Metropolitan era is also discussed in Karen Ahlquist, *Democracy at the Opera: Music, Theater, and Culture in New York City, 1815–60* (Urbana: University of Illinois Press, 1997).

7. "New York: Social Notes," in *The American Scene* (1907; Bloomington: Indiana University Press, 1968), 164.

8. Pierre Bourdieu, *Distinction: A Social Critique of the Judgement of Taste*, trans. Richard Nice (Cambridge, Mass.: Harvard University Press, 1984), 2; E. L. Godkin, editor of *Atlantic Monthly*, in 1871, quoted in Judith Freeman Clark, *America's Gilded Age: An Eyewitness History* (New York: Facts on File, 1992), 36.

longer to afford the aristocratic behaviors it had introduced into the city's social life.

On his American trip in 1904–5, his first return home from England in twenty years, James was horrified—if not particularly surprised—at what he considered the impoverishment of New York cultural life; "nowhere else does pecuniary power so beat its wings in the void," he observed elsewhere in the quoted passage. Part of the problem was that he found American culture grotesquely feminized. "If the men are not to be taken as contributing to it, but only the women, what new case is *that*, under the sun, and under what strange aggravations of difficulty is the problem not presented?" The resulting picture was one "poor in the male presence."[9]

The moral earnestness, at least relatively speaking, of the earlier society of the 1870s, as well as its blasé habituation to its privileges, is characteristically portrayed in Elizabeth Stuart Phelps's *The Silent Partner* (1871). We are introduced to the heroine, Perley Kelso of Boston, on her way to hear *Don Giovanni:* "a young lady . . . who is used to her gloves, and indifferent to her stone cameos; who has the score by heart, and is tired of the prima donna; who has had a season ticket every winter since she can remember."[10] But Perley's life is changed when, in a chapter pointedly entitled "Across the Gulf," she encounters another young woman on her way to a different musical entertainment. Sip Garth, a mill hand who works for Perley's father, is making her way through the January slush to the show at the Blue Plum.

Bostonian that she is, Perley is overcome with moral confusion at the blatant class differences between them, marked so explicitly by their musical choices; she seeks Sip's friendship, and ultimately she devotes her life to the betterment of social and cultural conditions at the mill that, as she comes to understand, pays for her gloves and her opera tickets. But as crucial to Phelps's point as the stark economic and cultural differences between the young women is the situation they share: not only the alignment with theatrical music, already feminized in American urban culture,[11] but the veiled

9. "New York: Social Notes," 159, 164, 165.

10. *The Silent Partner* (Boston: James R. Osgood, 1871), 16. Phelps is called "the first American novelist to treat the social problems of the Machine Age seriously and at length" by Walter Fuller Taylor in *The Economic Novel in America* (Chapel Hill: University of North Carolina Press, 1942), 58.

11. And perhaps not only in America. "The assumption that musical arousal brings out specifically feminine psychic characteristics in man and that music is—among all the arts—the most suggestive metaphor of femininity appears to a considerable number of novelists to be self-evident" (Aronson, *Music and the Novel*, 113).

and suggestive dangers it holds for them as well. Waiting for Perley outside the opera house after the performance, Sip challenges her: "Look here, young lady, I want to speak to you. I want to know why you tell *me* the Plum is no place for me? What kind of a place is this for you?" (29).

The assiduously self-seeking Undine Spragg, heroine of Wharton's *The Custom of the Country* (1913), knows exactly what kind of place the opera box is for her and understands the process of social certification only too well. Undine, whom a contemporary reviewer called "the most repellent heroine" in American literature, is the archetype of the parvenu social climber, one of a series of turn-of-the-century heroines who ceaselessly demand everything fashionable, and who impoverish any number of men in the project of acquisition. Her gloriously mismatched name enacts her social ambition: the poetic Undine constantly at pains to camouflage the ungainly midwestern Spragg.

"The great vessel of social salvation" is an early and obvious target of Undine's rampaging greed, though the ferocity of her demand marks her fatally as one to whom the experience is entirely novel—a newcomer. Thorstein Veblen, the contemporary analyst of "conspicuous consumption," would have recognized without difficulty Undine's construal of the opera box as commodity, along with the dresses, hats, and accessories she purchases by the truckload.[12]

It is to the staid old Academy of Music that Ellen Olenska is brought, in an attempt to recertify her as a respectable member of society. But Undine goes to the Metropolitan Opera, a distinction in more than chronology, and one intensely meaningful to Wharton and her readers. In the heat of the social fray between the Knickerbockers (among whom Wharton herself was raised) and the upstart robber barons of considerably greater fortune, the physical sites of spectacle themselves became game tokens. As the growing numbers of new rich—Vanderbilts, Roosevelts, Rockefellers, Morgans, Astors, Goulds, Whitneys, and their vast Victorian families—were unable to purchase boxes at the academy, they simply built their own theater, farther uptown. The Metropolitan Opera opened in 1883, with no fewer than 122 pique-inspired boxes for which the wealthy subscribers drew lots.[13] "As cer-

12. *The Theory of the Leisure Class: An Economic Study of Institutions* (1898; New York: B. W. Huebsch, 1922). The fact that, by tradition, nobody in the boxes actually listens to the opera—either in the novels or, apparently, in reality—makes the purchase doubly extravagant.
13. This story is well told in John Dizikes, *Opera in America: A Cultural History* (New Haven: Yale University Press, 1993), ch. 20, and in other accounts of opera in the United States. After a few years of what New Yorkers called the "opera wars"—

tainly as the pews of a church are ranged in lines ordained by the purpose of the structure, so the Metropolitan was built around the tiers of boxes which were its original sin."[14] Thus the two theaters were indelibly affiliated with warring factions of society and, by extension, with sharply contrasting attitudes toward the seriousness of high culture. The new house, with its unprecedented and in fact grotesque complement of boxes in a "golden horseshoe," served many an author as a concrete icon of conspicuous consumption and vulgar social display.[15]

And what happens when Undine finally gets to her coveted box? Unlike *The Age of Innocence*, with its fine historical details of performer, work, and language, this novel contains no music, no actual opera—and not by any oversight.[16]

> When the curtain fell on the first act she began to be aware of a subtle change in the house. In all the boxes cross-currents of movement had set in: groups were coalescing and breaking up, fans waving and heads twinkling, black coats emerging among white shoulders, late comers dropping their furs and laces in the red penumbra of the background. Undine, for the moment unconscious of herself, swept the house with her opera-glass. (39)

featuring a pitched battle between "old-fashioned" Italian opera at the academy and "modern" German (Wagnerian) opera at the Metropolitan—the Academy of Music succumbed. It became a venue for melodrama and finally closed its doors in 1926. On this antic (but artistically fateful) chapter in New York's social history see also Henry Krehbiel, *Chapters of Opera* (New York: Henry Holt, 1908); Edward Ringwood Hewitt, *Those Were the Days: Tales of a Long Life* (New York: Duell, Sloan and Pearce, 1943); Cone, *First Rival of the Met;* Louis Auchincloss, *The Vanderbilt Era: Profiles of a Gilded Age* (New York: Charles Scribner's Sons, 1989); and Joseph Horowitz, *Wagner Nights: An American History* (Berkeley: University of California Press, 1994).

14. Kolodin, *Metropolitan Opera,* 51.

15. An effort in 1940 to rectify this peculiarly motivated design exchanged the grand tier boxes for individual seats; some had already been removed in the renovation after an 1893 fire. See Frank Merkling et al., *The Golden Horseshoe: The Life and Times of the Metropolitan Opera House* (New York: Viking Press, 1965). New York's extensive German-American community was among the Met's large audience of serious music lovers, but novelists have not been so interested in this segment of the audience.

16. Wharton wryly describes the actual situation of New York opera production in the 1870s: "an unalterable and unquestioned law of the musical world required that the German text of French operas sung by Swedish artists should be translated into Italian for the clearer understanding of English-speaking audiences" (*The Age of Innocence* [New York: Charles Scribner's Sons, 1968], 5). Christine Nilsson did indeed sing Marguerite at the Academy of Music several times, first in 1870; ironically, she opened the Met in the same role on 22 October 1883; see note 13.

This, of course, is the spectacle for which she has been waiting, for which she has come. Undine is assisted in her surveillance by another operatic practice accurately detailed by Wharton, "that the numbers of the boxes and the names of their owners were given on the back of the programme" (40); for Undine the back of the program holds more meaning than anything inside it, as she peruses one of what Neil Harris has wonderfully called the period's "iconographies of possession."[17]

Wharton has some fun with her heroine's social pretensions—Undine insists that "Friday's the stylish night, and that new tenor's going to sing again in 'Cavaleeria'"[18]—but her authorial distress at the attitudes and behavior Undine epitomizes is dead serious. Pondering the puzzling behavior of the nouveau riche in a different context, Wharton and her coauthor Ogden Codman remark that "men, in these matters, are less exacting than women, because their demands, besides being simpler, are uncomplicated by the feminine tendency to want things because other people have them, rather than to have things because they are wanted."[19] And this is far from an idiosyncratic observation: author after author in this period portrays a woman in frantic and heedless pursuit of social status through the acquisition of fashionable goods, to the ultimate ruin of husband or father, however rapidly he is amassing cash. With help from Veblen, it is possible to understand this nexus of behaviors as a coordinated social campaign, despite the hortatory trappings of its moralizing surface: banned from the actual processes of capital accumulation by a century of "separate-spheres" gender ideology, the wife instead contributes her share by the energetic pursuit of cultural capital. She is her husband's accomplice and lieutenant in the public performance of the economic status he has labored to achieve.[20]

17. *Cultural Excursions: Marketing Appetites and Cultural Tastes in Modern America* (Chicago: University of Chicago Press, 1990), 178.

18. The *Custom of the Country,* ed. Stephen Orgel (Oxford: Oxford University Press, 1995), 27. In addition to Undine's obvious mispronunciation, it seems that her information is also wrong, since by this time Monday had become the most fashionable evening at the Met, as Wharton's readers would likely have known.

19. *The Decoration of Houses* (New York: Charles Scribner's Sons, 1897), 17.

20. "In order to gain or hold the esteem of men it is not sufficient merely to possess wealth or power. The wealth or power must be put in evidence, for esteem is awarded only on evidence" (Veblen, *Theory of the Leisure Class,* 36). See also the chapter "Conspicuous Consumption," where Veblen introduces the ideas of vicarious consumption and vicarious leisure, as performed by upper-middle-class wives. Discussing the historical development of these women's economically crucial role as shoppers, Ann Douglas memorably suggests that "women would operate as the subconscious of capitalist culture" (*The Feminization of American Culture* [New York: Alfred A. Knopf, 1977), 67.

ART, BUSINESS, AND THE LURE OF SPECULATION

"Buy May wheat. It'll beat art all hollow."
    FRANK NORRIS, *The Pit* (1903)

Like *The Age of Innocence*, Frank Norris's novel begins at the opera. We meet another young heroine, Laura Dearborn, with her sister and aunt, waiting for their hosts in the lobby of Chicago's Auditorium Theatre.[21] In this opening scene, as in the novel as a whole, Norris both sets up and cannily complicates a set of familiar alignments: thus male is to female as business is to culture, America to Europe, and Chicago to the older cities of the East Coast, especially New York and Boston.

The Pit, along with *The Octopus* part of a projected but unfinished trilogy to be called "The Epic of the Wheat," is more ambivalent about these dichotomies than most novels. An unabashed celebration of the muscular energy and apparently inexhaustible natural bounty of the New World—a typical fascination of Chicago writers—the dramatic action of the book nonetheless concerns the line between sound business and irresponsible speculation. That is, investment for profit, to build the wealth and institutions of the country, is exemplary (American male) behavior, but "speculation" as technically defined—investment in anticipation of the future direction of the market, like the "day-trading" that is its later avatar—is as disreputable as any other form of gambling. The problem, of course, is that the excitement of the one lures a man irresistibly to the other.

The abstraction of the enterprise is a matter of pride for the speculators; it is the essence of risk that no actual products are being bought and sold at all, but only fictive, heroic predictions as to the rise or fall of their price.[22] The reader is caught up in this excitement, in the implication of that unspeakable fate, addiction—"worse than liquor, worse than morphine," says a minor character (130)—and in the heat of the only slightly sublimated

21. *The Pit* (New York: Doubleday, Page, 1903), 255. Built by Adler and Sullivan, the Auditorium Theatre was completed in 1888.
22. This unproductivity renders speculation morally questionable in the post-Victorian realm. But a more concrete problem is that speculators inevitably make their profits at serious cost to some innocent party: as one conscience-stricken character in *The Pit* observes, "if we send the price of wheat down too far, the farmer suffers, the fellow who raises it; if we send it up too far, the poor man in Europe suffers, the fellow who eats it" (129). In reacting to Jadwin's statement that those people "over in Europe" will pay any price now, since a global short crop in wheat means "they've got to have the wheat," Laura signals her female innocence about business matters: "Oh, then why not give it to them? . . . That would be a godsend," Laura suggests. Her husband explains, "that isn't exactly how it works out" (233).

warfare between those zoological combatants peculiar to Wall Street, the bears and the bulls. In short, speculation itself is swashbuckling, amply suited to operatic treatment.

> One of those great manoeuvres of a fellow money-captain had that very day been concluded, the Helmick failure, and between the chords and bars of a famous opera men talked in excited whispers, and one great leader lay at that very moment, broken and spent, fighting with his last breath for bare existence. (34)

Within this context the actual opera must paradoxically play two apparently contradictory roles: on the one hand, it signifies that America is capable of maintaining high culture, even on the prairie, and that Chicago's businessmen as well as New York's are able to supply even that culture's most extravagant requirements; on the other hand, the guiding vision of the novel is the historic turnabout in which the New World feeds the Old, in which American mercantile culture supersedes the old museum life of Europe as the son outstrips the father. And so throughout the first chapter we hear the opera—an unidentified piece minutely described but probably the invention of Norris himself—in counterpoint with whispered gossip about Helmick's failed attempt to corner the corn market:

> as the music died away fainter and fainter, till voice and orchestra blended together in a single, barely audible murmur, vibrating with emotion, with romance, and with sentiment, she heard, in a hoarse, masculine whisper, the words:
> "The shortage is a million bushels at the very least. Two hundred carloads were to arrive from Milwaukee last night—"

Laura is no social climber, no Undine, but an earnest young woman recently arrived from New England, and so she is actually listening to the music; at first she attempts to silence the whisperers, to no avail.

> While [the soprano] declared that the stars and the night-bird together sang "He loves thee," the voices close at hand continued:
> "—one hundred and six carloads—"
> "—paralysed the bulls—"
> "—fifty thousand dollars—"

The counterpoint is precisely balanced; as Laura gradually recognizes, two dramas of equal power and attractive force are vying for her attention.

> And abruptly, midway between two phases of that music-drama, of passion and romance, there came to Laura the swift and vivid impression of that other drama that simultaneously—even at that very moment— was working itself out close at hand, equally picturesque, equally ro-

mantic, equally passionate; but more than that, real, actual, modern, a thing in the very heart of the very life in which she moved. (34)

It falls to Laura, as the principal female character, to evaluate the two dramas. Sentimental Victorian reasoning would require it, on the grounds that the woman's finer moral sensibilities make her the more fastidious judge, and so Laura must finally decide how to weigh the two realms. And two men with them: true to genre, Laura in her opera box faces the choice between two suitors, the artist Corthell and the financier Jadwin. Her decision represents an attempt to reach beyond her own allocated position in the aligned pair of opposites, opting for what seems at the moment a wider sphere. About Corthell she notices that "straightway he made her feel her sex. Now she was just a woman again, with all a woman's limitations, and her relations with Corthell could never be . . . any other than sex-relations."[23] But

> with Jadwin somehow it had been different. She had felt his manhood more than her womanhood, her sex side. And between them it was more a give-and-take affair, more equality, more companionship. Corthell spoke only of her heart and to her heart. But Jadwin made her feel—or rather she made herself feel when he talked to her—that she had a head as well as a heart. And the last act of the opera did not wholly absorb her attention. (35)

Laura's effort to escape the confines of her "sex side" must necessarily vitiate her absorption in the opera, since it disrupts the pattern of alignments as American authors used them. But other alignments are also in play: as Laura's gender stipulates a seat at the front of the opera box, so her gentility determines the sort of performance she watches.

Brander Matthews's 1896 novel of financial temptation, *His Father's Son*, is an intensely moralistic and old-fashioned novel in which a son "goes bad."[24] Apprenticed in his father's investment company, Winslow Pierce suddenly realizes that the entire business of Wall Street is "getting money for nothing," and in disillusionment he turns to drink, gambling (including stock speculation), and the company of bad women. "Bad women" in this case are represented by Miss Daisy Fostelle, the soprano and principal of the Daisy Fostelle Opera Comique Company; indeed, fifty thousand of the irresponsibly gambled dollars have been invested in the troupe, "formed

23. Nineteenth-century writers used the word "sex" where we would more likely use "gender." Laura has no intimate relations with Corthell but fears that she can never relate to him except *as* a woman.

24. *His Father's Son: A Novel of New York* (New York: Harper and Bros., 1896).

for the production of semi-spectacular light opera" (144). Suffering from bad conscience, Winslow takes his wife to see one of the shows—performed, irony of ironies, at the Academy of Music in its now reduced circumstances—but she is uneasy, shocked by the costumes and worried about the company her husband is keeping (110).

Here, the moral taint already evident in Winslow's crisis is both revealed and reinforced by his frequenting the wrong kind of entertainment; the virtuous woman aligns only with the highest form of cultural expression.[25] As Winslow's father tries to explain to him, great financial men like himself are different from

> the mere speculator, who is of very little account. . . . The men who rule Wall Street are the greatest benefactors of humanity the world has ever seen. They are the men who are developing this mighty country of ours, who are opening up new States to the oppressed millions of Europe, who are building the great railroads and bridging the great rivers. (17)

They are also, of course, building the great opera houses in which the truly powerful have left the now déclassé Academy of Music far behind them. Ultimately it is not clear whether the destruction threatening Winslow Pierce is moral decay or simply bad taste.[26]

But such failures of taste are part and parcel of the literary image of the Gilded Age, an era concisely named for a novel. When Mark Twain and Charles Dudley Warner wrote *The Gilded Age* (1873) from the genteel comfort of their adjacent homes at Nook Farm in Hartford, they intended above all to portray the hypocrisy and petty ignorance underlying the pretensions

25. Except in those cases where a greedy and corrupt woman is central to the plot, virtually every single novel of financial dealings contains some version of the line, "Your mother is a very good woman—but she knows nothing at all about business. . . . She wouldn't understand anything. Women never do see things clearly— you will learn that as you grow older" (ibid., 95). Inevitably, such disclaimers signal a virtuous and level-headed woman's attempt to extricate her husband from certain financial disaster; Persis Lapham comes to mind.

26. Social historians have noted characteristically American ironies in the fact that the same money—and thus the same names—dominated both the mercantile and cultural realms. See, e.g., Michael and Ariane Batterberry, *On the Town in New York: From 1776 to the Present* (New York: Charles Scribner's Sons, 1973), ch. 4; Richard Hofstadter, *Anti-Intellectualism in American Life* (New York: Vintage, 1963), ch. 9; and Sean Dennis Cashman, *America in the Gilded Age: From the Death of Lincoln to the Rise of Theodore Roosevelt* (New York: New York University Press, 1984). Cashman captures the transaction nicely by describing the impulse to art patronage as the effort "to celebrate the confidence of accumulated capital" (46).

of so many ambitious philistines. They knew, too, the crucial importance of operatic competence in the effort:

> Harry knew all about the opera, green room and all (at least he said so), and knew a good many of the operas, and could make very entertaining stories of their plots, telling how the soprano came in here, and the basso here, humming the beginning of their airs—tum-ti-tum-ti-ti—suggesting the profound dissatisfaction of the basso recitative—down-among-the-dead-men—and touching off the while with an airy grace quite captivating; though he couldn't have sung a single air through to save himself, and he hadn't an ear to know whether it was sung correctly. All the same he doted on the opera, and kept a box there, into which he lounged occasionally to hear a favourite scene and meet his society friends.[27]

Perhaps the "golden horseshoe" is only gilded after all.

SLUMMING

> Mr. Barnum . . . abandoning for a time his waxworks, wild beasts, and various kinds of human monstrosities, became for a brief season, in view of the money to be made out of the Swedish nightingale, a veritable impresario.
>
> H. SUTHERLAND EDWARDS, *The Prima Donna*

Part of the appeal opera had for upright Americans was its way of legitimating the exotic, the sensational, what would in everyday circumstances be not quite respectable. Henry Blake Fuller's *With the Procession* (1895) dwells in that familiar territory where an older, intensely proud society is losing both financial and fashionable ground to an upstart bevy of business titans. Truesdale Marshall, the scion of an old family just beginning to come to grips with change, has recently returned from his Grand Tour; the association with Europe and its high culture marks him as a member of his father's patrician class, but Truesdale's own vaporous artistic ambitions and the vaguely bohemian group he attempts to draw around himself upon his return signal something different. He misses the aesthetic aura of Europe.

> Mimi and Musette, the actual, the contemporaneous, once met at short range, were far, far from the *gracieuse* and *mignonne* creations of Murger and of 1830. And if disappointing in Paris, how much more so in

27. Ed. Herbert Van Thal (London: Cassell, 1967), 149.

Chicago?—where impropriety was still wholly incapable of presenting itself in a guise that could enlist the sympathies of the fastidious.[28]

Truesdale thinks operatically about slumming.

Operagoing, like other fixtures of high culture in turn-of-the-century America, encapsulated and focused an ambivalent relationship to Europe. Recognized as the source of artistic achievements that Americans had not yet matched, venerated as the reservoir of "civilized" life, and covertly eyed by ambitious mamas for those inherited titles and privileges that the American upper bourgeoisie was beginning to mourn, Europe and its artistic ways at the same time represented the effete, the effeminate, the disreputable, and—perhaps most reassuring—the commercially unsuccessful.

As a comedic turn, of course, this philistine world view is famously the territory of Sinclair Lewis, most especially in *Babbitt* (1922), where it is laid on with a trowel in George Babbitt's celebrated "boosting" speeches:

> In no country in the world will you find so many reproductions
> of the Old Masters and of well-known paintings on parlor walls as
> in these United States. No country has anything like our number
> of phonographs, with not only dance records and comic but also
> the best operas, such as Verdi, rendered by the world's highest-paid
> singers.
> In other countries, art and literature are left to a lot of shabby bums
> living in attics and feeding on booze and spaghetti, but in America the
> successful writer or picture-painter is indistinguishable from any other
> decent business man.[29]

In his little-known but piquant earlier novel, *The Job* (1917), Lewis traces the career of a small-town young woman who must move to New York in order to support her widowed mother and makes her way painfully from typist to business owner. Una Golden's negotiation of the city, and her eventual success in moving up to a slightly more leisured class (though Society is not within her grasp), require among many other things her ability to esteem cultural phenomena appropriately. She is briefly married to one of Lewis's quintessential vulgarians, Eddie Schwirtz, who momentarily distracts her with the knowingness of his aesthetic certainties:

28. (Chicago: University of Chicago Press, 1965), 77. This section's epigraph by H. Sutherland Edwards comes from *The Prima Donna: Her History and Surroundings from the Seventeenth to the Nineteenth Century* (London: Remington and Co., 1888), 2:16.

29. *Babbitt* (New York: New American Library, 1961), 150.

once I went to the grand opera—lot of fat Dutchmen all singing together like they was selling old rags ...

Own up. Don't you get more fun out of hearing Raymond Hitchcock sing than you do out of a bunch of fiddles and flutes fighting out a piece by Vaugner like they was Kilkenny cats? ... I notice that Hitchcock and George M. Cohan go on drawing big audiences every night—yes, and the swellest, best-dressed, smartest people in New York and Brooklyn, too—it's in the gallery at the opera that you find all these Wops and Swedes and Lord knows what-all.[30]

For others less ingenuous than George Babbitt and Eddie Schwirtz, though, the "shabby bums" had a certain appeal, and in the decades just around 1900 every urban center in the United States saw the development of indigenous bohemian circles attempting to capture something of the fabled aesthetic and personal freedom of the continental artist. At the same time a certain curiosity was developing among the "respectable" about what went on in the city's ethnic communities. "Little Germany" already existed in New York by the 1840s; it was followed in ensuing decades by a French quarter, Chinatown, and then by an increasing multitude of neighborhoods whose fascination was partly what Daniel Horowitz has called their "expressive ethnic traditions" and partly simple otherness.[31] Theatrical productions—plays and musicals—about various ethnic groups as well as other "city types" became wildly popular.[32]

Urban novels naturally rely heavily on the conspicuous and well understood social geography of cities; appropriate neighborhoods for family dwellings and permissible venues for shopping and entertainment are clearly and accurately demarcated in Wharton's New York, Norris's or Fuller's Chicago, and Howells's Boston. As cities changed, the movements of the respectable—particularly women—were increasingly restricted by their very respectability, and such restrictions chafed as much in real life as they did on some fictional characters. For the most reckless young, the slums became a tour site as suburbanization removed the well-to-do from daily contact with the poor, and new "scientific" theories of degeneracy in-

30. (New York: Harcourt Brace, 1917), 196–97.

31. *The Morality of Spending: Attitudes toward the Consumer Society in America, 1875–1940* (Baltimore: Johns Hopkins University Press, 1985), xviii. On the emergence of ethnic neighborhoods in New York, see Batterberry, *On the Town*, ch. 4. For some musical ramifications, see Nicholas Tawa, *A Sound of Strangers: Musical Culture, Acculturation, and the Post-Civil War Ethnic American* (Metuchen, N.J.: Scarecrow Press, 1982).

32. See Russel Nye, *The Unembarrassed Muse: The Popular Arts in America* (New York: Dial Press, 1970), ch. 5.

creasingly described them in terms of various colorfully pathological behaviors.[33]

But recreational slumming expeditions were often disappointing, as Lewis's Una Golden discovers:

> He took her to a Lithuanian restaurant, on a street which was a débâcle. One half of the restaurant was filled with shaggy Lithuanians playing cards at filthy tables; the other half was a clean haunt for tourists who came to see the slums, and here, in the heart of these "slums," saw only one another.[34]

The music critic James Huneker reports a similarly unsuccessful evening spent in searching for authentic tango, but finding "no spoor of delirium, and absolutely nothing bacchanalian"; rather, "all that I've witnessed thus far in New York is tame and so respectable."[35]

Opera, in glorious contrast, offered the opportunity to engage vicariously with bohemian, foreign, or otherwise exotic lives not admitted to fastidious bourgeois circles, and to experience supercharged emotions not otherwise permitted there:

> In mounting fervour the aria developed, trailing, as it climbed, words such as *amore, speranza, morir*. A breath of brutality passed.[36]

Another character in *With the Procession*, the socialite Susan Bates, has triumphed over her humble origins. Her mansion includes the luxurious music room and concert grand piano that certify her arrival, and her music stand is "laden with handsomely bound scores of all the German classics and the usual operas of the French and Italian schools" (47). But Sue Bates has a secret. In a shabby upstairs room behind an office, she hides another musical life, "a small upright piano whose top was littered with loose sheets of old music" (60), on which she plays "Old Dan Tucker" and the "Java March," singing at the top of her lungs. Fortunate Sue is wealthy enough to go slumming in her own house.

Henry James assuaged his misery over the state of American opera with visits to Bowery theaters, relishing the "so exotic audience" he saw at a "so domestic drama."

33. See David Ward, *Poverty, Ethnicity, and the American City, 1840–1925: Changing Conceptions of the Slum and the Ghetto* (Cambridge: Cambridge University Press, 1989).

34. *The Job*, 149.

35. *New Cosmopolis* (New York: Scribner's, 1915), 99, 102.

36. Saltus, *Monster*, 74.

No single face . . . but referred itself, by my interpretation, to some
such strange outland form as we had not dreamed of in my day.
There they all sat, the representatives of the races we have nothing
"in common" with, as naturally, as comfortably, as munchingly, as
if the theatre were their constant practice.[37]

The alienness he experiences is striking, considering that elsewhere it appears to be a more European sensibility toward opera that James wishes
American philistines would develop. On the Bowery, Europeans have somehow inscrutably become other "races."

But opera also provides the opportunity for figurative rejoinder. In the
opening scene of *The Pit*, Chicago's poor turn the tables, putting the wealthy
and well-born on exhibit as they make their way into the theater's lobby:

a crowd had collected about the awning on the sidewalk, and even upon
the opposite side of the street, peeping and peering from behind the
broad shoulders of policemen—a crowd of miserables, shivering in rags
and tattered comforters, who found, nevertheless, an unexplainable
satisfaction in watching this prolonged defile of millionaires. (7)

THE MATING GAME

On opera he doth fondly dote,
Though of its music, we confess,
He seldom hears a single note
With any real attentiveness.
From box to box he loves to float,
And there he finds us all the same;
Compared with him we promptly vote
Our favorite tenor tame.

The Buntling Ball (1885)

It is of particular interest that so many of these fictions dwell within the
sensibilities of young women, and that some *(Rose of Dutcher's Coolly, The
Job, The Silent Partner)* even represent that rarest of genres, the female *Bil-
dungsroman*. To a considerable extent this peculiarity reflects the alignments
I discussed above, especially the association of women with the maintenance

---

37. James, *The American Scene*, 198, 196. See also Gist Blair's letters to his aunts
Virginia Woodbury Fox and Ellen DeQuincey Woodbury on visits to Little Hungary and to the Jewish, Italian, and Chinese quarters of New York (1906), reprinted
in *The Gilded Age*, ed. Ari and Olive Hoogenboom (Englewood Cliffs: Prentice-Hall,
1967), 110–12.

of high culture.[38] But women also had, as male novelists fully recognized, much more at stake in those opera boxes than their brothers did. In an opera scene, it is a safe bet that some young woman's life course is about to be decided. Though the occasional heroine makes an obstreperous and resistant choice—perhaps under the influence of the music—much more often she meets or accepts her future husband in a murmured exchange in the box or during the promenade between acts. Opera boxes are for display, and most especially for the display of available young women.

In opera scenes, verbs of vision fairly bristle from the text. A single page in Henry James's *Portrait of a Lady* (1909) offers up "looked," "scanning," "perceived," "recognized," "appeared," "seen," "saw," "looked" again, "watch" twice, along with several occurrences of the noun "eyes."[39] Critics observe that vision is a central theme in the novel as a whole, and James himself has corroborated that interpretation,[40] but that is surely not the whole story. Rather, the thematic prominence of sight lines in all literary opera scenes makes the venue, with all its conventional associations, especially suitable to his larger purpose.

In *Portrait* James's characters, most of whom are Americans, are in Europe—in an unnamed "large, bare, ill-lighted house" in Rome, attending an unnamed "bare, familiar, trivial opera" that is later identified as one of Verdi's, although no music is represented in the scene. His doomed heroine, Isabel Archer, has come to the opera in a group that includes Gilbert Osmond, whom she has recently met and will disastrously marry. The insistence upon vision—candid or covert, insightful or morally blind— informs the tension of the scene and signals many of its consequences. Lord Warburton, a failed suitor, visits Isabel in her box when he notes that she has seen him enter the house; when the opera resumes after intermission, he hears nothing of the music and can see "nothing but the clear profile of this young lady defined against the dim illumination of the house." Watching Isabel, he finds that she "had, in operatic conditions, a radiance, even a slight exaltation." Osmond, by contrast, is prevented by his own self-

38. This section's epigraph—*The Buntling Ball: A Graeco-American Play*, published anonymously by Edgar Fawcett (New York: Funk and Wagnalls, 1885), 97–98—is recited by a "chorus of belles."

39. *The Portrait of a Lady* (New York: Bantam Books, 1983), 261. All quotations from the scene are taken from 261–62. Such terms are equally numerous in other scenes I discuss.

40. See, e.g., Stephen Koch's afterword in the 1983 ed., and several of the critical comments collected in *Portrait of a Lady: An Authoritative Text*, ed. Robert D. Bamberg (New York: W. W. Norton, 1975); James's preface to the 1909 ed. is included in both volumes.

involvement from observing much about others. "What's the character of that gentleman?" he asks her. "Irreproachable—don't you see it?" But Isabel herself, the reader notes, has not been seeing character particularly clearly. It is a sinister scene, on the whole, and we gather from it what is characteristic of these episodes: somehow a die has been cast, and Isabel's fate is *en train*.

Henry James's own discussion of this novel has become notorious to a degree and makes clear why the opera setting is so appropriate. He began, he says, with "a certain young woman affronting her destiny" but then wondered, what next?

> By what process of logical accretion was this slight "personality," the mere slim shade of an intelligent but presumptuous girl, to find itself endowed with the high attributes of a Subject? . . . Millions of presumptuous girls, intelligent or not intelligent, daily affront their destiny, and what is it open to their destiny to *be*, at the most, that we should make an ado about it?

To make an ado about Isabel, James considers, is an "extravagance," but a problem not without "charm."[41] The setting, as a response to the problem, may have taken on an increased zest for him after his American sojourn. In the original version of the novel (1881) Warburton only notices "that Miss Archer looked very pretty; he even thought she looked excited."[42] It is only in the 1909 revision that Isabel is fully realized in the "radiance" and "exaltation" of the "operatic conditions" in which she is set.

The situation has a certain prurience. In an opera box, as in James's novel, a young woman becomes the center of attention and the focus of all eyes, but her "charm" is that her destiny is firmly in the hands of others. Hamlin Garland acknowledges the ploy forthrightly—we might even say he exposes it—in *Rose of Dutcher's Coolly* (1895), in which a young woman from rural Wisconsin comes to Chicago and is brought to a performance at the Auditorium Theatre. Garland entitles the chapter "Rose Sits in the Blaze of a Thousand Eyes."

> [Mrs. Harvey] gave Rose the outside seat, and before she realized it the coolly girl was seated in plain view of a thousand people, under a soft but penetrating light.
> She shrank like some nocturnal insect suddenly brought into sunlight. She turned white, and then the blood flamed to her face and neck. She sprang up.

41. Preface to the 1983 ed., xi.
42. (Boston: Houghton, Mifflin, 1881), 260, and similarly at its first publication in *Macmillan's Magazine* 43 (1881): 423.

"Oh, Mrs. Harvey, I can't sit here," she gasped out.

"You must! ... The public welfare demands that you sit there ... "

Rose sank back into her seat, and stared straight ahead. She felt as if something hot and withering were blowing on that side of her face which was exposed to the audience. She wished she had not allowed the neck of her dress to be lowered an inch. She vowed never again to get into such a trap.[43]

In novels as in life, convention singled out the opera box as one of very few appropriate sites of heterosocial interaction for the offspring of the wealthy and respectable. The increasingly threatening urban environment and the apparent spread of questionable and "alien" moral values prompted high society to retrench and circle its wagons; social historians have observed that rituals of etiquette became more elaborate during this period, and practices of chaperonage that had fallen by the wayside were resumed with ferocious intensity. The identification of "the 400," the legendary list of approved insiders who could fit into Caroline Astor's ballroom, was less an amusing foible of the self-important than a frightened and rather desperate attempt to control the circles in which one's sons and daughters would associate and intermarry.[44]

In the real world outside that ballroom, cities were more diverse, more energetic, and more commercially alluring than ever before. In the United States as well as in Europe, that peculiarly urban character the *flâneur*—whom Bruce Mazlish refers to as "a kind of perambulating Panopticon"—strolled the city taking in the sights, consorting with the shop girls and chorus girls whose occupations and class status allowed them the freedom of the streets.[45] Even for them, such freedom had its cost. Theodore Dreiser

43. *Rose of Dutcher's Coolly* (New York: Harper and Bros., 1899), 230–31.

44. The contemporaneous formation of "the 400" and the passage of Jim Crow laws in the southern states express the same impulse to distinguish the acceptable from the outcast. On the social purity movement and "the 400," see Banner, *American Beauty,* esp. ch. 7.

45. "The *Flâneur:* From Spectator to Representation," in *The Flâneur,* ed. Keith Tester (London: Routledge, 1994), 50. The higher the class, the more stringent the restrictions "womanhood" required, though the streets were not always safe or pleasant for working-class women either. See Carole Klein, *Gramercy Park: An American Bloomsbury* (Boston: Houghton Mifflin, 1987), 125 ff.; Judith Walkowitz, *City of Dreadful Delight: Narratives of Sexual Danger in Late-Victorian London* (Chicago: University of Chicago Press, 1992), esp. chs. 1–2; and John Kasson, *Rudeness and Civility: Manners in Nineteenth-Century Urban America* (New York: Hill and Wang, 1990). Pierre Michot indicates that the situation was similar in eighteenth-century Europe: "Dans ce jeu infiniment repris des échanges de regards, la femme est en montre, elle vient s'offrir ... [à] cet oeil multiplié qu'est le parterre et que sont les loges" ("La Soirée ... L'opéra au xviiie siècle," in *Actes du Colloque*

tells us, in a rather charming essay about Broadway's days as the center of the popular music industry, that while the successful male author of the latest popular song is "a delicious presence,"

> In his coat lapel is a ruddy boutonnière, in his hand a novel walking-stick. His vest is of a gorgeous and affluent pattern, his shoes shiny-new and topped with pearl-gray spats. With dignity he carries his body and his chin. He is the cynosure of many eyes, the envy of all men, and he knows it.[46]

a young woman who arrives on the street with similar ambitions—one very like Dreiser's own Carrie Meeber, perhaps?—is perceived rather differently:

> a rouged and powdered little maiden, rich in feathers and ornaments of the latest vogue; gloved in blue and shod in yellow; pretty, self-assured, daring, and even bold. There has gone here all the traditional maidenly reserve you would expect to find in one so young and pleasing.(243)

One of the crueler clues Edith Wharton gives us to the social origins of Undine Spragg is her delight at being seen in public; not yet in possession of her opera box, "she had to content herself with the gaze of admiration which she left in her wake along the pavement; but she was used to the homage of the streets and her vanity craved a choicer fare" (31). Wharton's readers knew what "the homage of the streets" was worth.

Given all the enticements, serious measures were necessary to keep girls concealed. The pseudonymous George Ellington describes the care taken with girls at fashionable New York boarding schools:

> They are permitted to go to lectures and operas occasionally, at the desire of their parents. They are always sent off in closed carriages to the Academy of Music, have reserved seats and enter the edifice by a private doorway. This is to avoid coming in contact with those male wolves in "store clothes" who are always hanging about such places.[47]

The schoolgirls have reserved seats rather than boxes because they are not yet of an age to be on display. Eventually they will be, for if young men and women are ever to meet and marry, a time comes when the concealment must end and visibility be sought. The opera box seems an ideal site: paradoxically both private and public—private in that access to it is strictly con-

---

organisé . . . *Aix-en-Provence par le Centre aixois d'études et de recherches sur le* xviiie *siècle* [Aix-en-Provence: Presses de l'Université de Provence, 1982], 562).

46. "Whence the Song," in *The Color of a Great City* (New York: Boni and Liveright, 1923), 242.

47. *The Women of New York; or, Social Life in the Great City* (New York: New York Book, 1870), 538.

trolled, but nonetheless in public view—it functions as a glorious jewel box to set off its prize. At the same time it is a sort of luxuriously upholstered trap; many a girl, like Rose Dutcher, must have experienced the opera box as cul-de-sac. The New York diarist Philip Hone, explaining the situation in a rather genteel manner, described

> a beautiful *parterre*, in which our young ladies, the flower of New York society, are planted and flourish, not to "waste their sweetness on the desert air," but to expand in a congenial soil under the sunshine of admiration; and here also our young men may be initiated into the habits and forms of elegant social intercourse, and learn to acquire a taste for a science of the most refined and elegant nature, better—far better—than diving into oyster-cellars, or even in consuming night after night in the less exceptionable coteries of the clubs.[48]

Both young men and women are appropriately socialized in the parterre boxes, and there they are trained to prefer one another to any alternative companions. It stands to reason, then, that the box becomes a conventional site, and a literary topos, for the rituals of courtship.[49]

Let us return to Henry James, and to another American character in a European opera house. *The American* (1877) recapitulates many themes we have visited already, in particular the contest between American and European cultural attitudes, here presented in most excruciating form. Christopher Newman—whose name, of course, signifies a new Columbus setting out this time upon a reverse voyage of discovery to the Old World—is a Westerner, "the superlative American," a man of self-made wealth who, at the age of forty-two, considers that he has amassed a sufficient fortune and prepares to spend it.[50] He travels to Paris in a fit of cultural acquisitiveness that is only just this side of caricature; he wants to "see first-class pictures," and to "hear first-class music," and most significantly, he seeks a wife. "I want a great woman . . . the best article in the market" (49).

It soon becomes clear, though, that Newman is a serious and sympathetic character. His exposure to these "first-class" items quickly reveals him as one with genuine sensitivity to them; the woman he finds, Claire de Cintré, is not only "the best article in the market" but, alas, too far upmarket for the pretensions of any declassed American. Though she falls in love with

48. Diary entry for 21 January 1848, quoted in Vera Brodsky Lawrence, *Strong on Music: The New York Music Scene in the Days of George Templeton Strong, 1836–1875* (New York: Oxford University Press, 1988), 1:497.

49. See also Michel Leiris, "L'érotisme dans l'opéra," in his *Operratiques*, ed. Jean Jamin (Paris: P.O.L., 1992).

50. *The American* (Boston: Houghton Mifflin, 1907), 2.

him and agrees to marry him, her ancient and thoroughbred family, the Bellegardes, cannot be won over: "we really can't reconcile ourselves to a commercial person," Newman is told (371). James's American is a man of thoroughly American convictions, besides having sufficient fortune to purchase whatever he fancies, and he hears this verdict with disbelief; but James himself is under no such illusions. *The American* is one of his harshest stories; when Claire's father shows some sign of weakening and permitting the match, her mother in effect kills him to prevent it. A chastened Claire ends in a Carmelite convent.

The opera scene in this novel is unusual in that Claire does not attend. Newman takes an orchestra seat—where he now seems to belong, in relation to the Bellegardes, although we are pointedly told that a box was his usual venue[51]—at a performance of *Don Giovanni*. In the family box he sees Claire's brother Urbain, the marquis, and his wife; visiting them at intermission, he is asked by the marquise to take her to the students' ball in the Latin Quarter—slumming, that is—where her husband will not go.

> I'm bored to death. I've been to the opera twice a week for the last eight years. Whenever I ask for anything my mouth is stopped with that: Pray, madame, have n't you your *loge aux Italiens?* Could a woman of taste want more? In the first place my box was down in my *contrat;* they have to give it to me. (343)

The first-act drama, then, is the tensions in the marquis's marriage—a marriage in which opera was transacted as part of the dowry—and indeed in the entire Bellegarde household, which have been exacerbated by Newman's arrival among them and the ensuing contretemps.

At another level of the theater's social geography, "in that obscure region devoted to the small boxes that in French are called, not inaptly, bathtubs" (335), Newman spots Claire's younger brother Valentin, in the company of a young woman of dubious social origin to whom Newman has introduced him against his own better judgment, and another man.[52] More extended and more sensational drama ensues from this triangle, which eventually leads to a duel and to Valentin's death.

The choreography of the scene is laid out impeccably, the two women literally positioned at a vertical distance metaphoric of their discrete social or-

---

51. "Frequently he took a large box and invited a group of his compatriots; this was a mode of recreation to which he was much addicted" (334).

52. *Baignoires* was the common French term for ground-floor theatrical boxes and likewise applied (familiarly) to the large, rather ungainly lowest tier of boxes at the Met.

bits, and all of the men perambulating from box to *baignoire* to promenade, watching the women and one another and circulating status and information. Newman can see only too well the havoc he has wrought in the Bellegarde family, but he cannot see Claire, who is too respectable even for the opera box. In her absence the reader becomes uneasily aware that Christopher Newman will not, finally, fit into her world, that the marriage will not occur.

WAGNER AND THE SOULS OF WOMEN

It is not possible to go to an opera in any of our large cities without seeing more of the representatives of the highest type of female beauty than can be found in months of travel in any part of Europe.

GEORGE M. BEARD, *American Nervousness* (1881)

The alignment of women—women of a certain economic class and social pretension—not only with culture and social maneuvering but with emotional and aesthetic susceptibility, drives these fictions of the opera box. Doctor Beard is not, of course, speaking of the women on the opera stage, but of those on display in the boxes.[53] His observation, in a book on the parlous state of American health, is provocative because it combines themes not obviously germane to one another in precisely the way they are often found entwined in novelistic opera scenes. The trope upon opera as specular site— one goes to the opera to see young women, not necessarily to hear anything—accompanies the boastful yet anxious challenge to Europe just as usual. The insistence upon the "highest type" of beauty is easily decoded as an allusion to Anglo-Saxon racial superiority, an interpretation quickly verified by further reading in *American Nervousness*.

The most evolved human types, according to Beard, unfortunately must pay for their advanced condition through a "fineness of organization" that makes them especially vulnerable to nervous disease. Revealing his supposedly empirical observations to be somewhat under the sway of his belief system, Beard explains that the "nervous temperament," which also suffers increased susceptibility to stimulants and narcotics, can be identified by physical traits such as fine hair and "chiselled" features. "It is the organization of the civilized, refined, and educated, rather than of the barbarous and low-born and untrained—of women more than of men" (26).

53. *American Nervousness* (New York: G. P. Putnam's Sons, 1881), 67.

Beard was especially intrigued by young women:

The phenomenal beauty of the American girl of the highest type,
is a subject of the greatest interest both to the psychologist and the
sociologist, since it has no precedent, in recorded history, at least; and
it is very instructive in its relation to the character and the diseases
of America. (65)

We should be clear that Beard's ideas were not unusual but perfectly
typical of the era, in which the state of science encouraged a strong commitment to racial essentialism that is visible in virtually every cultural context.[54] The social fallout of Darwinian theory and the first glimmerings of
a Freudian construction of the psyche combined with an ideologically
charged understanding of human reproduction to yield an image of the well-
born young woman so extreme in her fragility that one marvels that she
ever lived to adulthood without falling into madness or moral depravity.

Carroll Smith-Rosenberg has written extensively on the biological understanding of young women during this period, making clear how, in the
case of nineteenth-century biology, a little knowledge was an extremely dangerous thing indeed.[55]

[Woman] was seen . . . as being both higher and lower, both innocent
and animal, pure yet quintessentially sexual. The central metaphor in
these formulations, central both emotionally and in content, pictures
the female as driven by the tidal currents of her cyclical reproductive
system. (183)

Because the menses then became a source of both physical and emotional
stress, young women in puberty and after were advised to avoid occasions
of strong emotion. That such advice had a sociological as well as a scientific
component is clear from the fulminations of some doctors who—turning
George Beard's argument on its head—complained that the idleness of
wealthy women gave them the "opportunity to cultivate the emotional and

54. However, Beard's penchant for argument from "scattergories" in an ineptly
Borgesian manner seems to have been idiosyncratic. He describes modern civilization as distinguished by five principal characteristics—steam power, the periodical
press, the telegraph, the sciences, and the mental activity of women—plus a number of subsidiary ones: "dryness of the air, extremes of heat and cold, civil and religious liberty, and the great mental activity made necessary and possible in a new
and productive country under such climatic conditions" (ibid., vi–vii).

55. In her *Disorderly Conduct: Visions of Gender in Victorian America* (New
York: Alfred A. Knopf, 1985), see esp. "Puberty to Menopause" and "The Hysteri-
cal Woman."

sensuous, to indulge the sentimental side of life," which in turn made them ill.[56] Such women were "morbidly suggestive."

Given this extraordinary susceptibility, the increased chaperonage and surveillance to which young women were subjected in the last decades of the nineteenth century come as no surprise. But for just the same reason, the social sanction that made the opera box a "safe haven" exposed them to a potentially greater danger: music. In fiction, it is just these young women of the "highest type" who prove most vulnerable to it; their "finer organizations" respond strongly, as indeed they must in order to prove their gentility and feminine sensibility.[57]

The particular state of American culture in these decades, along with the preoccupations of contemporary medical science, combined to form an atmosphere perfectly primed for the emotional "Wagner craze" that hit at the end of the century, as Joseph Horowitz has recently detailed: "Wagner offered an avenue of intense spiritual experience, a surrogate for religion or cocaine, a song of redemption to set beside Emerson and Whitman. It was both intellectually and emotionally vitalizing. It spoke to America's women."[58] Not only to the women, of course: Horowitz describes the general effects of the mania in the bourgeois population, along with such responses as the critic Henry Krehbiel's "warnings against surrendering to Wagnerian narcosis" (110). But it was primarily, and most alarmingly, women who both fell victim to it and at the same time drew from it a certain subversive sustenance. Horowitz is reporting on the impressions of actual women, many of them "of a certain age" and experiencing Wagner as "a consuming alternative to a world of marriage and men,"[59] but the nov-

---

56. George Preston, *Hysteria and Certain Allied Conditions* (1897), quoted in ibid., 205.

57. This topos survives into twentieth-century cinema, as in *Pretty Woman* or *Moonstruck;* both the 1933 and 1993 films of *Little Women* include such a scene—in which Professor Bhaer takes Jo to the opera—even though Louisa May Alcott did not (I am grateful to Susan Van Dyne for this observation). For relevant discussions of fictional opera as the site of passion and *jouissance,* see Lindenberger, *The Extravagant Art;* and Michel Poizat, *The Angel's Cry: Beyond the Pleasure Principle in Opera,* trans. Arthur Denner (Ithaca: Cornell University Press, 1992); both focus on the European situation.

58. Horowitz, *Wagner Nights,* 8.

59. Ibid., 215; and see his informative and highly important argument in ch. 12, "Protofeminism" (though I do not consider this episode of American women's experience merely "proto"feminism). M. Carey Thomas was already dean of Bryn Mawr College when she first heard *Tristan* and wrote the response recorded by Helen Lefkowitz Horowitz in *The Power and Passion of M. Carey Thomas* (New York: Knopf, 1994), 215. Also enlightening is Willa Cather's short story, "A Wagner Matinee."

elists naturally are more interested in the youngest and most "morbidly suggestible" of women, women whose sensibilities are yet to be tested in the crucible of opera. Often we find ourselves eavesdropping at virgin operatic excursions, and the titillation of these first Wagnerian swoons is too riveting a spectacle for authors to pass up.

Thus Rose Dutcher:

> The voice of Wagner came to her for the first time, and shook her and thrilled her and lifted her into wonderful regions where the green trees dripped golden moss, and the grasses were jewelled in very truth. Wistful young voices rose above the lazy lap of waves, sad with love and burdened with beauty which destroyed. Like a deep-purple cloud death came, slowly, resistlessly, closing down on those who sang, clasped in each other's arms. . . .
>
> When she rose to her feet the girl from the coolly staggered, and the brilliant, moving, murmuring house blurred into fluid color like a wheel of roses. (235)

Rose is observed, in her box, by Warren Mason—whom she will marry—and after watching her in the throes of this spasm, "he began to comprehend the soul of the girl" (239).

A considerably less pleasant young woman, the creation of a somewhat less pleasant author, has a similar experience, though hers cannot pass as a virgin encounter:

> Easter, her eyes closed, her face flushed, swam out on the muffled ecstasy of the prelude. The curtain rose. Soon Lilli passionately broke in upon the song of the seaman, and the glorious symphony of human desire and renunciation went swirling by. . . . Jean, warrior and lover, met his Isolde in the shock of passion and remorse, but did not flinch at the climax. . . . At moments Easter thought she couldn't longer stand the suspense. She wished to cry, to roll on the floor, to tear her hair, to press her aching eyeballs till they fell out. She was in the centre of an emotional typhoon.[60]

James Huneker's *Painted Veils* is a novel that more properly belongs to quite a different generic tradition, that of the budding diva, along with Willa Cather's *Song of the Lark* and George du Maurier's notorious *Trilby*. Easter Brandès (her name mutates unnervingly in the course of the story from Esther to Easter to Istar) comes to New York to study singing, and she wit-

---

60. *Painted Veils* (New York: Liveright, 1920), 59. Since Huneker was one of the city's most knowledgeable music critics, this insider's novel has unusually precise musical and historical details (in that era Lilli Lehmann and Jean de Reszke were New York's most lionized Isolde and Tristan).

nesses this performance not from a box but from an orchestra seat during a rehearsal conducted by Anton Seidl. Easter triumphs, opening her singing career in the role of Isolde herself, partnered just as she had fantasied by Jean de Reszke.

The story is a rather puerile, vaguely pornographic account of a bohemian circle, and in it Easter emerges as a woman without trace of moral scruple—and bisexually promiscuous, besides—who is toasted at the end as "the greatest Isolde since Lilli Lehmann . . . Istar, the Great Singing Whore of Modern Babylon" (306). But her reaction to Wagner is nonetheless the counterpart of Rose's: "music, the most sensual of the arts, . . . tells us of the hidden secrets of sex" (62).[61] The difference is only that Easter already knows the secrets.

Charles Dudley Warner's *A Little Journey in the World* (1889), part of a trilogy, tells the story of a young New England woman whose soul is lost through the acquisition of a fortune. Margaret Debree is a bluestocking, something of a feminist, and devoted to good works; she is loved and admired in a great circle of acquaintances. She scrupulously turns down an offer of marriage from the visiting John Lyon, an Englishman next in succession to an earldom, distrusting her own greedy interest in his future title. But in New York at the opera, alas, Margaret is introduced by her friends to Curtis Henderson, and her fate is sealed.

Warner is a sophisticate concerning opera and its uses by novelists of the period, as his narrator (impersonating one of the circle of Margaret's friends) alerts us:

> In youth, as at the opera, everything seems possible. Surely it is not necessary to choose between love and riches. One may have both, and the one all the more easily for having attained the other. . . . It was in some wholly legendary, perhaps spiritual, world that it was necessary to renounce love to gain the Rhine gold. The boxes at the Metropolitan did not believe this. . . . For was not beauty there seen shining in jewels that have a market value, and did not love visibly preside over the union, and make it known that his sweetest favors go with a prosperous world?[62]

61. This seems to be a trope for Huneker, who elsewhere writes that "music is too sexual—it reports in a more intense style the stories of our loves. Music is the memory of love" ("The Eighth Deadly Sin," in his collection of short stories, *Visionaries* [New York: Charles Scribner's Sons, 1905], 35). It is no accident that Easter chooses Isolde as her signature role; see Horowitz, *Wagner Nights*, ch. 6, on its problematic implications. Huneker does his best to undermine the sanitizing efforts of genteel New York.

62. Thomas R. Lounsbury, ed., *The Complete Writings of Charles Dudley Warner* (Hartford: American Publishing, 1904), 11:94.

This is a delusion, to be sure, that Margaret Debree had seen through perfectly well before she was introduced into the world of the opera box.

As ever, opera glasses and sight lines diagram the play of recognition and relationship throughout the episode.

> [T]he scene was brilliant, of course with republican simplicity. The imagination was helped by no titled names . . . but there was a certain glow of feeling, as the glass swept the circle, to know that there were ten millions in this box, and twenty in the next, and fifty in the next, attested well enough by the flash of jewels and the splendor of attire, and one might indulge a genuine pride in the prosperity of the republic. As for beauty, the world, surely, in this later time, had flowered here. . . . Here and there in the boxes was a thoroughbred portrait by Copley—the long shapely neck, the sloping shoulders, the drooping eyelids, even to the gown in which the great-grandmother danced with the French officers. (97–98)

Henderson is spotted in an opposite box, with Mr. Lyon and the beautiful Carmen Eschelle, a young woman of faintly sinister nature who will play a significant role throughout the trilogy. Henderson is brought to the box in which Margaret sits, takes a seat beside her, and is "quite content while the act was going on to watch its progress in the play of her responsive features. How quickly she felt, how the frown followed the smile, how she seemed to weigh and try to apprehend the meaning of what went on" (101). Margaret's responsiveness is a healthy sign, a sign of her feminine competence and appropriate aesthetic susceptibility; to the knowledgeable reader, however, it also portends suggestibility to other influences.

And so it proves. Margaret marries the financier—and railroad speculator—Henderson, and becomes intimate with the stylish Carmen. Her decline is long and slow, sometimes almost imperceptible, and is punctuated by her strenuous efforts to retain her original integrity:

> "You see, Margaret," Morgan explained, "when people in trade buy anything, they expect to sell it for more than they gave for it."
>
> "It seems to me," Margaret replied, . . . "that a great deal of what you men call business is just trying to get other people's money, and doesn't help anybody or produce anything."
>
> "Oh, that is keeping up the circulation, preventing stagnation."
>
> "And that is the use of brokers in grain and stocks?"
>
> "Partly. They are commonly the agents that others use to keep themselves from stagnation."
>
> "I cannot see any good in it," Margaret persisted. "No one seems to have the things he buys or sells. I don't understand it."
>
> "That is because you are a woman. . . . " (153)

Margaret knows better, just like Laura Dearborn, picturing in her mind what she elsewhere calls "the thousands who have been reduced to poverty by this operation" (149), but she carries her point no further. Finally, the transformation has been completed and even her friends sadly conclude that "she was valuing people by the money they had, by the social position they had attained" (342).

Margaret dies in childbirth near the end of this novel, along with her infant, because what Warner wishes his readers to trace is Henderson's fortune itself; its life span is the most significant influence upon his characters. The last page of *A Little Journey* sees the narrator, with his wife, at a performance of *Siegfried* at the Metropolitan. In one of the boxes they spot Henderson and Carmen, married now: we are alerted that neither the story nor the fortune's curse is ended, that the twilight of these particular gods is yet in the offing.

In these scenes, then, we might go so far as to say that women lose their souls; more precisely, they and we first see how they are destined to be lost in the course of their stories. Isabel Archer, Laura Dearborn, and Margaret Debree are just about to enter upon their dark nights of the soul. May Welland and Ellen Olenska are embroiled in a tragedy from which neither emerges unscathed. Claire de Cintré is sacrificed—or, rather, is forced through the inexorable logic of blood to sacrifice herself. Even Olive Chancellor, Henry James's Brahmin feminist, ponders her next move in the terrible struggle for the soul of Verena Tarrant at a performance of *Lohengrin*, about which Verena speaks "only of Wagner's music, of the singers, the orchestra, the immensity of the house, her tremendous pleasure."[63] Their stories have a certain operatic quality, conforming to Catherine Clément's characterization of opera itself as "the undoing of women."[64]

But, very occasionally, a woman comes along who escapes the common fate through sheer purity, Parsifal-like. In *That Fortune* (1899), the third of Warner's trilogy, the narrative contortions necessary to create such a woman and to keep her credibly up to the task are remarkable: readers understood the stakes. Evelyn Mavick, the daughter of Carmen Eschelle and her second husband, has been raised in a millionaire's castle on Fifth Avenue, under the care of a rather radical Scottish governess; to explain Evelyn's isolation and ensuing hyperinnocence, Warner is driven to contrive a childhood kidnap-

---

63. Henry James, *The Bostonians*, ed. R. D. Gooder (Oxford: Oxford University Press, 1984), 285–86.

64. Catherine Clément, *Opera, or the Undoing of Women*, trans. Betsy Wing (Minneapolis: University of Minnesota Press, 1988). Undine Spragg is irredeemable long before we meet her.

ping attempt after which she was kept quarantined from all society. Ultimately, of course, Evelyn must be presented in public or all the care and expense of her upbringing will be for naught. Philip Burnett—from whose poverty, integrity, literary ambition, and altogether unsuitable social origins we are to understand that he is the suitor who will enable Evelyn's redemption—has been longing to get a glimpse of her now that she is emerging from her seclusion. "Watch for a Wagner night," he is advised (93), and so he does. In fact, it is a *Siegfried* night, and as Philip watches her box there

> appeared a gentleman who looked as if he were performing a public duty, a lady who looked as if she were receiving a public welcome, and seated between them a dark slender girl, who looked as if she did not see the public at all, but only the orchestra.[65]

Evelyn's utter dissimilarity to her bowing and smiling mother is the first thing about her that Philip is privileged to see: she becomes absorbed in the music. Like Curtis Henderson before him, he traces "the progress of the drama repeated in her face." But Evelyn is able to survive spiritually because she does not analyze the drama and its moral efficacy, as Margaret Debree proceeded to do in her bluestocking way. Evelyn is all experience.

> But presently something more was evident to this sympathetic student of her face. She was not merely discovering the poet's world, she was finding out herself. As the drama unfolded, Philip was more interested in this phase than in the observation of her enjoyment and appreciation. To see her eyes sparkle and her cheeks glow with enthusiasm during the sword-song was one thing, but it was quite another when Siegfried began his idyl, that nature and bird song of the awakening of the whole being to the passion of love. Then it was that Evelyn's face had a look of surprise, of pain, of profound disturbance; it was suffused with blushes, coming and going in passionate emotion; the eyes no longer blazed, but were softened in a melting tenderness of sympathy, and her whole person seemed to be carried into the stream of the great life passion. (96)

Evelyn's long virginity is ended. Later, after her father's financial ruin has broken the curse and enabled the lovers to marry, Philip understands that "the soul of the woman [had been] perfectly revealed to him that night of 'Siegfried.'"

The conventional fiction of the opera box did not, of course, outlive the particular social negotiation it had so mercilessly illuminated. In one of its last

65. Lounsbury, *Charles Dudley Warner*, 13:93.

avatars, *Not on the Screen* (1930), Henry Blake Fuller traces the frenetic social quest of a young woman in chapters successively situated at a prize fight,
a football game, and then, somewhat archaically, "At the Opera." But the
erstwhile glamour has become mere tabloid fodder, and Fuller furnishes the
trope with its epitaph:

> The only persons who know how to grade and present the occupants
> of opera-boxes are the discriminating young women who make note of
> them for the daily papers. . . . To the casual observer in the parquet or
> the balcony, all the box-people may seem to be participating on equal
> terms in a brave spectacle; but when it comes to the acute dissection of
> the spectacle's component parts by these inquirers with note-books and
> pencils, it will be found that they know, they know.[66]

66. *Not on the Screen* (New York: Knopf, 1930), 95. Opera scenes continue to
occur, of course, in historical novels; but Fuller's is the latest I found that represents
contemporary experience.

Index

Text: 10/13 Aldus
Display: Aldus
Compositor: Integrated Composition Systems
Printer and binder: Malloy, Inc.